Zend Enterprise PHP Patterns

John Coggeshall with Morgan Tocker

Apress®

Zend Enterprise PHP Patterns

Copyright © 2009 by John Coggeshall

ISBN-13 (pbk): 978-1-4302-1974-3

ISBN-13 (electronic): 978-1-4302-1975-0

Lead Editor: Matt Wade
Technical Reviewer: Kevin Schroeder
Editorial Board: Clay Andres, Steve Anglin, Mark Beckner, Ewan Buckingham, Tony Campbell, Gary Cornell, Jonathan Gennick, Jonathan Hassell, Michelle Lowman, Matthew Moodie, Jeffrey Pepper, Frank Pohlmann, Douglas Pundick, Ben Renow-Clarke, Dominic Shakeshaft, Matt Wade, Tom Welsh
Project Managers: Sofia Marchant and Kylie Johnston
Copy Editor: Hastings Hart
Associate Production Director: Kari Brooks-Copony
Production Editor: April Eddy
Compositor: Lynn L'Heureux
Proofreader: Liz Welch
Indexer: BIM Indexing & Proofreading Services
Artist: April Milne
Cover Designer: Anna Ishchenko
Manufacturing Director: Tom Debolski

Distributed to the book trade worldwide by Springer-Verlag New York, Inc., 233 Spring Street, 6th Floor, New York, NY 10013. Phone 1-800-SPRINGER, fax 201-348-4505, e-mail orders-ny@springer-sbm.com, or visit http://www.springeronline.com.

For information on translations, please contact Apress directly at 233 Spring Street, New York, NY 10013. E-mail info@apress.com or visit http://www.apress.com.

Apress and friends of ED books may be purchased in bulk for academic, corporate, or promotional use. eBook versions and licenses are also available for most titles. For more information, reference our Special Bulk Sales–eBook Licensing web page at http://www.apress.com/info/bulksales.

The source code for this book is available to readers at http://www.apress.com.

To my daughter, Diana Katheryn Coggeshall, who continues to be the single steadfast reason I have to do more and be more in my life

John Coggeshall

Contents at a Glance

Contents

Foreword

Seat 5D, Continental Flight 449B, someplace over North America

In the late '90s, PHP was still referred to mockingly by many computer science graduates as a "scripting language." Lack of strict typing was the number one reason it was not viewed as ready for prime time. At that time most computer science graduates were developing either in C or C++, or picking up Java, and therefore there was a strong bias in the IT community. Although PHP grew rapidly during this period and among other things displaced Perl on the Web, it still was not widely considered an enterprise-ready solution.

During the dot-com boom venture capitalists expected startups to build their solutions on the latest and greatest Oracle/Solaris/WebLogic combo. It was very much a culture of "Java is the solution. What's the problem?" Paying ridiculous prices such as tens of thousands of dollars per CPU did not stop anyone from buying these solutions, and the majority of projects really weren't using the enterprise features they paid for. This was very familiar to the well-known saying, "No one gets fired for buying IBM."

With the dot-com bust, companies started to realize they needed to get the most out of their investment. PHP went through a very strong period of growth during those years, including early penetration within business-critical enterprise applications. The perception of "scripting languages" changed, and they were even given a new more professional-sounding name, "dynamic languages." It was now OK for a computer science graduate to add dynamic languages to their toolbox.

Over the past five years PHP adoption within the enterprise has accelerated, and it is now going mainstream within IT. In addition to the already mentioned reasons for this change, there were additional factors that drove this change. The ecosystem and the solutions around PHP have matured to make it a strong contender for driving standardization within corporate IT. With the investments by the likes of IBM, Oracle, Adobe, and Microsoft ensuring that PHP runs well with their solutions, there are few solutions that are as cross-platform and interoperable as PHP.

In addition, application servers, application frameworks, tools, many available prebuilt applications, and other solutions are now readily available as part of the PHP ecosystem. Add five million to six million developers to that, and it becomes a very compelling value proposition for enterprises.

With the financial crises that started in 2007 we are seeing the same trends as we did with the dot-com bust. Companies are looking to do more with less as that is the only way for them to continue to be competitive and grow. Yet again a perfect setup for yet another acceleration in PHP adoption, but this time with the full-blown ecosystem.

Strategic adoption of PHP in mainstream IT continues to accelerate, and there are few other solutions out there that can compete on the same ease of use, cross-platform support, huge developer community, large ecosystem, and corporate support.

PHP is in the enterprise because it is faster, cheaper, and I also claim better!

I have known John, the author of this book, for over five years. In fact, first time I started working with John was when we had a significant enterprise opportunity that we had to engage with, and I asked John to join that effort. Over the years he has worked with many enterprises, helping them build business-critical PHP applications. I have no doubt that you will find this book a valuable resource for building and deploying enterprise-ready PHP applications.

Andi Gutmans
Cofounder and Chief Executive Officer of Zend Technologies
July 10, 2009

About the Authors

JOHN COGGESHALL is CEO of Internet Technology Solutions, a PHP-focused technology consultancy. The former Senior Architect of Zend Technologies' Global Services team, he got started with PHP in 1997 and is the author of three published books and over 100 articles on PHP technologies with some of the biggest names in the industry such as Sams Publishing, Apress, and O'Reilly. John also is an active contributor to the PHP core as the author of the Tidy extension, a member of the Zend Education Advisory Board, and a frequent speaker at PHP-related conferences worldwide. His web site, http://www.coggeshall.org/, is an excellent resource for any PHP developer, and you can follow him on Twitter by adding @coogle.

MORGAN TOCKER is a Consultant at Percona, a company that provides consulting and custom development for MySQL.

Before joining Percona, Morgan worked as a Technical Instructor for MySQL (and then Sun Microsystems) in Canada, where he taught courses on high availability, performance tuning, and database administration. He is a frequent conference speaker in the United States and Canada.

Morgan has also previously worked as a MySQL Support Engineer and claims that he can look at complex problems and answer with a bug number, without having to ever look it up.

About the Technical Reviewer

KEVIN SCHROEDER, Technical Consultant for Zend Technologies, is well versed in technologies pertinent to small- and large-scale web-application deployments. He has developed production software using PHP and several other languages and also has extensive experience in system administration on Linux, Solaris, and Windows. He is the author of *The IBM i Programmer's Guide to PHP* (MC Press, 2009).

Acknowledgments

I'd like to give a special thanks to Morgan Tocker, who so willingly agreed to lend his amazing wealth of MySQL knowledge to this book. Without him the book most certainly would have suffered.

John Coggeshall

I can remember the day I told my dad I was going to be working remotely for a Swedish database company called MySQL AB. To him, the idea of someone putting money in my bank account each month while I sat at home in Australia sounded like a scam. It turned out to be a big career break.

I would like to acknowledge my former colleagues at the MySQL AB (now Sun Microsystems) Support and Training teams. It was through your patience and willingness to share that I began picking up the pieces to place in this book (with a special thanks to Tobias Asplund, who provided many of the examples I used).

I would also like to thank Percona, my current employer, for continuing to enhance MySQL and adding the demanding performance features that escape Sun Microsystems' eyes. We'd all be at a loss without you.

Morgan Tocker

Introduction

The idea for this book came to me years ago after about a year and a half of working in the Zend Global Services group. Being "on the front lines" of solving the problems of some of the most complex PHP application implementations on the planet, it quickly became clear to me that there was a real need for a text that captures the solutions and techniques we were discovering from one client to the next. Unfortunately when you're in the services business time is scarce, and while I had written the table of contents for the book, that TOC sat gathering dust in my archives until the day I had the time and energy to pursue it.

That opportunity came years later, after I resigned my position at Zend to pursue other challenges. As it turned out, Zend was interested in creating a branded series of books as part of a series through Apress ("Zend Press") and was in search of qualified authors. Suddenly that TOC that had been stagnant for years once again had legs. Of course it took a few revisions to factor in things that have changed over the years, but ultimately I was surprised to find how many of the solutions we had worked with years ago still were not only relevant today but also unknown to many PHP developers.

Of all of the books I have worked on over the years, I have enjoyed writing this one the most. Partly because it's a bit smaller than my previous works (*grin*), but mostly because I really feel like the content has so much value that doesn't get a lot of attention even today. I hope you enjoy the book as much as I enjoyed writing it! As you get started with this book, I strongly recommend that you visit the companion web site (`http://www.zendenterprisephp.com/`), where you will find an errata, the VMware virtual machine that is a complete self-contained environment for the examples and demos found in this book, as well as other resources you may find useful.

Thank you for purchasing my book! Enjoy!

Who This Book Is For

This book is for intermediate PHP developers who work with large, extremely complex code bases and have a significant amount of traffic to deal with. It is also for technical leaders within organizations charged with managing those developers.

How This Book Is Structured

Each chapter in this book for the most part is independent from the next, although they are all structured in such a way that it can be read cover to cover without issue. This makes the book not only a great read start to finish but also a great reference guide to some of the more challenging aspects of PHP application development.

Prerequisites

This book was written against PHP 5.2 and Zend Framework 1.8. That said, the provided VMware image on the book web site (http://www.zendenterprisephp.com/) is a fully functional, self-contained environment to work with the code in this book.

Downloading the Code

The source code for this book is available to readers at www.apress.com in the Downloads section of this book's home page. Please feel free to visit the Apress web site and download all the code there. You can also find the book's source code at http://www.zendenterprisephp.com/ (recommended).

Contacting the Author

E-mail: john@coggeshall.org
Web site: http://www.coggeshall.org/
Book site: http://www.zendenterprisephp.com/
Twitter: @coogle

CHAPTER 1

Introduction to Zend Framework

When developing an enterprise application in any language, tooling is almost as important to you as the way you use the tools. If you look at the success of languages such as Java you see an entire ecosystem of tools to make the lives of the developers, managers, and team as a whole better.

When it comes to tooling, the PHP world is no different. While I'll admit there are decidedly fewer options available to a PHP development team, those options that do exist are impressively robust and easy to use. One such category of tools is frameworks that help ease the pain of development and maintenance of applications for their entire lifetime while promoting best practices. One such framework is Zend Framework (ZF), where we will begin our voyage into the development of enterprise-class PHP applications.

Introduction to Zend Framework Library

Zend Framework, while a relatively new framework to the PHP space, has quickly become the de facto standard of enterprise PHP development. This is due in no small part to Zend Technologies, which has used its considerable resources to research, develop, and actively grow the framework into the powerhouse it is today. Philosophically, Zend Framework is quite different than most other PHP-based frameworks in the sense that your commitment to using the framework is left entirely to you. Where most frameworks force you into a specific coding practice or impose on you a specific way the framework must be used to be effective, Zend Framework is based on the notion that each component can be used completely independently of the rest of the framework. This not only makes each component a more interesting piece of technology on its own but also allows you to cherry-pick those pieces of the framework that solve your development problems without committing to an entire way of development. In fact, Zend Framework can be used piecemeal in existing PHP applications to accomplish development tasks as easily as it can be used to develop incredibly complex applications from the ground up.

Looking at the framework itself, its component nature is reflected in its organizational structure and class-naming conventions. Let's take a look at an abbreviated directory and file listing (showing only the `Zend_Acl` component) for the framework (see Listing 1-1).

Listing 1-1. *The Zend_Acl Component File Structure*

```
|-- Acl
|   |-- Assert
|   |   '-- Interface.php
|   |-- Exception.php
|   |-- Resource
|   |   '-- Interface.php
|   |-- Resource.php
|   |-- Role
|   |   |-- Interface.php
|   |   |-- Registry
|   |   |   '-- Exception.php
|   |   '-- Registry.php
|   '-- Role.php
|   |   |-- Digest.php
|   |   |-- Exception.php
|   |   |-- Http
|   |   |   '-- Resolver
|   |   |       |-- Exception.php
|   |   |       |-- File.php
|   |   |       '-- Interface.php
|   |   |-- Http.php
|   |   |-- InfoCard.php
|   |   |-- Interface.php
|   |   |-- Ldap.php
|   |   '-- OpenId.php
|   |-- Exception.php
|   |-- Result.php
|   '-- Storage
|       |-- Exception.php
|       |-- Interface.php
|       |-- NonPersistent.php
|       '-- Session.php
|-- Acl.php
```

Being an entirely object-oriented framework, Zend Framework classes follow naming conventions that reflect their location in the file system. For example, the primary class for the Zend_Acl component is found in the top-level Acl.php file within the file structure, where the interface that defines the ACL data store object Zend_Acl_Storage_Interface can be found in the Acl/Storage/Interface.php file.

CLASS STRUCTURE VS. CLASS LOCATION IN ZEND FRAMEWORK

The relationship between a class name and its location within Zend Framework directory structure is no accident! Besides being a very logical approach, there is a component within the framework Zend_Loader that can be used to automatically include as necessary classes that follow this convention without any further effort on the part of the developer. So use this convention to your advantage by organizing your libraries of object-oriented code in the same fashion to save time and effort writing complex applications.

Now that we know a little about how Zend Framework is structured, let's talk a little about how Zend Framework is designed to be implemented. In general, there are two approaches to using Zend Framework. The first is to simply use its components within your application—ideal if you already have an existing code base you must integrate with. The second option is to build an application from start to finish using Zend Framework, and to do that you'll need to understand Zend Framework MVC (model-view-controller) subsystem of the framework.

Zend Framework MVC

When building a new application in Zend Framework, the recommended approach is to use Zend Framework MVC subsystem to do so. Structured as a collection of loosely bound components, Zend Framework MVC implements the model-view-controller design pattern. To understand how to use this aspect of Zend Framework, you need to understand this pattern, so let's begin there.

Model, View, and Controller

In recent years the MVC pattern has gained wide acceptance within the web development community as a powerful approach to web application design. However, not many developers realize that the MVC pattern has roots deep within the world of computer science and was created well before the Internet was even conceived. The MVC was introduced in 1979 by Trygve Reenskaug and was implemented in the Smalltalk programming language.

Note Did you know: Besides the origins of the MVC design pattern being an interesting piece of history, this fact has relevance when we discuss the modern version of MVC now used on the Web because while many aspects of this pattern are similar, the modern MVC is actually not the same implementation as the pattern of old due to the differences in web application implementation. In the original MVC pattern there was a direct logical connection between the model object and view object whereby the model could directly notify the view when its data was modified. Since the view in MVC applications on the Web is in the browser (while the model resides on the server), the pattern requires modification to be effective in this space.

The acronym MVC stands for model, view, and controller. These three distinct components of the pattern represent the data model, the rendering of that data model (the view), and the logic that accepts input and contains the logic to manipulate the model and view (the controller). The relationship between these three components is shown in Figure 1-1.

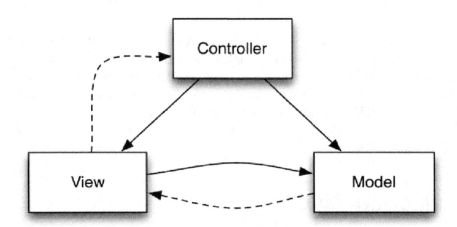

Figure 1-1. *The high-level relationship between a model, view, and controller within an MVC framework*

Before we begin our discussion around the specifics of the MVC pattern, let us take a moment to describe Figure 1-1 in more detail. The diagram has the three components of the MVC framework represented as boxes. An important aspect, however, is the nature of the lines that connect them. These lines represent the relationship (concrete or abstract) between the various components represented by dashed or solid lines, where solid lines represent a concrete reference and dashed lines represent an abstract relationship. These relationships are a cornerstone of the MVC framework and can be expressed in the following terms:

Controllers handle all input and manipulate specific instances of both models and views.

Models represent the data used by the application and know nothing of controllers, although they do have access to an abstract view interface.

Views render data of specific instances of models to the user and have an abstract access to the controller that created them.

So what does it mean to have an abstract access to another component? In practical programming terms for a view, this means in many cases that the view simply knows about one specific interface implemented by the controller and can call those methods alone. Likewise for models, while they have no access to call a controller whatsoever, they do know of an interface implemented by the view that renders it. For example, a model may notify the view if its data has changed as the result of an action by the controller.

What we have described is the MVC design pattern as created by Reenskaug back in 1979. For web applications, such a design pattern doesn't make sense holistically. For starters, in the traditional Web 2.0 application, the view is of course the browser window and not some sort of object that can be easily bound to a model or a controller, simply because its logic (implemented usually in JavaScript) is not the same as the server-side PHP. Furthermore, view logic is almost entirely executed on the client-side machine, which makes it a real problem for a model and controller (implemented on the server side in PHP) to have the sorts of relationships as described in the original pattern.

These facts introduce some interesting complexities to the theoretical design of the MVC pattern for web applications, which is of course reflected in the design of the various so-called MVC implementations available in web development languages today. For instance, in most if not all MVC implementations (including Zend Framework), there is a fourth component to the MVC architecture called the front controller. While labeled a controller by name, the purpose of this critical component is to marshal what fundamentally is a simple HTTP request from the browser into a form that can be mapped into the MVC architecture we introduced in this section. Let's examine the front controller and the various components it harnesses to breathe life into your applications.

The Front Controller and Friends

For a Zend Framework application, the front controller serves as the launch point for a Zend Framework MVC application and abstracts a multitude of complexities away from the end developer. The front controller's responsibility is to accept the input of a web request received from a client and use various related components to identify and execute a specific controller to be executed as represented in Figure 1-2.

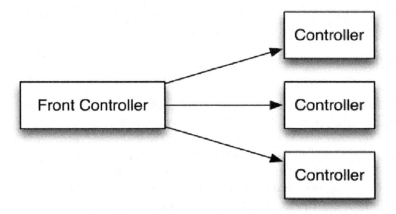

Figure 1-2. *Front controllers create instances and execute logic contained within controllers.*

However, while this is the basic idea behind the purpose of the front controller, there are many subcomponents the front controller utilizes that play a key role in what otherwise seems a relatively simple task. In fact, if you were to draw Figure 1-2 to include all of its elements you would arrive at something that looked closer to Figure 1-3.

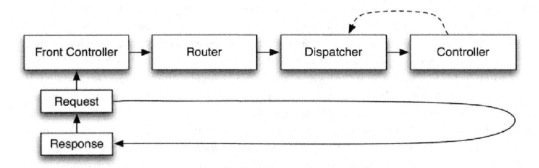

Figure 1-3. *An expanded view of the relationship between the front controller and controller*

In order to understand how these components all work together, let's go through each of them in order, starting with the front controller. As you might imagine, the front controller's responsibility is to initialize the MVC system of the framework (including creating the router and dispatcher) and prepare and pass along the input provided by the standard PHP superglobals into the system as a more structured object (the request object). By definition the front controller is implemented as a singleton (meaning there is only one instance of it ever in an application) and can be referenced from anywhere in the application if necessary. Note, however, while it is always possible to retrieve an instance of the front controller in all but the most complex situations, such an action should not be necessary.

Note We use the term "superglobals" to refer to those arrays that are available in PHP regardless of scope, such as $_SERVER, $_GET, $_POST, $_REQUEST, and $_COOKIE.

Ultimately, the outcome of the execution of the front controller is to create instances of the router and dispatcher and to pass execution control of the request into the router for further processing. Note that, as Figure 1-3 indicates, from this point forward all input and output of the request is contained within the request and response objects, respectively, which are created by the front controller.

Once the router has received the request object from the front controller, its task is to examine the request data as received from the user and determine the proper controller and action to execute. How does this determination happen? Such behavior is entirely definable by the user through the implementation of a custom router component. Since most users will never have a need to write their own custom routers, Zend Framework of course provides a default router that maps a given URL to a controller and action by following the structure shown in Figure 1-4.

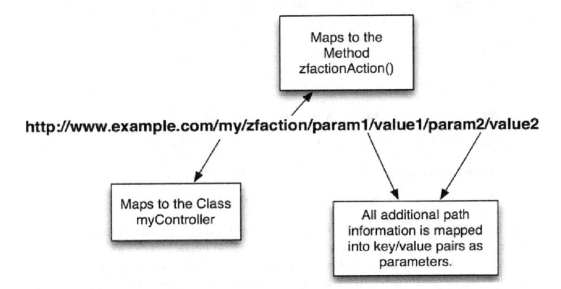

Figure 1-4. *How the default Zend Framework router routes requests to controllers and actions*

■**Note** You might be wondering how the router always gets executed every request. This is a necessary configuration step we haven't discussed in detail, but basically you need to set up a mod_rewrite rule (if you are using the Apache server) to map all URL requests that don't refer to concrete files to index.php—called the bootstrap file. This file is where you will fire up the ZF front controller and start the process we're describing.

Once the router has fulfilled its sole purpose of mapping the request to a controller and action, this information is stored within the request object that is then passed into the dispatcher—our next subject of discussion. If no routing information is provided, the ZF router will automatically default the controller to "index" and the action to "index," making IndexController::indexAction() comparable to an index.php file of a directory.

After the request has started, the front controller has initialized the MVC framework, and the router has properly identified and added the necessary controller and action information into the request, the next step is for the request itself to be dispatched to an action within a controller. This is done by the dispatcher object that, like the router, you can replace with your own class if so desired.

The vast majority of your development efforts will be spent in writing the controllers that are dispatched by the dispatcher object. The job of the dispatcher object is to execute business logic by executing a method within your controller object based on the routing information provided by the router object. Furthermore, depending on the logic of your controllers, multiple actions across multiple controllers can be executed within a single request (called chaining of actions)—also the responsibility of the dispatch object to manage.

For every action that is executed, the dispatcher goes through multiple steps:

1. The controller class is instantiated.

2. The init() method is called (overridden by developer).

3. The preDispatch() method is called (overridden by developer).

4. The requested action is called (implemented by developer).

5. The postDispatch() method is called (overridden by developer).

In the simplest implementation of a controller, only an action within the controller class must be implemented. However, depending on your needs you can also implement the init(), preDispatch(), or postDispatch() methods to execute code on initialization of the controller, before dispatch to the action, or after dispatch to the action.

Note What is the difference between the `init()` and `preDispatch()` methods? It refers to when you chain multiple controllers together. Think of the `init()` method as a replacement for the class constructor—if you have action A that forwards to action B within the same class, `init()` will be called only once before the execution of A while `preDispatch()` will be called before both action A and action B.

So now that we have an understanding of how controllers are executed by the dispatcher, how are they actually implemented? Controllers and the actions within them follow a strict naming convention, which allows them to be executed dynamically by the dispatcher. Assuming you are using the standard Zend Framework router and dispatcher, the following rules define the name of the controller class, file name, and an action within a controller:

Controllers are named in the form of `ExampleController`, where the controller action is "Example." The name is capitalized, followed by a capitalized "Controller" suffix.

Actions are named in the form of `myAction`, where the action name is "my." The action method name is lowercase, followed by a capitalized "Action" suffix.

Referring to Figure 1-4, if the URL of the request was as follows:

```
http://www.example.com/myexample/foo
```

the corresponding controller and method that must be implemented to execute on that URL would be `MyexampleController::fooAction()`.

So where do controllers live in the file system? Well, that is mostly up to you. Later in the chapter we will make recommendations as to where you might want to put them, but the front controller's `addControllerDirectory()` method defines where Zend Framework will look for them.

"Hello World" in Zend Framework

Now that we understand at least at a high level how Zend Framework MVC works, let's dive into some code and write our first ZF-powered application: a simple "Hello, World!" program. In fact we will look at two examples of a Hello World application. The first will be the simplest approach that only implements a controller, and the second a slightly more complex example that uses layouts, views, and controllers. While both are valid ZF applications, the first exists only to show you the bare-bones setup and to illustrate an important architectual point—the only required component of a web-based MVC is the controller from which everything else builds off of.

To create our most basic MVC application in ZF there are a few steps we have to go through:

1. Create a document root and point our web server to it.

2. Create a rewrite rule that redirects every non-static request to our index.php file.

3. Create and set up an instance of the front controller (Zend_Controller_Front).

4. Dispatch the request.

■Tip Typically the basic rewrite rule used for Zend Framework applications is !\.(js|ico|gif|jpg| png|css)$ index.php, which routes all requests for files that don't end in .js, .ico, .gif, and so on to index.php to be handled by Zend Framework. You can put this rule in your Apache httpd.conf file, but most people simply use the .htaccess file. If you elect to use the .htaccess file, make sure you enable overrides by setting AllowOverride All in your httpd.conf file first! From a performance perspective using the httpd.conf is a better choice since the server will check the status of the .htaccess file for every request if it exists, but the .htaccess file is often much more convenient.

Listing 1-2 gives us an idea of how our simple Hello World program is structured.

Listing 1-2. *The Simplest Zend Framework Application*

```
.
|-- application
|    '-- default
|         '-- controllers
|              '-- IndexController.php
'-- public
     '-- .htaccess
     '-- index.php
```

Now that we have that out of the way, let's take a look inside the index.php file for the application and see how we kick off a Zend Framework request. The contents of index.php are shown in Listing 1-3.

Listing 1-3. *A Simple "Hello World" Zend Framework index.php Bootstrap File*

```php
<?php

require_once 'Zend/Controller/Front.php';

// Turn on errors being displayed
ini_set("display_errors", true);

// Set the error reporting level to its highest setting
error_reporting(E_ALL | E_STRICT);

// Grab the instance of the Front Controller
$frontController = Zend_Controller_Front::getInstance();


/*
 * ZF needs to know where to find the controllers for the application so
 * we call this method to set the controller path.
 */
$frontController->addControllerDirectory("./../application/default/controllers",
                                    "default");
/*
 * By default ZF will catch exceptions during execution and route them into
 * an error handler. This changes the default behavior to let them bubble
 * into a fatal error.
 */
$frontController->throwExceptions(true);

/*
 * Now that the environment is set up, dispatch the request into the ZF
 * MVC architecture
 */
$frontController->dispatch();
?>
```

Looking at Listing 1-3 you should be able to follow along fairly easily with the steps I described earlier on building a Zend Framework application. We start the bootstrap by first turning on error reporting. You will find that in all of the code examples in this book we elect to have the maximum error reporting enabled for the purpose of demonstration.

The first real step in our Zend Framework application is to retrieve an instance of the front controller class `Zend_Controller_Front`. Since the front controller is a singleton we don't simply use the `new` operator to create an instance but rather let the class itself retrieve the instance by calling the static `getInstance()` method. Now that we have our instance we can begin to configure it by calling a variety of different methods of the object. For the simplest ZF applications the only required configuration is a call to the `addControllerDirectory()` method, which sets up the path where the dispatcher may find the controllers needed for the application. In our example we take this one small step further and make a call to the `throwExceptions()` method as well. This is an unnecessary step but one we do for purpose of demonstration. Finally, once our front controller is configured we can pass the request into the MVC architecture by calling the `dispatch()` method.

■**Note** By default Zend Framework comes preconfigured not to allow exceptions that may be thrown during the course of the request to bubble up to the main execution frame and to cause a fatal error to occur. If such a thing was allowed it would encourage developers to expose stack traces in production systems and cause a serious potential security concern by exposing application internals to an end user. What happens instead will be discussed shortly. For now be content in knowing that all we have done is force ZF to not stop a fatal error if one was to occur for debugging and demonstration purposes.

Once the call to `dispatch()` has been made, we have officially entered the workflow described in Figure 1-3 and begun the process of routing and dispatching the request to a controller for execution. From this point forward you can now attempt to make a request against any URL and map it to a controller and action. Since we have turned off some error handling for this example if the controller doesn't exist, you'll see an exception that looks something like the following:

```
Fatal error: Uncaught exception 'Zend_Controller_Dispatcher_Exception' with ➡
message 'Invalid controller specified (foo)' in /usr/local/zend/share/ ➡
ZendFramework/library/Zend/Controller/Dispatcher/Standard.php:241 ➡
Stack trace: ➡
#0/usr/local/zend/share/ZendFramework/library/Zend/Controller/ ➡
Front.php(934):Zend_Controller_Dispatcher_Standard->dispatch (Object(Zend_➡
Controller_Request_Http), Object(Zend_Controller_Response_Http)) ➡
#1/mnt/hgfs/EnterprisePHP/HelloWorldBasic/public/index.php(31): ➡
Zend_Controller_Front->dispatch() ➡
#2 {main} thrown in /usr/local/zend/share/ZendFramework/library/Zend/ ➡
Controller/Dispatcher/Standard.php on line 241
```

Since obviously we'd like to avoid this we need to create controllers that can handle our requests. For this, we're going to need to create controller classes in the directory we specified when we set up the front controller in the bootstrap file. For our example this controller is the IndexController and is shown in Listing 1-4.

Listing 1-4. *The Simple "Hello World" IndexController Class*

```php
<?php

require_once 'Zend/Controller/Action.php';

/**
 * The Index Controller
 */
class IndexController extends Zend_Controller_Action
{
    /**
     * The default index action
     */
    public function indexAction()
    {
        // Disable the automatic view renderer enabled by default in a ZF project
        // for the sake of a simplified example
        $this->_helper->viewRenderer->setNoRender(true);

        print "Hello, World!";
    }
}
?>
```

As far as controllers go, the IndexController of Listing 1-4 is about as bare-bones as it can be. Like all controllers, the IndexController extends the base controller class Zend_Controller_Action. Since this is a simple example we don't bother implementing any of the workflow functions such as preDispatch() or postDispatch() and instead only implement a single indexAction() method.

In the indexAction() method we have two lines of code. The first line of code is generally omitted (included here to simplify the example by removing the coupling to a formal view), and the second simply prints "Hello, World!" to the screen. The result should be fairly predictable. When you execute this application without specifying a controller or action, it should print "Hello, World!" to the screen.

Hopefully that seems simple enough, because now we are going to look at a more complex (yet arguably easier to use) example that effectively does the same thing. However, it introduces a few more core Zend Framework tools and concepts: error handling, views/layouts, unit testing, and a more effective bootstrapping mechanism.

Let's start by looking at the structure at the file system level, shown in Listing 1-5.

Listing 1-5. *The Complete Structure of a Zend Framework Application*

```
|-- application
|   |-- Initializer.php
|   |-- bootstrap.php
|   '-- default
|       |-- controllers
|       |   |-- ErrorController.php
|       |   '-- IndexController.php
|       |-- helpers
|       |-- layouts
|       |   '-- main.phtml
|       |-- models
|       '-- views
|           |-- filters
|           |-- helpers
|           '-- scripts
|               |-- error
|               |   '-- error.phtml
|               '-- index
|                   '-- index.phtml
|-- bin
|-- library
|-- public
|   |-- .htaccess
|   |-- images
|   |-- index.php
|   |-- scripts
|   '-- styles
'-- test
    |-- AllTests.php
    '-- application
        '-- default
            '-- controllers
                '-- IndexControllerTest.php
```

Comparing Listing 1-5 with our original Hello World structure in Listing 1-2, we can see that we've certainly added a lot of things. Let's take a look at how our bootstrap system works now in this more complex example.

In our original Hello World application we created and set up our front controller class in the `index.php` file. In our new version we have moved this setup phase into two files, the first defining the `Initializer` class and the second a `bootstrap.php` that loads that class (along with other tasks originally in the old `index.php` file). As a result, we now can replace the code in `index.php` with a single line of code (see Listing 1-6).

Listing 1-6. *The New Hello World* `index.php` *File*

```
require '../application/bootstrap.php';
```

So what is now in our `bootstrap.php` file? Let's take a look at it in Listing 1-7.

Listing 1-7. *The* `bootstrap.php` *File of a Zend Framework Application*

```php
<?php

set_include_path('.' . PATH_SEPARATOR . '../library' .
                         PATH_SEPARATOR . '../application/default/models/' .
                         PATH_SEPARATOR . get_include_path());

require_once 'Initializer.php';
require_once 'Zend/Loader.php';

// Set up autoload.
Zend_Loader::registerAutoload();

// Prepare the front controller.
$frontController = Zend_Controller_Front::getInstance();

// Change to 'production' parameter under production environment
$frontController->registerPlugin(new Initializer('development'));

// Dispatch the request using the front controller.
$frontController->dispatch();
?>
```

As you can see from Listing 1-7 there are many similarities between the bootstrap file and what was originally in the `index.php` of Listing 1-3. There are a few notable differences, however, that warrant discussion. For starters we now add three new paths to our include path—one for the `library/` directory (where you can put your own library files or extensions to Zend Framework) and the other for the models of your application used for data access. We also introduce our first official Zend Framework component, the Zend_Loader component. This component's purpose is to simplify the loading of the various classes used within Zend Framework by automatically loading class files for classes without requiring you to include them manually using a require_once statement. Rather, class files can now be automatically resolved based on their name. For instance, Zend_Controller_Action will automatically be loaded from the Zend/Controller/Action. php file thanks to the Zend_Loader component. This functionality is enabled by calling the Zend_Loader::registerAutoload() method.

Note It is strongly recommended that this class- and file-naming convention be maintained for your own library classes and extensions to Zend Framework! Doing so will allow you to harness tools such as Zend_Loader as easily as Zend Framework does internally. Furthermore, from a performance perspective, it is significantly faster to use the auto-loading facilities of Zend_Loader.

The next new thing in our bootstrap file is registering a front controller plug-in that is used to initialize the application. This is done by calling the Zend_Controller_ Front::registerPlugin() method and passing it an instance of the next class we'll discuss: the Initializer class.

Before we discuss the Initializer class, however, first we must discuss the notion of a front controller plug-in. Just as controllers have a series of workflow steps that can have logic attached to them such as preDispatch() and postDispatch(), the front controller's workflow (shown in Figure 1-3) can have custom logic attached to it at various points through the use of front controller plug-ins. To create a plug-in, all you have to do is create a class that extends the Zend_Controller_Plugin_Abstract class and override the implemented methods to your desires. Following is a listing of the methods you can override from this class and their purpose:

- setRequest()/getRequest(): Sets or returns the request object

- setResponse()/getResponse(): Sets or returns the response object

- routeStartup(): Called before evaluating the request against the application's routes

- routeShutdown(): Called immediately after routing is complete

- dispatchLoopStartup(): Called before the application enters its dispatch loop

- preDispatch(): Called before every dispatch to an action

- postDispatch(): Called after every action dispatch returns

- dispatchLoopShutdown(): Called after the application exists the dispatch loop

This workflow is depicted in Figure 1-5 as an extension of the original flowchart described in Figure 1-3.

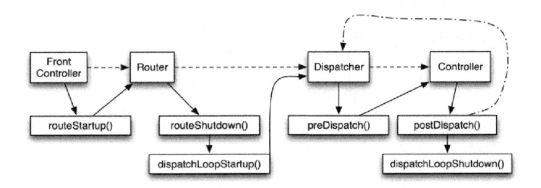

Figure 1-5. *Zend Framework MVC workflow including plug-in calls*

For the purposes of our `Initializer` plug-in we will only override one method from this base class, the `routeStartup()` method, which will be used to initialize the application before we begin the official request. The `Initializer` class is shown in Listing 1-8.

Listing 1-8. *The Initializer Front Controller Plug-in*

```php
<?php

require_once 'Zend/Controller/Plugin/Abstract.php';
require_once 'Zend/Controller/Front.php';
require_once 'Zend/Controller/Request/Abstract.php';
require_once 'Zend/Controller/Action/HelperBroker.php';

/**
 *
 * Initializes configuration depending on the type of environment
 * (test, development, production, etc.)
 *
 * This can be used to configure environment variables, databases,
 * layouts, routers, helpers, and more
 *
 */
```

```php
class Initializer extends Zend_Controller_Plugin_Abstract
{
    /**
     * @var Zend_Config
     */
    protected static $_config;

    /**
     * @var string Current environment
     */
    protected $_env;

    /**
     * @var Zend_Controller_Front
     */
    protected $_front;

    /**
     * @var string Path to application root
     */
    protected $_root;

    /**
     * Constructor
     *
     * Initialize environment, root path, and configuration.
     *
     * @param  string $env
     * @param  string|null $root
     * @return void
     */
    public function __construct($env, $root = null)
    {
        $this->_setEnv($env);
        if (null === $root) {
            $root = realpath(dirname(__FILE__) . '/../');
        }
        $this->_root = $root;

        $this->initPhpConfig();

        $this->_front = Zend_Controller_Front::getInstance();
```

```php
        // set the test environment parameters
        if ($env == 'test') {
            // Enable all errors so we'll know when something goes wrong.
            error_reporting(E_ALL | E_STRICT);
            ini_set('display_startup_errors', 1);
            ini_set('display_errors', 1);
            $this->_front->throwExceptions(true);
        }
    }

    /**
     * Initialize environment
     *
     * @param  string $env
     * @return void
     */
    protected function _setEnv($env)
    {
        $this->_env = $env;
    }


    /**
     * Initialize any PHP Configuration
     *
     * @return void
     */
    public function initPhpConfig()
    {
    }

    /**
     * Route startup
     *
     * @return void
     */
    public function routeStartup(Zend_Controller_Request_Abstract $request)
    {
        $this->initDb();
        $this->initHelpers();
        $this->initView();
```

```php
        $this->initPlugins();
        $this->initRoutes();
        $this->initControllers();
    }

    /**
     * Initialize databases
     *
     * @return void
     */
    public function initDb()
    {

    }

    /**
     * Initialize action helpers
     *
     * @return void
     */
    public function initHelpers()
    {
        // register the default action helpers
        Zend_Controller_Action_HelperBroker::addPath(
        '../application/default/helpers', 'Zend_Controller_Action_Helper');
    }

    /**
     * Initialize view
     *
     * @return void
     */
    public function initView()
    {
        // Bootstrap layouts
        Zend_Layout::startMvc(array(
            'layoutPath' => $this->_root . '/application/default/layouts',
            'layout' => 'main'
        ));

    }
```

```php
    /**
     * Initialize plugins
     *
     * @return void
     */
    public function initPlugins()
    {

    }

    /**
     * Initialize routes
     *
     * @return void
     */
    public function initRoutes()
    {

    }

    /**
     * Initialize Controller paths
     *
     * @return void
     */
    public function initControllers()
    {
        $this->_front->addControllerDirectory($this->_root .
                            '/application/default/controllers', 'default');
    }
}
?>
```

For the purposes of this book, consider the Initializer class shown in Listing 1-8 as a skeleton for a much bigger project to initialize configuration files, database connections, and so on, prior to the start of the routing process (triggered by a call to the Initializer::routeStartup() method). However, there are a few things about it that are worth mentioning. Note that the constructor of this class accomplishes a few key things. First, it establishes the root of the application directory structure (used in various areas of the application). Second, it introduces the notion of different application modes such as a production and development mode, each of which in theory could respond differently than the next. This mode is set when the `Initializer` plug-in is instantiated by passing in a mode string from the bootstrap file.

Since this is a simple Hello World application without database access requirements, configuration files, more plug-ins, or custom routes, we won't discuss what might go into the `initDb()`, `initHelpers()`, `initPlugins()` or `initRoutes()` methods. We will, however, look into the `initView()` method, which sets up the `Zend_Layout` component—a critical piece of the view of the MVC architecture in Zend Framework.

Views in Zend Framework are broken into two distinct components representing a classic two-step view design pattern, with the layout of the view encapsulated by the `Zend_Layout` component and the actual templates that populate the layout encapsulated by the `Zend_View` component.

Note The two-step view design pattern is used in web application development to allow you to separate the layout of a web page (e.g., a two-column or three-column layout) from the actual formatted content of the page. By using a two-step view design pattern, you can make global changes to the layout of your web site without altering the format of the content itself, and you can change the specific content without affecting layout.

While we will not be discussing the details of layouts and views in this book (please consult Zend Framework reference guide for details), let's take a minute to at least understand how they work in this simple application. When using the `Zend_Layout` component in a ZF MVC application, the layout component must be initialized by calling the `Zend_Layout::startMvc()` method and passing into it any necessary configuration values in the form of an associative array. For our particular application, we are setting two configuration values: the path to where we can find the layout templates ("layoutPath")and the specific layout we are interested in rendering ("main"). While we won't be discussing layouts and views in extensive depth in this book, we will come back to the rendering of the content of our application later in this chapter.

With our bootstrapping and application initialization now completed, we are ready to execute a controller and perform some business logic. As with our original Hello World application, we will be implementing an `IndexController` and its corresponding `IndexController::indexAction()` method. This class is shown in Listing 1-9.

Listing 1-9. *The IndexController for Hello World Version 2.0*

```php
<?php

/**
 * IndexController - The default controller class
 */
```

```php
require_once 'Zend/Controller/Action.php';

class IndexController extends Zend_Controller_Action
{
    /**
     * The default action - show the home page
     */
    public function indexAction()
    {

    }
}
?>
```

Examining this version of the `IndexController`, you might notice in comparison to the original controller we implemented in Listing 1-4 that this version of the controller has no business logic at all! This is not in error but rather due to the fact that we are now utilizing the full Zend Framework MVC architecture, and static text such as a simple "Hello World!" message is no longer implemented in business logic but as a part of the view.

In Zend Framework's two-step view approach we use a combination of the `Zend_Layout` and `Zend_View` component to render the output of any given request. Since in a Hello World application we do not have any business logic to implement, our controller is empty, and we implement it in the view. Recall that in the `Initializer::initView()` method we kicked off the `Zend_Layout` with a layout path of `application/default/layouts` and specified the layout "main" as the one we will be using to render our output. This corresponds to the layout in the `application/defaults/layouts/main.phtml` file, shown in Listing 1-10.

Listing 1-10. *The Hello World Layout for Zend_Layout*

```php
<?php
/**
 * Default Main Layout
 */
echo '<?xml version="1.0" encoding="UTF-8" ?>';
echo $this->doctype()
?>

<html>
    <head>
        <meta http-equiv="Content-Type" content="text/html; charset=UTF-8" />
        <?php
        echo $this->headTitle();
```

```
        echo $this->headScript();
        echo $this->headStyle();
        ?>
    </head>

    <body>
        <h1><?php echo $this->placeholder('title') ?></h1>
        <?php echo $this->layout()->content ?>
        <br />
        <br />
    </body>
</html>
```

The layout defined in Listing 1-10 represents the structure of the request response without specifying the actual content or formatting of the content the response contains. Rather, Zend_Layout is designed instead to indicate placeholders for content that can be populated at any time during the execution of the rest of the framework. These content segments are then assembled into a holistic response by the Zend_Layout component before they are returned to the request issuer.

■Note The full functionality of the Zend_Layout and Zend_View components is out of the scope of this book. While we will continue to discuss it in some degree of detail, please consult Zend Framework documentation at http://framework.zend.com/manual/en/ for a more complete reference.

With the foundation layout for Zend_Layout constructed, we have to next look at the role that Zend_View plays in our application (for populating the placeholders in the layout). For this, we need to discuss how views are related to controllers at the file system level.

Referring back to our file system structure for the application in Listing 1-5, notice the application/default/views/ directory. This directory contains all of the view scripts for the application organized into two distinct groups: view filters (our application has none) and action view templates. Action view templates are simply content templates implemented in the template engine provided by the Zend_View component, one for each action implemented inside a controller of the application. Thus, since we have a IndexController::indexAction method (MVC action) we must have an index/ directory (for IndexController) and an index.phtml file (for IndexController::indexAction) within it. This index.phtml file is shown in Listing 1-11.

Listing 1-11. *The IndexController::indexAction() View index/index.phtml*

```php
<?php

/**
 * Default home page view
 */

$this->headTitle('Example Zend Framework Project');
$this->placeholder('title')->set('Welcome');
?>

Hello, world!
```

In Listing 1-11, you can see how it ties itself to the Zend_Layout main.phtml through its use of the headTitle() and placeholder() methods available within a Zend_View template. The headTitle() method is a Zend_Layout placeholder helper that was installed into the Zend_View template engine during the call to Zend_Layout::startMvc() within the Initializer::initView() method call discussed earlier. This method sets the placeholder to the value of "Hello World Zend Framework Project" used in the Zend_Layout main. phtml headTitle() call. Likewise, the call in the Zend_View index.phtml to the placeholder() method maps to the identical method found in the Zend_Layout main.phtml file.

With that explained, let's move on to the non-PHP component of our index.phtml file—our actual "Hello, World!" string. To understand how this string ultimately makes its way into the response, let's revisit the Zend_Layout component and discuss the notion of named segments.

One of the cornerstones of the two-step view design pattern is the notion that the layout script can define blocks (or segments) of content that can be juggled and shifted around the layout of the page at will. For example, one may have a navigation bar that in one layout view is on the left side of the page and in another layout is on the right. In both cases the exact same controller produced that navigational segment (along with its corresponding view). To fulfill this functionality within Zend Framework MVC, Zend_Layout implements the notion of named segments. These named segments can be named whatever you would like, but where are they set?

To answer that question, we have to go back to a detail about Zend Framework MVC that we glossed over: why and how does Zend Framework map IndexController::indexAction() to the index/index.phtml view file? The answer to this question is an important one, as it explains the last missing pieces in our Zend_Layout and Zend_View discussion.

By default, when a controller's action is executed by Zend Framework and returns, Zend Framework ultimately seeks to render the view it associates with it by name as previously demonstrated by the `IndexController::indexAction()/index/index.phtml` controller/view relationship. However, this behavior can be overridden entirely by calling the `Zend_Controller_Action::render()` method from within your controller's actions. This method has two purposes. The first purpose of this mention is to, if you so choose, change the view script rendered for that action from the default (based on the controller and action name) to another template within the same controller. The second behavior, which is much more relevant to our current discussion, is to provide a named segment to which the execution of the controller should be rendered.

Consider Listing 1-12, which uses the `Zend_Controller_Action::render()` method in both ways described.

Listing 1-12. *An Example of Using the Zend_Controller_Action::render() Method*

```php
<?php

/**
 * IndexController - The default controller class
 */

require_once 'Zend/Controller/Action.php';

class IndexController extends Zend_Controller_Action
{
    /**
     * The default action - show the home page
     */
    public function indexAction()
    {
        $this->render('myview');
        $this->render(null, 'indexcontent');
    }
}
?>
```

In the two examples of the `Zend_Controller_Action::render()` method in Listing 1-12, the first call, `$this->render('myview')`, changes the default rendering behavior from rendering `index/index.phtml` to rendering `index/myview.phtml` instead. The second behavior renders based on the default behavior and thus uses `index/index.phtml` as its view. However, that view is rendered into the "indexcontent" segment that must be specified in the layout to be rendered.

For actions that do not specify a segment, Zend Framework automatically appends them in the order they were rendered to the named segment "content." Since our new version of Hello World specifies no rendering segment in Listing 1-9, the content of the render is displayed in the "content" segment of our layout shown in Listing 1-10.

Zend Framework Request/Response Objects and Error Handling

With the detailed explanation of a full Zend Framework MVC execution out of the way, let's now talk about how you write something a bit more complex than a simple Hello World application. To do that, you'll need to understand a bit more about how Zend Framework treats two important subjects: I/O operations and error handling.

In the previous section we discussed in detail the basics of how Zend Framework handles output through the use of the `Zend_Layout` and `Zend_View` components. Recall, however, from Figure 1-3 that all input and output are handled through a set of request and response objects. These objects by default are created by the framework for you and are members of the `Zend_Controller_Request_*` and `Zend_Controller_Response_*` family of objects. We'll be looking briefly at one specific set from this family, the `Zend_Controller_Request_Http` and `Zend_Controller_Response_Http` objects.

Note We describe the request/response objects in Zend Framework as a family because Zend Framework can be used to write more than web applications! Applications that are based on the console have different requirements for I/O than applications written for the Web, and thus any object that extends from `Zend_Controller_Request_Abstract` or `Zend_Controller_Response_Abstract` can be used as request/response objects and set during the initialization of Zend Framework front controller.

As has been mentioned throughout this chapter, the `Zend_Controller_Request_Http` and `Zend_Controller_Response_Http` objects serve to provide context to the application during the web request. As such, you can access these objects from almost any aspect of the MVC framework. In most cases within the framework (such as from controllers) this is as simple as calling the `getRequest()` or `getResponse()` methods available to you. Since we have already discussed output in significant detail, we will be focusing on how input is received into the application through the `Zend_Controller_Request_Http` object.

The intention behind the request object within the framework is to centralize into an object-oriented interface all input the application has received from the outside world. For an HTTP version of this object you can access all GET/POST/COOKIE data you would normally have access to from a PHP script as well as server variables, environment variables, the request URI, base URL, path information, and more. Beyond that, the ZF request object also contains the current controller and action being executed as well as any controller and action parameters that may have been passed along. Since there are far too many functions and helper methods that extend and enhance PHP's abilities to process input, please refer to Zend Framework reference on the request object online at http://framework.zend.com/manual/en/zend.controller.request.html.

Listing 1-13 demonstrates the use of the request object from within the context of the controller to access GET, POST, and the current controller action name.

Listing 1-13. *Retrieving Input Data from a ZF Request Object*

```php
<?php

require_once 'Zend/Controller/Action.php';

class IndexController extends Zend_Controller_Action
{
    /**
     * The default action - show the home page
     */
    public function indexAction()
    {
        // Retrieve the 'myvar' from GET, if it doesn't exist set it to false
        $myGETvar = $this->getRequest()
                            ->getQuery('myvar', false);

        // Retrieve from POST, if it doesn't exist set it to the value 10
        $myPOSTvar = $this->getRequest()
                            ->getPost('myvar', 10);

        // Retrieve the action name, in this case 'index'
        $action = $this->getRequest()
                        ->getActionName();
    }
}
?>
```

Like the request object, which serves the purpose of providing context to Zend Framework application, the response object gathers all relevant output data to be displayed to the user. Returning to one of our first code examples in Listing 1-3, the reason it was important to call the front controller's throwExceptions() method was because, by default, Zend Framework will catch all exceptions that occur in the framework and place them into the response object of the execution instead. That's ideal behavior if you understand the framework but potentially confusing behavior for those being introduced to it. Like the request object, we will skip an in-depth discussion of all of its functionality other than to refer you to Zend Framework reference, which provides a detailed explanation of all of its abilities: http://framework.zend.com/manual/en/zend.controller.response.html.

Speaking of error handling, looking back to our previous section on the Hello World application recall that we demonstrated what would happen in our first example if we attempted to go to a controller or action that did not exist. Doing so caused Zend Framework to throw an exception that bubbled to the top of the execution stack and resulted in a fatal PHP error. Since by default Zend Framework puts exceptions into the response object, how do you handle them? To understand how Zend Framework MVC expects to see and will deal with errors, we need to revisit an untouched aspect of our very first application and discuss the ErrorController.

Zend Framework MVC, unless you have specified otherwise by a call to the front controller throwExceptions() method, will require all of your MVC applications to implement a special controller and action—the ErrorController::errorAction() action/method. In the event of an exception within your application that is caught by the front controller, the front controller will automatically route the request to this action for error handling instead of causing an unsightly PHP error message. Once in this action, it is up to you to handle the error gracefully.

Note It is worth mentioning that Zend Framework, in every situation that it is possible to do so, will use exceptions to indicate an error (rather than a normal PHP error, through a trigger_error() call) that has a base class of Zend_Exception. It is strongly recommended that your Zend Framework applications also rely on exceptions as well instead of traditional PHP error-handling facilities.

Let's take a look at an example ErrorController implementation (controller only) in Listing 1-14.

Listing 1-14. *An Example Zend Framework* ErrorController

```php
<?php

/**
 * ErrorController - The default error controller class
 */
require_once 'Zend/Controller/Action.php';

class ErrorController extends Zend_Controller_Action
{
```

```
    /**
     * This action handles
     *      - Application errors
     *      - Errors in the controller chain arising from missing
     *        controller classes and/or action methods
     */
    public function errorAction()
    {
        $errors = $this->_getParam('error_handler');
        switch ($errors->type) {
            case Zend_Controller_Plugin_ErrorHandler::EXCEPTION_NO_CONTROLLER:
            case Zend_Controller_Plugin_ErrorHandler::EXCEPTION_NO_ACTION:
                // 404 error -- controller or action not found
                $this->getResponse()->setRawHeader('HTTP/1.1 404 Not Found');
                $this->view->title = 'HTTP/1.1 404 Not Found';
                break;
            default:
                // application error; display error page, but don't change
                // status code
                $this->view->title = 'Application Error';
                break;
        }

        $this->view->message = $errors->exception;
    }
}
?>
```

Examining Listing 1-14, you'll notice a call we have previously not discussed specifically in the first line of the action: $this->_getParam('error_handler'). This call is a shorthand call to the request object to retrieve the parameter identified by the key "error_handler" from the request ("error_handler" is the key used by Zend Framework to store the context of the error when it routed it to the ErrorController). This error object is a simple ArrayObject class instance that contains any exception that was thrown, a copy of the original request that caused the error, and the type of the error.

Following Listing 1-14, the first step we take in this example is to determine the nature of the error by checking its type through the type property. This property can be extended to suit your own needs, but within Zend Framework itself there are a total of three possible values for this value defined as constants within the Zend_Controller_Plugin_ErrorHandler class: EXCEPTION_NO_CONTROLLER, EXCEPTION_NO_ACTION, or EXCEPTION_OTHER. These type constants should be self-evident based on their names, the first occurring when the controller class was not found, the second when the controller was found but not the method name within it, and the third for all other exceptions caught by the framework.

Based on these error types you can see in Listing 1-14 how they are used to differentiate between HTTP 404 errors and true exceptions through the use of a simple `switch()` statement.

Conclusion

In this chapter we've discussed a great deal in terms of concepts, starting with the way Zend Framework is organized both in a class and a file structure (including the relationship between them) and everything you will need to know to build an application from scratch using Zend Framework MVC. It will serve you well to remember the relationships between the front controller, dispatcher, router, and controllers when developing your business logic, so do spend the time to learn them correctly. Once you have a solid grasp there, leveraging the ability to create complex responses using components like `Zend_Layout` and `Zend_View` will be paramount in turning that business logic into useful responses when the request is returned.

That's it for our introduction to Zend Framework. We have barely scratched the surface of the framework as a whole, but even so we have laid a great foundation for writing Zend Framework applications. If you are interested in learning more about the details of the framework, the best resource is Zend Framework web site at `http://framework.zend.com` or Beginning Zend Framework by Armando Padilla (Apress, forthcoming).

## CHAPTER 2

Introduction to Zend Studio for Eclipse

Now that we have introduced you in Chapter 1 to the fundamental concepts behind writing a Zend Framework application, let's now look at one tool that will help you significantly in the development of Zend Framework applications—Zend Studio for Eclipse (ZSE).

Zend Studio for Eclipse is the premier IDE (integrated development environment) for development for both Zend Framework and PHP projects. Here are just a few of the features that separate ZSE from your everyday text editor:

- Remote debugging and profiling of PHP applications

- Importing of Web Services Description Language (WSDL)-based web services

- Type hinting for PHP 4, PHP 5, Zend Framework, Java, and JavaScript

- Color-highlighting support for all web application document types

- Integration with the entire suite of Zend Technologies products

- Eclipse-based features, allowing for extensive customization and enhancement through plug-ins

In this section, we will explore ZSE and how to use it to not only become a more effective PHP developer but also a more effective Zend Framework developer.

Getting Started Zend Studio for Eclipse

As the name implies, Zend Studio for Eclipse is based on Eclipse (http://www.eclipse.org), an IBM-backed open source development environment written in Java. Technically, Zend Studio is a collection of Eclipse plug-ins that provides PHP-specific functionality such as syntax highlighting to the base Eclipse tool set. Of the plug-ins, some are a part of an open source project backed by both IBM and Zend known as PHP Development Tools (PDT, see http://www.eclipse.org/pdt/) while some of the more commercially focused features constitute the commercial offerings contained within the ZSE products.

Because of the architecture used by Eclipse and ZSE, one of the biggest advantages is its ability to be extended. Countless extensions and plug-ins exist for Eclipse (both open source and commercial) that can be added directly to ZSE, making it an almost limitless platform for application development. Note that although ZSE can be extensively customized, it is far from useless as a stand-alone IDE, as we will see now. To download Zend Studio, visit the Zend Technologies' web site at http://www.zend.com/studio/.

To get started, let's introduce you to the Eclipse interface, shown in Figure 2-1.

Note Because of differences in versions between ZSE, do not be alarmed if your screen does not look identical to the screenshots displayed in this book, although it should be fairly close.

Figure 2-1. *A typical Zend Studio for Eclipse workspace*

An Eclipse-based development environment has a number of conceptual differences in application development compared to other IDEs. First, while in most IDEs the highest-level collection of an application is a project, in Eclipse you will find that there is one higher: the workspace. Workspaces can contain collections of projects, and, if desired, these projects can be associated to one another through the workspace configuration. This can be very useful organizationally for web developers who often work across multiple different development contexts and languages in the course of delivering one real project. For example, within a single workspace for a rich Internet application you may have at least three projects: a project for the front end of the application based in a technology such as Adobe Flex, a server-side project that is a Zend Framework project, and a third project that contains the DocBook XML for the documentation of the application.

The next thing you will need to get accustomed to when working in an Eclipse environment is the notion of views and perspectives. In Eclipse, a view is simply a windowpane that may or may not be docked into one of the various edges of the Eclipse IDE window. Looking at Figure 2-1, PHP Explorer, Outline, and Problems are all examples of Eclipse IDE views. At any time you can remove, move, or add new views to the screen by simply going to the Window ➤ Show View menu and adding a new view from the available collection (keep in mind that many plug-ins represent themselves as views). Perspectives on the other hand can be thought of as a collection of views that are organized in both size and location to perform a certain task. In Figure 2-1 we are looking at the PHP perspective. Figure 2-2 is identical in every way to Figure 2-1, except we have changed into the PHP Debug perspective.

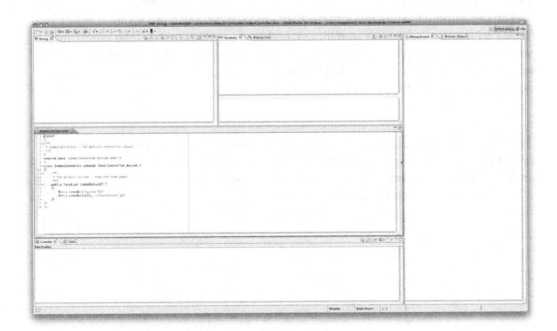

Figure 2-2. *The PHP Debug development perspective in ZSE*

As you can see, the PHP Debug perspective looks considerably different than the PHP perspective shown in Figure 2-1. Not only have the various views been shifted around, but some have been added (such as Debug and Breakpoints views), and some have been removed. To make perspectives even more powerful in Zend Studio, they can also be customized and created. Look in the Window menu for available perspectives to add and change.

Creating Projects in Zend Studio for Eclipse

Now that we have some of the fundamentals in our minds, let's create our first PHP project in Zend Studio for Eclipse. Zend Studio supports creating numerous different types of projects, but for our purposes we'll be creating a Zend Framework project. To do this, click File ➤ New ➤ Zend Framework Project, which will bring up the New Zend Framework project dialog shown in Figure 2-3.

When creating a new Zend Framework dialog project, you will have a number of choices to make such as Zend Framework version to use, whether to include Dojo support, and the PHP version you will use. In the following steps of the wizard you will also have the ability to add additional libraries (Zend Framework is included by default) and to choose the version of Java you will use (if using the Zend Java Bridge). For our needs, simply click Finish to create the project once you have given it a name.

You can explore the project from the PHP Finder view, and chances are you will find it feels very familiar—at least it should, as it is almost identical to the Hello World application we walked through in the last chapter! As we have already explored that aspect earlier in the chapter, let's instead build a simple new application to test the debugging and profiling aspects of Zend Studio for Eclipse.

Tip When writing applications in Zend Studio for Eclipse, it pays to use comments! By using phpDocumentor-style comments for classes and functions, ZSE will automatically parse them as you code and provide type hinting for your own application APIs. For more information on phpDocumentor-style comments, see the phpDocumentor web site at `http://www.phpdoc.org/`.

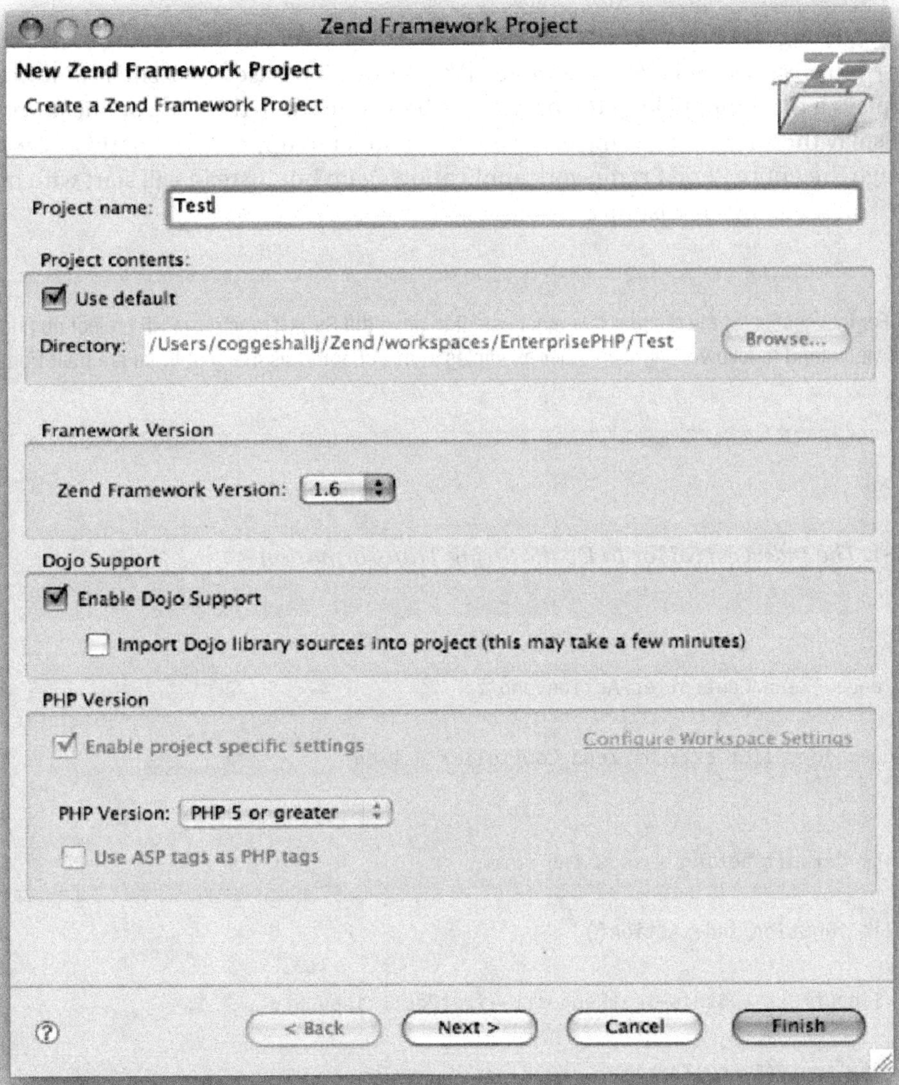

Figure 2-3. *The New Zend Framework Project dialog*

Debugging in Zend Studio for Eclipse

To test the debugging functionality of ZSE, first we need to create something to debug. For these purposes we will create a simple MVC application based on Zend Framework that displays a text input field in the browser. When submitted, the MVC application will redisplay the string converting every other character to uppercase. For this we won't go through the entire Zend Framework application again but instead will start with our IndexController shown in Listing 2-1.

■**Note** For this section of the chapter it is most useful to have the StringTransform PHP project up and running if you intend to follow along with other examples in this chapter, as many of them are built from this base.

Listing 2-1. *The IndexController to Do the String Transformation*

```php
<?php

require_once 'Zend/Controller/Action.php';

class IndexController extends Zend_Controller_Action
{
    /**
     * The default action. - show the form
     */
    public function indexAction()
    {
        $inputText = $this->getRequest()->getPost('inputStr', "");

        if(!empty($inputText))
        {
            $this->view->inputText = $inputText;
            $this->render('transform', 'transformedText');
        }

        $this->render('index', 'form');
    }
}
```

As you can see, for this application our `IndexController` accepts a `POST` parameter `inputStr` that contains the string to transform. If such a string is provided, we pass it along to the `inputText` view variable and render the `transform.phtml` template into the `transformedText` layout segment. Regardless of whether there was input data or not, we always render the `index.phtml` template into the `form` layout segment to be displayed.

The actual transform of our text is implemented as a view template, specifically `index/transform.phtml` shown in Listing 2-2.

Listing 2-2. *The* `transform.phtml` *Template*

```php
<?php
    if($this->inputText)
    {
        $upperCase = false;
        $len = strlen($this->inputText);
        for($i = 0; $i < $len; $i++)
        {
            print ($upperCase) ? strtoupper($this->inputText{$i}) :
                                 strtolower($this->inputText{$i});
            $upperCase = !$upperCase;
        }
    }
?>
```

Finally there is the `index.phtml` file that displays the form, shown in Listing 2-3.

Listing 2-3. *The* `index.phtml` *Template*

```php
<?php

$this->headTitle('String Transformation');
?>
Type in a string:
<form method="post" action="<?php print $this->escape($_SERVER['PHP_SELF']);?>">
<input type="text" name="inputStr" size="40"/>
<input type="submit" value="Transform!"/>
</form>
```

When this application is run from a browser, you should see something that looks like Figure 2-4.

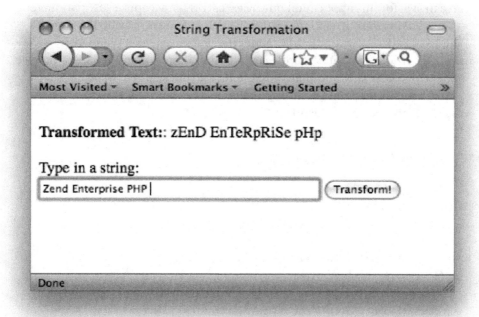

Figure 2-4. *The running StringTransform application*

To demonstrate the debugging capabilities of Zend Studio, let's introduce a small bug into Listing 2-2 by reversing the qualifying condition of the for() statement from less than to greater than by changing this line:

```
for($i = 0; $i < $len; $i++)
```

to

```
for($i = 0; $i > $len; $i++)
```

This subtle change to the logic will prevent the transformation from working without causing any obvious error messages.

Now that we have introduced a bug into our application, let's set up our project to be debugged. To do this the following tasks must be completed:

1. Set up the Zend Debugger extension on the server.

2. Set up the access control of the debugger to allow connections.

3. Configure a debugger within the IDE.

4. Configure a Debugging Profile for the project.

This book assumes that you are using one of the following products from Zend Technologies, which will provide the Zend Debugger functionality required:

- Zend Core

- Zend Platform

- Zend Server

Note Using the provided virtual machine, you already have the debugger available as part of the Zend Core package. If you already have a PHP server set up, you can download the Zend Debugger PHP extension from the Zend Technologies web site: `http://www.zend.com/products/studio/downloads`. This book will only discuss setting up debugging on Zend Core. For other possible configurations please consult the Zend Debugger documentation.

Once the Zend Debugger is installed in your PHP server, you will need to set up the server to allow your local machine to connect to it. For Zend Core, this is done from the configuration interface available at the following URL: `https://<serveraddress>/ZendCore`, which will present you with the Zend Core login page shown in Figure 2-5.

If you are using the virtual machine provided with this book, you can log in to the Zend Core interface by using the password "zend"; otherwise you should use whatever password you set up or enter a new password if it is a new installation.

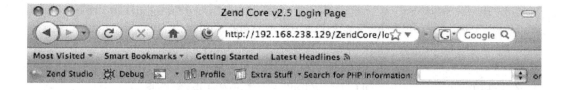

Figure 2-5. *The Zend Core login page*

Once logged into Zend Core, go to the Configuration tab and click the Zend Debugger link, which will bring you to the Zend Studio Server Settings page shown in Figure 2-6.

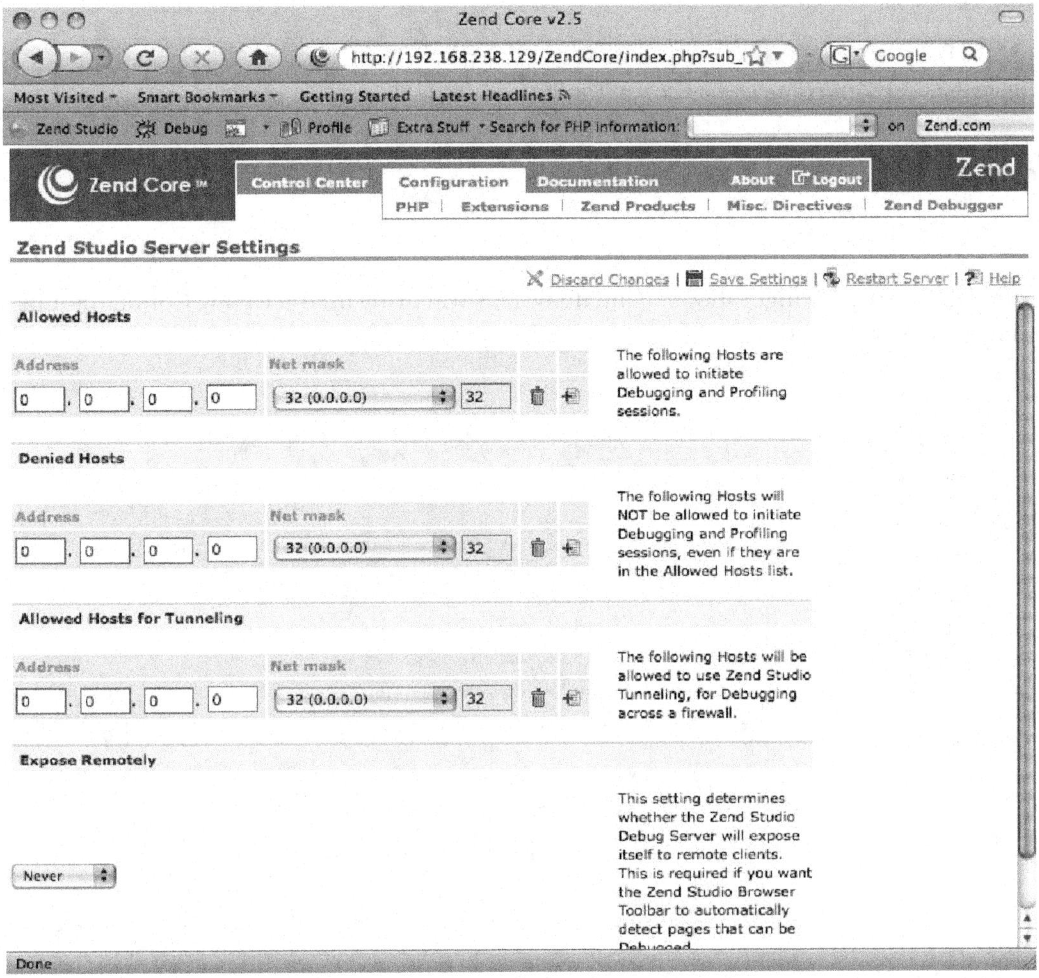

Figure 2-6. *Zend Studio Server Settings in Zend Core*

If you are using the virtual machine provided with this book, the server should be automatically configured to allow a debugging connection from any IP address within the 192.*.*.* subnet. If this configuration is unacceptable to you, you can add a new IP address in a variety of ranges using this interface or remove any IP address currently enabled. Once you have altered this configuration, the server will inform you that you must restart the server for the changes to take effect. To do this, click the Restart Server button at the bottom of the page.

With the debugger itself set up, now it is time to set up debugging for our String-Transform project. To do this, we will need to configure a PHP debugging server and a debugging profile that uses it within Zend Studio for Eclipse. To do this, find the Zend Studio toolbar shown in Figure 2-7.

Figure 2-7. *The Zend Studio for Eclipse Toolbar*

Click the submenu under the debugging icon.

Select the Debug Configurations menu item. This will bring up the Debug Configurations window shown in Figure 2-8.

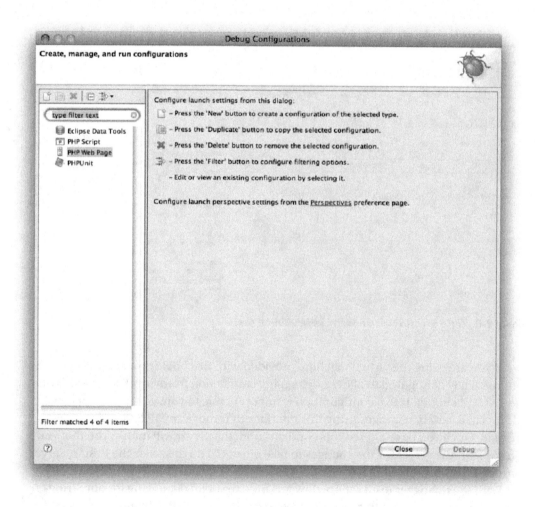

Figure 2-8. *The Zend Studio for Eclipse Debug Configurations window*

The window shown in Figure 2-8 is used to set up the various ways a given project can be run. To set up our StringTransform project to be debugged from the server, we will need to create a new PHP Web Page profile by right-clicking on it from the menu on the left and selecting New, which will bring you to a new window shown in Figure 2-9.

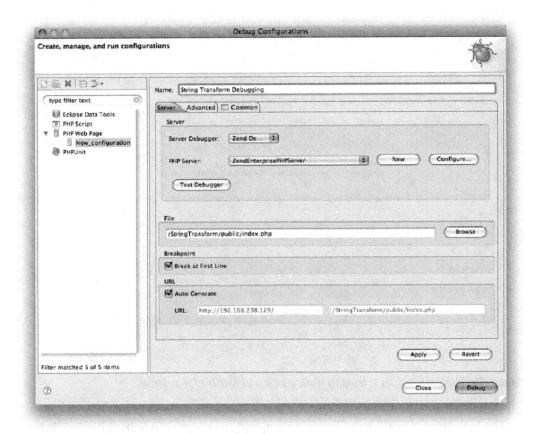

Figure 2-9. *Setting up a new PHP Web Page configuration*

Setting up a new PHP Web Page configuration involves giving it a useful name (in this case, "String Transform Debugging"), specifying the file within a project you want this execution profile to be connected to (in this case it is our public/index.php file within the StringTransform project), if necessary specifying the URL for the request, and setting up a new PHP Server. To set up a new PHP server, click the button labeled New, which will bring up the PHP Server Creation dialog shown in Figure 2-10.

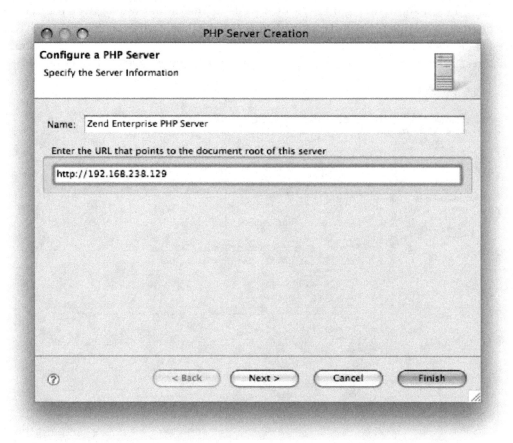

Figure 2-10. *The PHP Server Creation dialog in Zend Studio for Eclipse*

The PHP Server Creation dialog is a critical part to setting up a debugging profile for Zend Studio, as it allows you to do three things:

- Specify the end point URL of the web server you are debugging

- Map web-server file paths for PHP scripts to their corresponding local file system paths

- Set up integration with Zend Platform (if being used)

From the dialog shown in Figure 2-10, enter a unique name for the PHP Server (such as "Zend Enterprise PHP Server") and click Next. This will bring you to the Edit Server dialog, Path Mapping tab. This list maps file system paths for files on the web server to file system paths located in your local file system. For the purposes of the StringTransform project running on the virtual machine, we need to set up two path maps. The first is for Zend Framework, which maps /usr/local/zend/share/ZendFramework/library to <path to your workspaces>/EnterprisePHP/ZendFramework. The second is mapping the path of the StringTransform project on the web server to the local copy. Both of these maps (using the virtual machine as the server) are shown in Figure 2-11.

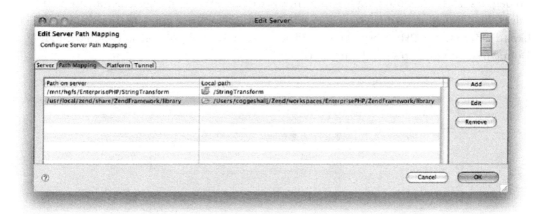

Figure 2-11. *Server path mapping for the StringTransform project*

With the server paths mapped we can now move forward and test our debugging connection by clicking the Test Debugger button with your new PHP server selected, shown in Figure 2-9. If all goes well, Zend Studio will be able to successfully communicate with the server, and you can move on to debugging your application.

■**Tip** If you have problems getting the debugging server to connect, please re-step through these instructions and test it against the virtual machine provided with this book first. If you are still having trouble please contact Zend Technologies for support or visit the Zend Enterprise PHP web site at http://www.zendenterprisephp.com/ for more assistance.

Recalling the bug we introduced into Listing 2-2 of our StringTransform project, we can now attempt to debug this through two different methods:

• Debug the entire execution of the application

• Set a breakpoint at one specific place in the application

Typically for a Zend Framework project attempting to debug the application from start to finish is a lengthy and inefficient task as there are countless lines of code that are executed in the bowels of the framework you likely have no interest in reviewing. It is, however, a good place to introduce the Zend Studio for Eclipse PHP Debug perspective. To begin, select the debugging menu from the toolbar shown in Figure 2-7 again, and select the debugging profile you just created. Doing so will ask you whether you would like to switch to the PHP Debug perspective (select Yes). This will bring you to the PHP Debug perspective shown in Figure 2-12.

Figure 2-12. *The Zend Studio for Eclipse PHP Debug perspective*

There are a few things to note about this perspective. First, you should now be executing the StringTransform project as is indicated by the Debug view in the upper-right-hand corner of the perspective. The line of code you are on (which has not yet executed) is shown in the code view directly below the Debug view. To the right of the Debug view you have a listing of all of the current variables that are in scope as well as a view that shows you all of the current breakpoints you have set.

For our purposes, we will be focusing on the toolbar just to the right of the Debug view shown in Figure 2-13. This toolbar allows us to navigate through the execution of the code base line by line if desired, inspecting the values of variables and the behavior of the application every step of the way.

Figure 2-13. *The debugging toolbar*

Going from left to right in Figure 2-13, the purpose of each icon is as follows:

- *Remove All Terminated Launches*: Removes launched from previous debug sessions

- *Resume*: Resume normal script execution (until next breakpoint)

- *Suspend*: Pause script execution

- *Terminate*: Stop script execution

- *Disconnect*: Disconnect from the debugging server

- *Step Into*: Step into the next statement code branch

- *Step Over*: Step over the next statement code branch

- *Step Return*: Step out of the current code branch

- *Drop To Frame*: Drop to frame

- *Use Step Filters*: Toggle the use of step filters

For most debugging operations you will only be interested in resuming and stopping the application and using the step functions to traverse your script's execution line by line.

To begin debugging the StringTransform application from the first line (the require statement), click the Step Into button. This will cause you to execute the require statement and dive into the next line of code that would be executed, and this can be done until every single line of code is executed. Since this can be a very time-consuming process, you can use the Step Over button to execute all of the code below the next statement (meaning the next function and all of the code the next function executes) until the function returns. The third option, the Step Out button, will allow you to return to the higher-level code branch once you have stepped into it. Once you have played with the stepping features of Zend Studio enough to be comfortable with them, click the Terminate button and return to the normal PHP development perspective by going to Window ➤ Open Perspective ➤ PHP.

For a Zend Framework application, while you could step through each line of framework code, this is tedious at best. The more useful approach is to use breakpoints. Breakpoints are mechanisms by which you can flag one or more lines of code within your application that, prior to being executed, will suspend the execution of the application and allow you to review the variable values and step through the code from that point forward.

That said, let's open up our StringTransform project and debug it. In this case we know exactly where the bug is, so for the sake of demonstration let's open the `application/default/views/scripts/index/transform.phtml` view file. From here, right-click on the line number 2 of the code view to bring up a menu and select Toggle Breakpoints. This action should cause you to set a breakpoint on line 2 of the script as indicated by a small blue circle next to the line number. From here, restart the debugging of the project, and instead of stepping through each line of code simply click the Resume button of the debugging toolbar. This will cause the script to execute normally until it reaches the breakpoint. Once it has reached the breakpoint, Zend Studio for Eclipse will load the relevant file and pause the execution prior to executing the breakpoint.

Tip Instead of right-clicking on the line number, a simple double-click of the line number will turn a breakpoint on or off for that line as well.

The first time you run the StringTransform with the breakpoint set in the `transform.phtml` script, you will notice something peculiar—the debugger didn't pause the execution! This was to be expected, because the first time you execute the application the code within the `transform.phtml` file never gets executed. For this code to execute we will need to provide it with input data. Thankfully, Zend Studio for Eclipse supports this situation by rendering the output of the debug execution into an integrated browser. This browser view (shown in Figure 2-14) is configured to trigger another debugging session for any request it generates. Thus, to actually hit our breakpoint we will need to enter some text into the form, submit it, and then click Resume again to land at our breakpoint shown in Figure 2-15.

Now that we have hit our breakpoint, we can debug, view variable values, and determine where the bug in our application is.

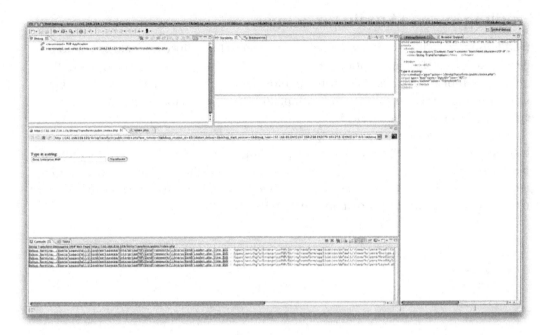

Figure 2-14. *The PHP Debug Perspective with the integrated debugging browser*

Figure 2-15. *Hitting the breakpoint on the second request*

Profiling in Zend Studio for Eclipse

In addition to profiling of an application, Zend Studio for Eclipse also allows you to profile the execution of an application and determine how long the various aspects of the application took to execute. This profiling information is critical in determining where best to optimize a slow-running application, and Zend Studio for Eclipse makes it very easy to get this information quickly.

Using the same StringTransform project (make sure you correct the bug we introduced in the last section!) we will now use profiling to determine how long the request took and determine where all that time was spent. To get started, switch to the profiler perspective by clicking Window ➤ Open Perspective ➤ PHP Profile, which will bring you to the profiling perspective shown in Figure 2-16.

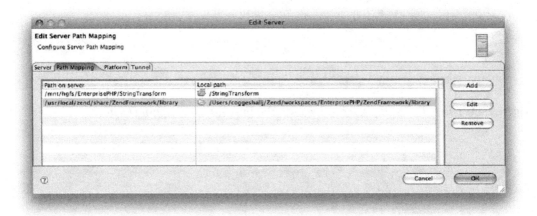

Figure 2-16. *The Zend Studio for Eclipse PHP Profile perspective*

Unlike debugging, there isn't much to do while profiling a request other than simply doing it. Since we already set everything up when we were debugging our application, you can simply click the Profile button.

Select the same profile you set up for debugging. This will perform a request and profile it, resulting in a very informative report shown in Figure 2-17.

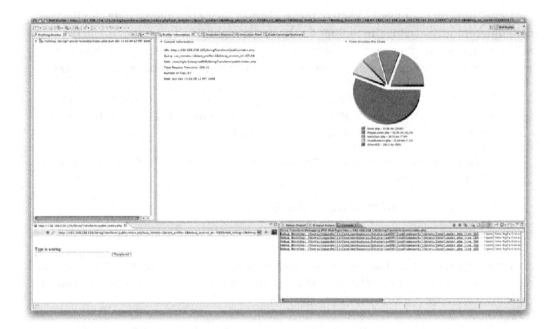

Figure 2-17. *A profiling report produced by Zend Studio for Eclipse*

Once a profiling report has been created, you have a wealth of information on the execution of your application. For starters, you are given a nice pie chart that gives you a high-level view of how the total execution time of the script was broken down into various aspects of your application. While this chart tends to be different for every server, in our example you can see that short of the generic "other" category "Front.php" (Zend Framework front controller class) represented 19.4% of our total execution time for the request.

This is by far not all the profile report can tell you. Notice that there are three additional tabs of information, each providing more details into the performance details of your application:

- *Execution Statistics*: A breakdown of the execution times, organized by file, class, and method

- *Execution Flow*: A breakdown of the execution times, organized by the order in which they were executed in the application as a tree

- *Code Coverage Summary*: A list of all of the PHP files executed, and which lines of code where actually executed from each of those files

Depending on your needs, each of these views of the performance data can be useful in different ways. Using the toolbar on the upper-right-hand corner of the PHP Profile perspective, you can filter each of these views on "own time," "calls," "total time," and "average time." Following is a description of each of these data points and the others:

- *Own Time*: The amount of time it took to execute this segment of the application, not counting the amount of time spent executing low-level PHP internals (which can't be changed without a custom PHP binary)

- *Calls*: The number of times the specified function was executed during the course of the entire request

- *Total Time*: The total amount of time the segment took

- *Others Time*: The total amount of time the segment took waiting on other files

Filtering the execution statistics for the application is an invaluable tool in determining where your bottleneck exists in the request and correcting it. Following are a few tips to produce effective performance optimization:

- There is only ever one bottleneck in a request that is keeping it from performing better. Of course, once you fix that bottleneck another will take its place.

- Understand your performance requirements before you begin the project and test your performance frequently to ensure that you meet your performance goals.

- Remember that it isn't always PHP that makes the application slow! Network latency, I/O latency, or memory limitations also can have a drastic impact.

- Amdahl's Law says that improving code execution time by 50 percent when the code only executes 2 percent of the time will result in a 1 percent overall improvement. On the other hand, improving execution time by 10 percent when the code executes 80 percent of the time will result in an 8 percent overall improvement. Keep an eye on the Calls figure!

Note These and many more performance-related discussions on PHP can be found later in the book or in the various talks I (John) have given at conferences worldwide published on my web site: http://www.coggeshall.org/resources/.

Conclusion

In this chapter you have been introduced to a lot of great tools available to you as a PHP developer to make your applications easier to develop, less bug prone, and more efficient. While many seasoned developers tend to choose development tools that they are accustomed to such as vim, if you have yet to make a choice I strongly recommend that you start in the Zend Studio environment. By taking advantage of the way Zend Studio sets up Zend Framework projects and using the tools such as the debugger and profiler introduced in this chapter you will be well on your way to fast, efficient development that will benefit you for projects and projects to come.

With that we've completed our introduction to Zend Studio for Eclipse. With the basics of both Zend Framework and Zend Studio out of the way, we are now ready to dive into the real good stuff—performance, databases, and production server farms to name a few. If you'd like to learn more about Zend Studio for Eclipse, I suggest both the Zend Studio for Eclipse User manual (see the Help menu) or the book *Zend Studio for Eclipse Developer's Guide* by Peter MacIntyre and Ian Morse (Sams, 2008).

CHAPTER 3

Web Application Performance and Analysis

In this chapter and the ones to follow we will discuss the various techniques you can use to improve the performance and responsiveness of your web-based applications. You will see that each technique has a set of pros and cons and that nearly all of them add at least some complexities to your application.

Before we discuss these strategies, let's first discuss what performance means to a web application. Unlike a traditional application running on a single machine, a web-based application (especially a browser application) has many different variables that will affect the overall performance of the application. This is because, to the end user using your application, the performance of your application isn't measured just by how fast your PHP script executes, as Figure 3-1 illustrates.

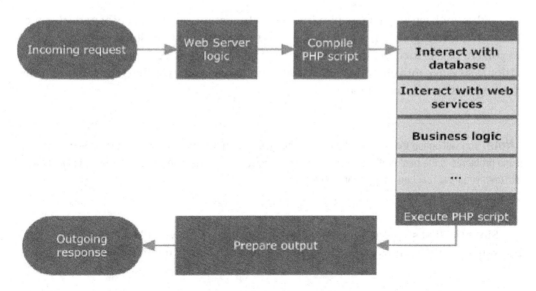

Figure 3-1. *A high-level view of a typical PHP web request life cycle*

As shown in Figure 3-1, there is a lot more to the performance of your web application than just how quickly your PHP script executes. For every step, from when the request comes in to when the response is returned, there are performance-enhancement techniques, many of which we will discuss in the course of this book.

While many performance discussions rightly center on the idea of statistics and figures showing decreased execution times and faster queries, it is often forgotten that to the end user none of these measurements are in any way relevant. To the end user, the only performance metric that ever matters is how quickly the page they requested loads, and how quickly they can do whatever they want to do. This is what Figure 3-1 is designed to introduce you to—the notion that it is the *entire* time between the incoming request and the outgoing response that makes up a significant portion of the user experience, not just how fast your PHP script itself does or does not execute.

Note We say a "significant portion of the user experience" intentionally, as Figure 3-1 only represents the dynamic aspect of the web request through PHP. Once PHP is finished, typically its output is an HTML document that very likely contains references to other resources such as JavaScript code, images, and CSS that must also be loaded if we are using user experience as the ruler by which to measure performance. Don't discount these additional steps either, as they are important in high-traffic web sites as we will see later in the book. Tools such as Firebug (http://getfirebug.com/) and YSlow (http://developer.yahoo.com/yslow/) can go a long way to providing visibility into the entire transaction of a web request and help you identify where things can be improved.

In this book we will in large part frame our discussion of the aspects of performance as they relate to Figure 3-1, and we will start by asking the million-dollar question: how do you effectively increase the performance of an application? As it turns out, the process of doing so is deceptively simple: identify the bottleneck, address the bottleneck, identify the next bottleneck, and repeat.

Note You will notice that we intentionally use "bottleneck" in the singular. Using a top-down approach to fixing problems is the best methodology to use. This process can be repeated as you continue to "find and fix" until you have reached your performance goals.

Since the first step is to identify where the bottleneck is, we will start our discussion by examining the various ways to identify where a bottleneck might be lurking.

Locating the Bottleneck

We'll admit—locating the bottleneck in a web application is not necessarily that easy. Even with the most modern tool set there is a certain amount of experience and intuition that comes into play that allow someone to quickly identify the bottleneck in an environment. However, as we've experienced time and time again in our own lives, understanding what tools are available and how they work can go a very long way to developing effective diagnostic conclusions. We'll look at a few of the most common tools and discuss how they work.

How Are You Bound?

At the end of the day all optimization techniques basically boil down to three high-level categories of computational performance that reveal where the bottleneck lies. The first is CPU-bound, meaning that your server doesn't have enough processor power to do the tasks asked of it. The second is memory-bound, meaning that the server doesn't have enough memory to accomplish the tasks. The third is input/output (I/O)-bound, meaning that the rate of data transfer from one point to the other over a variety of media (to and from disk, to and from a network destination, and so on) is not sufficient for the task at hand. Knowing which of these three categories your performance problem falls into is the first step in determining where the bottleneck of your application is.

On most web server platforms (UNIX-based), the most consistent way to determine your bounding influence is to measure it using tools such as vmstat and iostat. These system-level commands allow you to monitor the status of your server's various bounding influences, which can be invaluable when displayed over time before, during, and after a performance event (such as a web stress test).

Using vmstat

Typically when using this approach you would start with vmstat, as it is the more general-purpose of the two tools, and only come back to iostat if you find that vmstat indicates that you need to examine I/O in more detail. The following usage should work in most Linux-based implementations of vmstat:

```
# vmstat  [delay [ count]]
# vmstat  1 86400 > vmstat.log &
```

This command, executed from a shell, will begin the vmstat process and begin recording data in one-second intervals to the log file vmstat.log. The second argument indicates that the recording will be performed for 86,400 intervals (one day). We could have also left this argument blank to record indefinitely.

By running this command on a server that is either immediately experiencing a suitable amount of load to cause a performance issue (or will predictably experience one during the time we are recording data) you can quickly ascertain which of the major bounding factors your performance issue belongs to.

Listing 3-1 provides an example output from a typical vmstat call as shown previously.

Listing 3-1. *Typical Output from a vmstat Execution*

```
procs -----------memory---------- ---swap-- -----io---- -system-- ----cpu----
 r  b   swpd   free   buff  cache   si   so    bi    bo   in   cs us sy id wa
 2  0  32712  10444   5152  9245?    0    1    60    77   47  105  1  0 99  0
 0  0  32712  10436   5152  92452    0    0     0     0   40   90  0  0 100  0
 0  0  32712  10436   5152  92452    0    0     0     0   41   88  0  0 100  0
 0  0  32712  10436   5152  92452    0    0     0     0   41   84  0  0 100  0
 0  0  32712  10436   5152  92452    0    0     0     0   43  104  0  0 100  0
 0  0  32712  10436   5152  92452    0    0     0     0   42   84  0  0 100  0
```

■**Note** Don't be alarmed if you are seeing different columns being output when you run vmstat. While many UNIX-like operating systems now implement vmstat, the options available, and resulting output, will differ between each. One key reason for this is that you are getting closer to the "bare metal" in how memory management works inside the kernel. For example, the point at which one operating system decides to start swapping memory might not be the same as that point on another server. On the same note, the metrics used to calculate how CPU wait time is determined are also going to differ (or might not even be available). It is best to consult the man page for vmstat for more detail regarding your particular flavor of operating system.

As you can see, the output of the vmstat utility is a table of data where every line represents the activity that occurred within a one-second interval (assuming you used the same parameters we used in the previous example). Since the idea here is that you would run this command throughout a performance event, it is quite possible that the amount of data you capture can get into the thousands of lines—much too much for a person to read and make much sense out of. Instead, we have always found it most useful to take this data and parse it out into a comma-separated file and load it into a spreadsheet program to graph the data visually. We'll show you how that is done in a moment, but for now we'd like to point out something that is missing from the outline in Listing 3-1—a timestamp indicating when each sample of data was collected. This is an important thing to know for a number of reasons:

- It's very difficult to accurately correlate `vmstat` data across multiple machines without a timestamp for each sample.

- Under extremely high loads it's possible that the `vmstat` poll for data may not execute every second as instructed to make room for higher-priority needs in the system. Without a timestamp per poll, it's impossible to tell whether this happens.

Unfortunately there isn't any version of `vmstat` we are aware of that will display the timestamp along with the polling data, so instead we will have to do it ourselves using a little shell-scripting magic. Assuming you are using `/bin/bash` or `/bin/sh` as your shell, we'll start by creating a simple shell script `add_timestamp.sh` as shown in Listing 3-2.

Listing 3-2. *The add_timestamp.sh Script*

```
 #!/bin/sh
while read line
do
     printf "$line"
     date '+ %m-%d-%Y %H:%M:%S'
done
```

Once you've made it executable (by typing **chmod +x add_timestamp.sh**) you can then pipe the output of `vmstat` into the `add_timestamp.sh` script to add the necessary time-stamps before writing it to a log file as shown in the following command:

```
# vmstat -n 1 100000 | ./add_timestamp.sh>vmstat.log
```

That command will append to each line of output from `vmstat` the date and timestamp, as shown in Listing 3-3.

Listing 3-3. *Partial Output of the vmstat Call with the add_timestamp.sh Shell Script*

```
... mory---------- ---swap-- -----io---- -system-- ----cpu---- 12-22-2008 13:57:25
... buff  cache   si   so    bi    bo    in   cs us sy id wa 12-22-2008 13:57:25
... 5364  91308    0    1    58    75    47  105  1  0 99  0 12-22-2008 13:57:25
... 5364  91308    0    0     0     0    55  123  0  1 99  0 12-22-2008 13:57:26
```

Finally we would like this data to be in some sort of comma-separated format so we can import it into a spreadsheet application. For this, we use a little more shell magic by adding the `tr` command to the mix:

```
# vmstat -n 1 5 | ./add_timestamp.sh | tr -s " " ',' >vmstat.log
```

This finally makes our log file something we can directly import into Excel, shown in Listing 3-4.

Listing 3-4. *The Final Version of Our vmstat Output (truncated)*

```
... --memory--------,---swap--,-----io----,-system--,----cpu----,12-22-2008,04:11:11
... uff,cache,si,so,bi,bo,in,cs,us,sy,id,wa,12-22-2008,04:11:11
... ,5428,89764,0,1,57,73,47,104,1,0,99,0,12-22-2008,04:11:11
... ,5428,89764,0,0,0,0,51,128,0,1,99,0,12-22-2008,04:11:12
```

■**Note** You'll likely want to give the various column headings a better label once the data has been loaded into Excel.

Now that we have the data in some sort of useful format, let's talk a little bit about how the data should be interpreted to determine our bounding influence.

Determining Whether You Are CPU-Bound

In terms of performance tuning, the ideal situation for a few reasons is that our bounding influence is the CPU. First, it is a problem that can be solved by simply increasing the processor capacity of the server, and second, it indicates that direct performance improvements to our PHP scripts will increase the overall capacity of the server. To determine whether the server is CPU-bound, you will want to look at five columns from a given line of vmstat output: r, us, sy, id, and wa. These figures are defined in the order presented:

- *Run-queue*: A rotating queue of processes being executed by the CPU, or more specifically, the number of processes currently waiting for CPU time.

- *User*: User time is "good" time, meaning that it is the percentage of time the server is spending executing user-space code such as a PHP script.

- *System*: System time is the percentage of time the server is spending executing tasks within the kernel. As some of your code may in turn make system calls, you may see this rise slightly when user time rises. This figure also includes pulling cached data from RAM, which means it has an aspect to it that pertains to I/O operations.

- *Idle*: The percentage of CPU resources that aren't doing anything at all. This percentage can be considered your breathing room.

- *Wait I/O*: The percentage of time the CPU was left waiting unable to complete a task because it was dependent on an I/O operation that had not yet completed.

Looking at these figures in a properly performing PHP application, you would expect to see a processor that is rarely idle and spends most of its time executing a combination of user-space and system code, which means (assuming the only significant thing running on the server is your web server) that you are spending most of the CPU resources executing PHP code. If your server is spending a large percentage of time waiting for I/O, that indicates that I/O operations could be the primary bottleneck, and it warrants further examination using iostat. If vmstat shows a higher run-queue value than the total number of processors in the server, this typically indicates that the system is CPU-bound and would benefit from increased CPU capacity.

Note You should allow enough extra capacity to survive spikes in load. One simple way to do this might be to look out for user plus system CPU times that sustain themselves above 70 percent total capacity with spikes into the 90 percent range as an indication that you might be CPU-bound. A more advanced technique would be to trend this information (with a script similar to the previous example) and capacity plan over a longer period of time.

Determining Whether You Are Memory-Bound

Determining whether you are memory-bound in a Linux system is a more difficult task to execute than it really should be, if only because the information you need isn't entirely available inside of the output of vmstat and thus is difficult to correlate over time. Perhaps someone will make a better utility, but for now we will introduce the best solution we are aware of. To determine whether you might have a memory-based bounding influence, we will start like we did with the CPU—by checking the vmstat output under the following columns: si and so. These two columns are defined in the same order as follows:

- *Swap-In*: The amount of memory swapped in from disk per second

- *Swap-Out*: The amount of memory swapped to disk per second

When looking at si and so, you should note whether either has a value above zero. While swap is not always a cause for concern, swap-in correlation to high load indicates that your server is running out of memory and is trying to juggle resources in order to complete the current work at hand.

In the cases where the swap is very low and not related to high load, the operating system kernel may choose to move infrequently accessed pages to disk in the hope that it will have more memory available for handling sudden spikes in load or will be able to use the memory for a file-system cache.

That said, if you do see increasing swaps happening under high load, you should investigate further by checking the vmstat virtual file (/proc/vmstat on a Linux system) as follows:

```
# cat /proc/vmstat | egrep 'scan|steal'
```

This command will produce an output similar to that shown in Listing 3-5.

Listing 3-5. *Page-Scanning Output from /proc/vmstat*

```
nr_vmscan_write 21765
pgsteal_dma 65362
pgsteal_normal 792043
pgsteal_high 0
pgsteal_movable 0
pgscan_kswapd_dma 37296
pgscan_kswapd_normal 518833
pgscan_kswapd_high 0
pgscan_kswapd_movable 0
pgscan_direct_dma 38049
pgscan_direct_normal 362019
pgscan_direct_high 0
pgscan_direct_movable 0
pginodesteal 23055
slabs_scanned 196736
kswapd_steal 511807
kswapd_inodesteal 119178
```

Unfortunately, because this output is not produced automatically during a vmstat call, diagnosing this means you will likely have to run the vmstat in real time from one terminal and watch for the swap numbers to rise. When they start rising, you'll be interested in the pgscan_kswapd_high and pgscan_direct_high values (indicating scan rate and page reclaim rate), which indicate that the system is swapping more heavily. If you notice high scan and reclaim rates while also noticing high swap-in rates, it is a good bet that your server is memory-bound and that steps should be taken to either increase the available RAM or decrease the demand.

Determining Whether You Are I/O-Bound

As mentioned when discussing CPU bounding influences, the wa column of the vmstat output is an important indicator that your server may be held up because it is reading or writing too much data to disk. However, that figure alone doesn't tell you the complete story. To investigate further, you should also make note of the bi and bo columns defined as follows:

- *Blocks In*: The number of blocks read during the vmstat poll

- *Blocks Out*: The number of blocks written during the vmstat poll

A high CPU percentage spent waiting for I/O operations coupled with high blocks in or blocks out can indicate that your server's bounding influence is I/O operations.

If you suspect that your system is I/O-bound and if you have the tool available (not all Linux systems do), the next step is to investigate why you are I/O-bound by looking at the output of iostat. An example output of iostat shown in Listing 3-6 includes the optional -x option for extended statistics.

Listing 3-6. *Output from a Call to iostat (Truncated)*

```
# iostat -x 1 2
Linux 2.6.18-92.el5 (centos-mon)        03/22/2009

avg-cpu:  %user   %nice %system %iowait  %steal   %idle
           0.95    0.04    8.76    0.12    0.00     90.13

Device:   rrqm/s   wrqm/s   r/s   w/s   rsec/s   wsec/s  avgrq-sz  avgqu-sz ...
hda        0.04     8.92    0.45  1.00  45.70    79.35    86.35      0.08 ...
dm-0       0.00     0.00    0.48  9.92  45.68    79.35    12.03      2.34 ...
dm-1       0.00     0.00    0.00  0.00  0.00     0.00      8.00      0.00 ...

avg-cpu:  %user   %nice %system %iowait  %steal   %idle
          38.14    0.00   61.86    0.00    0.00     0.00

Device:  rrqm/s  wrqm/s  r/s      w/s    rsec/s     wsec/s  avgrq-sz  avgqu-sz ...
hda      31.96    0.00   419.59  0.00   74548.45   0.00    177.67    0.57 ...
dm-0      0.00    0.00   451.55  0.00   74548.45   0.00    165.10    0.58 ...
dm-1      0.00    0.00   0.00    0.00   0.00       0.00    0.00      0.00 ...
```

While much more detail could be gleaned from the output of iostat, for the purposes of this book we are interested in understanding the proportion of I/O operations as they happen across the various devices in the system. For example, if the majority of I/O is happening on a swap device, then this indicates that the problem might actually be memory, not I/O. If the majority of I/O is happening on a normal partition coupled with a high wait I/O CPU time, then this indicates an I/O bounding influence. Some key columns to point out in the previous `iostat` example are

- *iowait*: The percentage of time the CPU was left waiting unable to complete a task because it was dependent on an I/O operation that had not yet completed.

- *% util*: The percentage of time the I/O subsystem was busy working. Note that on a busy system with RAID, this figure may always appear near 100 percent since it only takes one spindle to be busy to be "under utilization."

- *svctm*: Average service time for an I/O request in milliseconds. On a loaded system, this number should trend upwards.

- *avggu-sz*: How many outstanding requests there are in the request queue.

Tip It isn't a bad idea in a major environment to create a device specifically for PHP to read and write only if possible. While it is extra work, being able to clearly identify PHP as the root cause for any I/O performance issues can not only be handy but also make the system much more robust. For instance, putting heavy write operations that are known in advance, such as log files, onto spindles different than those used by your data can increase the performance of your system by keeping the disk heads from having to physically move as much to perform their operations (creating a reduction in seek times).

Where to Start Looking

Once you have determined your high-level bounding influence, the next obvious question is where to go next. Let's take a look at each of the bounding influences and name some of the usual suspects that cause them in a web application. For the purposes of this discussion we will assume that PHP is running alone on the web server (with no other major processes such as a MySQL database).

CPU Bounding Influence

If you find yourself with the CPU as the bottleneck, the best place to start trying to improve performance of PHP is by installing an opcode cache and a opcode optimizer, both provided by Zend Platform. If that still isn't enough, you can begin improving the performance of the application logic itself using the Zend Studio for Eclipse profiler against your application and determining the best place to improve application performance in terms of processing time. (See Chapter 2 for information regarding the use of Zend Studio for Eclipse's PHP Profiler.) It's important here to remember Amdahl's Law: improving code execution time by 50 percent when the code executes 2 percent of the time will result in a 1 percent overall improvement, while improving execution time by 10 percent when the code executes 80 percent of the time will result in a 8 percent overall improvement. This means you should identify code segments that are executed on almost every request and that can be improved before improving aspects of the application that are possibly very inefficient but rarely executed.

As an even more drastic step, consider reimplementing aspects of your application that do not have to happen within the context of the web request itself (such as sending an e-mail) as asynchronous operations using Zend Platform's Job Queue, discussed later in this book.

Memory Bounding Influence

If the problem you are having is memory-bound, chances are you that are likely performing memory-extensive tasks in your application that need to be streamlined. To identify where the memory hog is, you can use various techniques. The most available technique is to toy with the `memory_limit` `php.ini` configuration value used to limit the amount of memory any given PHP script can consume. Through experimentation with this value (starting low and moving up, or starting high and moving low) you can identify the aspects of your application that are consuming the most memory (as they will cause out-of-memory errors when the limit is reached). Once you have determined the amount of memory PHP needs to execute your application per request, you should solidify the memory limit using the following formula:

$$(total\ RAM - non\text{-}Apache\ memory\ needs)\ /\ number\ of\ Apache\ children$$

Once you know exactly which requests are eating up all the available memory, you will likely have to reimplement those aspects to be more memory-friendly by doing whatever processing is necessary in chunks (i.e., streaming) or taking the processing off the web server using Zend Platform's Job Queue. Depending on the nature of your application, it may also be helpful to be sure PHP frees up large memory chunks no longer being used by setting their respective variable(s) to null after the operation is complete. (Although due to the nature of the Zend Engine powering PHP, other references to the data contained within the variable may prevent it from being freed immediately even if you explicitly set the variable to `null` in a script.)

I/O Bounding Influence

If your application is I/O-bound, the first obvious candidate is the application itself. If your application's logic doesn't write to the disk at all, or if it is determined that whatever writing is being done couldn't account for the significant I/O bounds you are experiencing, then another possibility is to look at PHP sessions. By default, PHP sessions will write to the file system and under heavy load could potentially cause I/O bounding influences. If that is the case, consider either using a RAM disk for session storage (much faster) or Zend Platform's Session Clustering feature to improve session performance across your application.

Tip Interestingly enough, most PHP applications are not I/O bound in performance, but database servers often are. The advice listed here for finding your bottleneck is equally as valid for debugging problems in MySQL.

When the Bottleneck Is a Remote Procedure Call

One of the reasons that PHP applications scale so well is that a large part of the environment does not maintain state (provided that session storage is not handled by Zend Session Clustering). What this means from a practical standpoint is that as you add additional web servers to your topology, your capacity to serve requests will increase at an approximately linear rate.

There will, however, be some components of your architecture that will not have this ad hoc scalability property, and they tend to be the components that have to guarantee some sort of persistence of data, such as databases, or calls to external APIs, which in turn hit their own limits before PHP or the web server itself does.

To determine whether a remote procedure call (RPC) is a bottleneck requires finding where the PHP script itself is being hung up waiting for a response, which is best done with the Zend Studio Profiler covered in detail in Chapter 2 in the "Profiling in Zend Studio for Eclipse" section.

Simulating Load to Identify Future Bottlenecks

Stress testing or simulating load turns out to be a very difficult problem for web applications. The reason for this is that it's almost impossible to create the perfect test to represent exactly what the access patterns of your application are going to be.

If the test does not represent what visitors are going to be doing, then it leaves potential edge cases where you do not get to see the bottlenecks you had hoped would arise. Some examples are as follows:

- *The stress test does not have high enough concurrency*: Not having enough concurrency prevents some database bottlenecks such as deadlocks and MyISAM table locking from appearing. Tests in a single thread do not help identify bottlenecks well at all.

- *The database size during the stress test is too small*: A test with too small a database prevents showing how performance may differ as soon as data is too big to fit in caches.

- *The database does not contain realistic data*: Repeating the name "test customer" 10,000 times may lead MySQL to execute queries differently than what was expected.

- *The stress test is disproportionately read-heavy:* Tests need to include a number of write operations similar to the number the real application would receive. This ensures that not every request is served by a cache.

- *The stress test does not access enough unique resources*: A test that hits only the home page will show a skew in high cache hits, which might not be the same for the rest of your application.

The best tools we are aware of to use as the basis of these stress tests are `ab` (an Apache benchmarking tool available to `http://httpd.apache.org/docs/2.0/programs/ab.html`) and `http_load` (`http://www.acme.com/software/http_load/`). Both are similar in usage, with `http_load` having the added feature of accepting an input file of URLs. Having said that, Selenium is one tool we are watching closely, as it has the ability to record tests that can be replayed directly within the browser environment. The one major advantage of using such a test is that it will stress the complete stack of technologies, since it also requires images to be loaded and JavaScript to be rendered. The downside of Selenium is that it's more difficult to generate enough load from one client machine to trigger performance issues on the server. This problem is addressed by Selenium Grid, which allows the tests to be distributed across multiple nodes and executed in parallel. Note that Selenium is not the only option available. Apache JMeter is also a very powerful load-generation tool to consider.

■**Note** The main purpose of Selenium is actually for test-driven-development. Stress testing is just a side effect of its functionality. The Selenium IDE Firefox plug-in is available at `http://seleniumhq.org/projects/ide/`.

Conclusion

In this chapter we discussed an extensive collection of system-level tools for the Linux platform for identifying potential bottlenecks in your web applications. Combined with the profiler tools provided by Zend Studio discussed in Chapter 2, you have a very powerful arsenal at your disposal for locating the most problematic performance issues.

As we said in the beginning of the chapter, the act of identifying a server-performance bottleneck is based as much on experience as it is technique. But let's face it—technique helps a lot. Hopefully after reading this chapter you have a much better grasp of how to analyze the data available to you and can make some intelligent conclusions as to why your application is slow. Once you understand the major bounding influence of your application, you can then apply the techniques in the rest of this book to that problem to solve it.

We'll introduce more information on MySQL in Chapter 10. In the next chapter we will examine data-caching techniques, an invaluable set of tools for improving application performance when the bottleneck lies in the CPU or in interactions with the database.

CHAPTER 4

Data-Caching Strategies in PHP

The first and easiest-to-implement caching technique for your PHP applications is something called opcode caching. Also known as a compiler cache, this technique corrects a rather obvious inefficiency in the way out-of-the-box PHP executes its code. This technique increases the performance of your PHP scripts anywhere from 50 percent to 200 percent with no other code changes. To understand how it works, let's take a look at what happens when PHP executes a script.

The PHP Execution Cycle

Every time a PHP script executes, it goes through a number of steps to get from the version you wrote into something the PHP engine can understand and execute as logic. This process is expensive from a performance perspective, and it has to happen for not only for the main script that was executed but also every script the main script references, as shown in Figure 4-1.

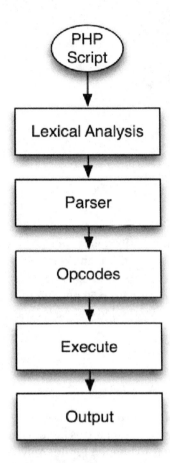

Figure 4-1. *The standard execution of a PHP script*

While completely functional, what makes the process outlined in Figure 4-1 so inefficient is the reality that there is a deterministic relationship between the original PHP script and the opcodes it produces. To say that another way, any given input script will always produce the same output opcodes and thus shouldn't have to be re-created every single request. Furthermore, since the opcodes are re-created every execution, a normally highly beneficial step of optimizing the opcodes created after parsing cannot be realized since the efficiency gained would be totally lost having to do it every time. Thus, there are many various opcode caches available for PHP that change the flow of Figure 4-1 as shown in Figure 4-2.

Note It is worthwhile to note that caching opcodes and optimizing opcodes are two very distinct steps. In fact, optimizing opcodes *without* caching them actually reduces performance! You can, however, cache unoptimized opcodes and still see a significant performance boost.

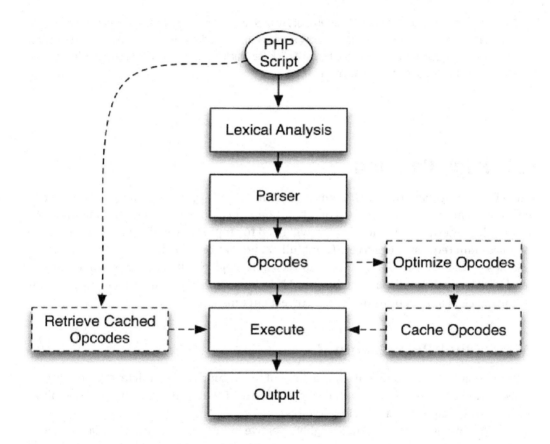

Figure 4-2. *Optimizer/opcode cache in the execution of a PHP script*

Simply by introducing an opcode cache into your PHP technology stack, it is possible to increase the speed of your script executions from anywhere to 50 percent to 200 percent! So how do you take advantage of this performance boost? There are many options available, both open source and commercial. If you are interested in open source technologies, you should take a look at APC (`http://pecl.php.net/apc`), but for the purposes of this book we will be focusing on the PHP stack provided by Zend Technologies through Zend Platform, which provides both the opcode optimization and caching technology out of box.

Tip If for whatever reason you want to disable the opcode cache for a specific file, you can do so from the Zend Platform admin panel under the File View submenu of the Performance tab. Select the file for which you would like to disable the opcode cache file, and click the Blacklist icon to disable opcode caching (called Acceleration in the GUI), output compression, or both.

Full-Page Caching

When it comes to caching in PHP, nothing is simpler than opcode caching. It is so simple in fact, you can forget there are lots of other different caching strategies and techniques that any high-performance application will need to employ correctly in order to handle the maximum requests per server. Thankfully Zend Platform provides all of these technologies in easy-to-use APIs and web interfaces. To begin we'll take a look at a feature of Zend Platform called full-page caching and how it can help you dramatically increase the performance of applications under the correct circumstances.

What Is Full-Page Caching?

Full-page caching is, simply put, the caching of the output of a complete PHP request based on input parameters from that request. Figure 4-3 outlines how full-page caching fits into the execution cycle of a PHP request.

While full-page caching can be highly effective in increasing the performance of a web site, there are many caveats that must be taken into consideration before this style of caching can be employed. Full-page caching works by caching the output of a PHP script based on the input data it receives from an outside source, including HTTP, GET, or POST requests; cookies provided by the request; or variables stored within the session of the request. Effectively, when using a full-page caching mechanism, a dynamic PHP request is turned into a static request with no PHP logic whatsoever based on the criterion specified. This can be extremely useful when there is no need to place any dynamic content on the page (such as perhaps a page of a product catalog), but it should be used with care! For instance, if you are attempting to optimize a blog it probably doesn't make sense to use full-page caching on the main landing page of the blog (which displays multiple blog posts) as that page is mostly based on highly dynamic content. On the other hand, on the individual pages that display only a single, mostly static blog post, full-page caching could be used to create a significant performance gain. In both cases it is critical to ensure that you craft your cache criteria carefully by making them generic enough to have a high percentage of cache hits and specific enough to not create errors (such as caching the user's name and displaying that name to another person who isn't that user).

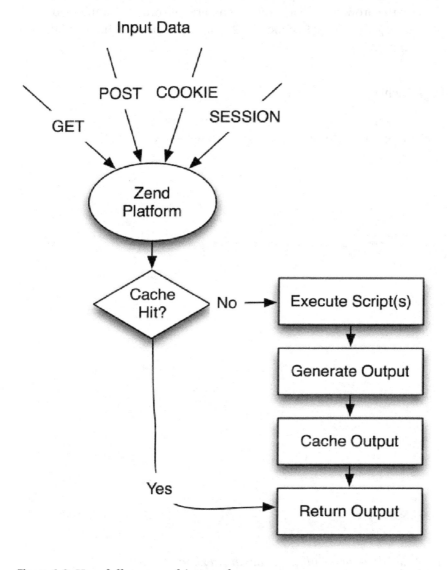

Figure 4-3. *How full-page caching works*

Setting Up Full-Page Caching

Setting up full-page caching is quite simple thanks to the Zend Platform admin console. To get started, first you must choose the way you will cache the output of a request by selecting either file-based or URL-based caching. File-based caching is useful when the PHP script that is executed for a request is directly requested from an URL entered into a browser such as `http://www.example.com/index.php?page=foo`. On the other hand, URL-based caching is useful when the PHP script that is executed isn't directly connected to the URL entered into the browser such as from a Zend Framework MVC application: `http://www.example.com/page/foo`. We'll first look at file-based full-page caching and then move on to the URL variety.

File-Based Full-Page Caching

File-based full-page caching can be accessed from the Zend Platform GUI by clicking on the File View link under the Performance tab. You can see an example of this view in Figure 4-4.

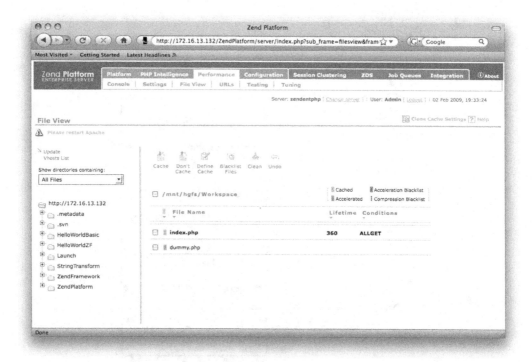

Figure 4-4. *The File View tab showing full-page caching in Zend Platform*

From this interface you can browse the document root of your web server (using the file navigation on the left) and set up specific PHP scripts that should be cached and how that caching should take place. To enabling caching of a specific PHP script, select it by placing a check next to the file and click the Cache icon above the file list. This will enable caching for this file using the default caching setup (found under the Settings link in the Performance tab). Once the script has been set up to be cached you can select the file again and click Define Cache, bringing up the interface shown in Figure 4-5, allowing you to define the particulars of one or more cached files.

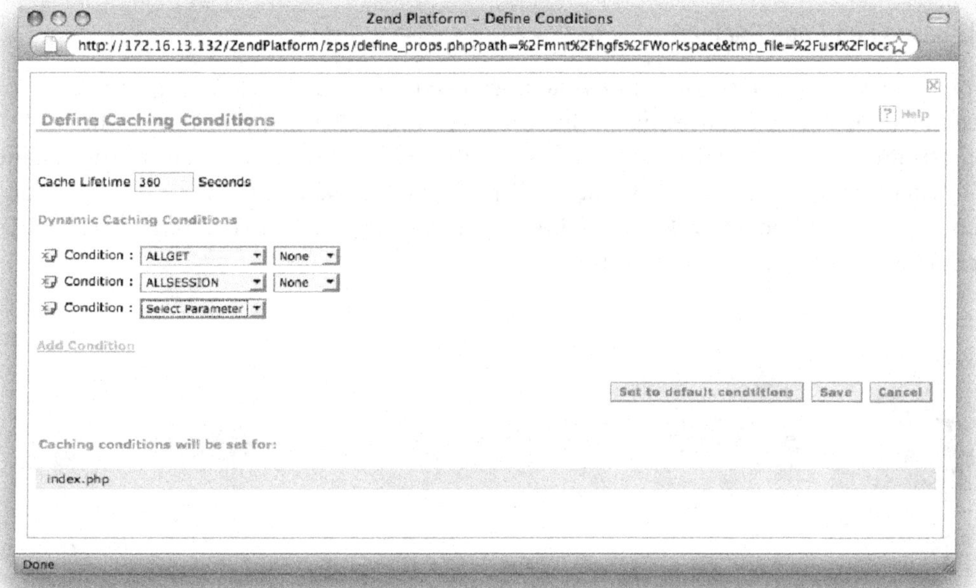

Figure 4-5. *Caching conditions setup screen in Zend Platform*

As you can see in Figure 4-5, for each file being cached you can define not only the lifetime of the cached file (how long it will remain cached before it is considered stale and will be automatically refreshed) but also create one or more caching conditions that define the criteria used to determine whether a cached version of the request exists or not.

Once you have completed the setup of your cache you will need to restart the web server for the new settings to take effect. You can do this either manually or by clicking the Restart Webserver link in the Zend Core interface.

▪**Tip** Set your caching conditions wisely! We have personally seen numerous people create completely ineffective caches of their data because they mistakenly either misused full-page caching when it wasn't a good option or included a variable in their conditions that changed nearly every request and thus only served to fill the cache with megabytes of cached outputs that never were used. Besides being a huge waste of disk space, a cache polluted in this way can actually slow down the application in a big way, defeating the purpose of the cache in the first place.

URL-Based Full-Page Caching

As previously mentioned, sometimes caching based on the literal PHP script to be executed doesn't make sense such as in Zend Framework MVC applications, where all requests are routed through a single bootstrap PHP script. For these circumstances Zend Platform provides the ability to define a full-page cache based on the request URL to be cached. To get started, click the URLs link on the Performance tab, bringing up the URLs caching interface shown in Figure 4-6.

Figure 4-6. *The URLs full-page caching interface*

Like the File View interface shown in Figure 4-4, the URL-based interface allows you to manage the various URLs that you are interested in caching. When adding a new URL, however, keep in mind that the URL by default will be a wildcard and thus `http://www.example.com/foo/` will cache not only that URL but `http://www.example.com/foo/bar/` as well. To prevent this behavior, make sure you select the Exact Match check box when entering the URL to be cached.

Final Thoughts on Full-Page Caching

Full-page caching is a significant performance booster, but as we previously mentioned, if it is improperly set up, it can actually do more harm than good (or even worse—break your application)! Be very mindful of your caching conditions and only select conditions that will result in the greatest number of cache hits without breaking the application. If for whatever reason you would like to flush your cache, you can do so by clicking the Clean icon in the File View tab or the URLs tab.

Semi-Full-Page Caching

While full-page caching is highly effective at improving the performance of an application there are times when the criteria available in Zend Platform are not sufficient to make it a viable option. An example of such a situation is a blog post that contains an advertisement—while the vast majority of the page is a prime candidate for a full-page cache, it can't be used since the advertisement image shown has no connection at all to any input parameter given to the page. While Zend Platform itself does not address this issue, if you are using the Apache web server there is a technique you can employ that achieves the same caching effects as Zend Platform with a relatively minimal amount of code.

■**Warning** This section requires that you to be running the Apache web server and to have the mod_rewrite server module installed. Please refer to the Apache HTTP server documentation at `http://httpd.apache.org/` for information on enabling mod_rewrite.

To achieve semi-full-page caching you will have to leave the comfortable GUI interface of Zend Platform and instead develop your application to employ the caching mechanism defined in this section. For the purposes of this explanation we will assume that the page you are interested in caching is the aforementioned blog post, wherein all of the content except a single advertisement can be cached. To get started, let's assume that the following URL can reach your blog post:

```
http://www.example.com/blog/getPost.php?id=4
```

To achieve a semi-full-page cache for this request, you could use the data-caching techniques described later in this chapter—at best a cumbersome effort—or you could harness the `mod_rewrite` module to make the solution much more elegant. To get started we will assume the creation of a new top-level directory in the document root called "posts" (writable by the web server), within which we create a `mod_rewrite` rule such that the following URL:

```
http://www.example.com/posts/4.php
```

is mapped back to our original URL, automatically populating the ID parameter of the `getPost.php` request with the file name from the URL (without the suffix, in this case "4"). So far, so good—doing so has created a secondary way to reach the same content, but the original `getPost.php` script all still dynamically generates it. To achieve a performance gain, we must now look at the `getPost.php` script itself and change its logic. Typically in a script with the behavior of `getPost.php` you can assume safely a basic pattern of operation:

1. Execute business logic and queries that do not need to change every request.

2. Execute the business logic and queries to generate the advertisement code (must change every request).

3. Generate the output HTML and display to the user.

Rather than do this every request, what if we instead created a `getPost.php` script that behaves as follows?

1. Execute the business logic and queries that do not need to change every request.

2. Generate a new PHP script that contains static HTML for all cacheable aspects of the output and includes PHP code for the business logic and queries to generate the advertisement code.

3. Write the generated PHP script to the `/posts/<ID>.php` file, where `<ID>` is the requested ID given by the user.

4. Include `/posts/<ID>.php` at the end of the request.

Again, by changing the flow of this logic as shown, we have returned our hypothetical application back to a fully functional status. However, we have introduced a major performance benefit. While on the first request everything will happen as expected and the `getPost.php` script will execute, on the second request you will find that you no longer need to execute this script to generate the page. To understand why, you need to realize an important detail about the `mod_rewrite` module—rewrite rules can be crafted to *not be* executed if the URL requested resolves to a real file to be served. Thus, while on the first request the `mod_rewrite` rule caused the `getPost.php` script to execute when that execution was complete, the `getPost.php` script wrote the semicached version of its output back to the file system. This file was then served on the second and every future request, bypassing all of the unnecessary actions, including only those that were deemed absolutely necessary. To make this behavior a little easier to understand, we've included a flowchart of its function in Figure 4-7.

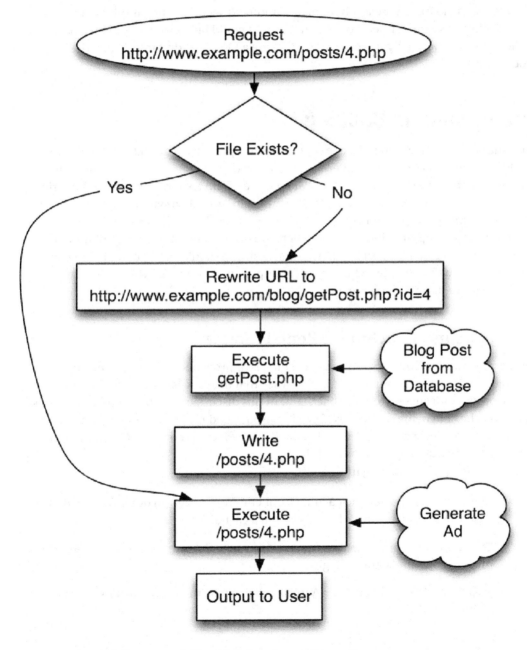

Figure 4-7. *Semi-full-page caching using Apache mod_rewrite*

Using this pattern can be incredibly powerful for complex sites where standard full-page caching doesn't quite provide the flexibility needed and also fits into a paradigm of output generation some developers find more comfortable than data-caching techniques. Incidentally, if you ever wanted to invalidate the cached entry you could do that as well very simply—just delete the generated file from the directory and the next request will regenerate it! In either case though, be mindful of security when implementing this sort of solution as write access to a document root could be abused by a malicious user if they can somehow get your application to write a file you didn't intend to write into document root.

Programmatic Caching

In some circumstances, no full-page caching technique will accomplish the necessary goals for a particular PHP script. Perhaps there is too much logic, or the logic that does exist within the script is dependent on data received from a source outside of the script itself such as a database or web service. For these circumstances you must use some form of programmatic caching or the introduction of caching logic as part of the overall operation of your application or script. There are many different implementations and approaches you can use to cache data at this level, and thankfully all of them are encapsulated nicely within the Zend Framework component Zend_Cache, which will be our tool of choice as we discuss the subject.

Components of Caching in Zend Framework

When you examine how programmatic caching is approached in Zend Framework through the Zend_Cache component, you will see that the process is broken down into two aspects: the front end and the back end. In this discussion the front end refers to the nature of the data being cached itself, while the back end refers to the storage medium used to store the cached data. The following is a brief introduction to each of the supported caching front ends and back ends.

The following are caching front ends:

- Zend_Cache_Core: A generic caching front end from which all other front ends are based; useful for storing arbitrary data in a cache

- Zend_Cache_Frontend_Output: A front end to cache the output of a particular segment of your application's logic

- Zend_Cache_Frontend_Function: A front end to cache the output of a function call

- `Zend_Cache_Frontend_Class`: **Similar to** `Zend_Cache_Frontend_Function`, a front end that allows you to cache static and non-static method calls of classes

- `Zend_Cache_Frontend_File`: A front end for caching data based on the status of a file in the file system

The following are caching back ends:

- `Zend_Cache_Backend_File`: A file-based cache-storage engine

- `Zend_Cache_Backend_Sqlite`: A SQLite database–based cache-storage engine

- `Zend_Cache_Backend_Memcached`: A Memcached-based cache-storage engine

- `Zend_Cache_Backend_Apc`: An APC-based cache-storage engine

- `Zend_Cache_Backend_Xcache`: An Xcache-based cache-storage engine

- `Zend_Cache_Backend_ZendPlatform`: A Zend Platform–based cache-storage engine

- `Zend_Cache_Backend_TwoLevels`: A special cache-storage engine designed to allow you to store the same cached data in two different storage back ends

---

Note We have intentionally omitted `Zend_Cache_Frontend_Page` from the list of available front-end cache mechanisms. If you desire to use full-page caching it is strongly recommended that you use the GUI provided by Zend Platform.

Because the usage of `Zend_Cache` is already extremely well documented both in printed text as well as on the Zend Framework web site (`http://framework.zend.com/`), we will forego an in-depth explanation of the syntax and usage of the component itself. Rather, we will focus on the characteristics of a successful caching implementation from a variety of angles interesting to enterprise applications. These characteristics are the correct identification of a caching opportunity, correctly choosing caching keys, and the various strengths and weaknesses of the various caching back ends.

You Can (Almost) Always Cache Things

Before you can ever hope to truly benefit in any measurable way from any caching tool, you first must know what in your application both can be cached and what will benefit from caching. The first is surprisingly simple and can be answered using a single

question: under a given time frame can the operation acceptably be described as deterministic? We have mentioned the notion of determinism before, but now that we are
discussing the implementation of caching mechanisms on a programming level, it is
worth hammering out in explicit terms. In computer science, calling an operation deterministic is another way of saying that the operation is predictable. For example, the
function call add(2,2) is deterministic if you will always receive "4" given those input
parameters. Unfortunately, when you look at a practical application's performance, the
bottleneck within the application (remember, there is only *one* bottleneck in any particular logic path of an application) is almost never the result of a deterministic function
series of operations. So how does this issue get addressed? By introducing a time frame
to the discussion. While most bottlenecks in applications are not caused by deterministic
operations, most bottlenecks can be considered deterministic operations under a short
enough time frame.

For example, consider a popular web script that receives 300 requests per second, and
for each request the script must perform an expensive query against the database. This
means that over the course of a minute this application will perform this single constant
query 18,000 times. You may argue that such a query is necessary, and we personally have
heard all too often the argument that real-time updates of data eliminate any possibility
of a performance boost through caching, but we disagree. As a matter of practicality when
dealing with humans, the difference of a few seconds of delay between updates rarely has
any impact at all on user experience (even live television has a seven-second delay!) yet
can yield significant performance improvements. In the original hypothetical example of
a script receiving 300 requests per second (18,000 requests per minute) we could cut down
our queries from 18,000 per minute to 2,572 per minute (18,000 divided by 7) or improve
the overall performance of the query by 85 percent! Even a two-second cache on the query
would yield an overall performance improvement of 50 percent. The point here should
be obvious: it is extremely rare that the developer of a real-time application can't still find
places to cache data, even for short periods of time, that produces a benefit—especially in
heavy-load applications.

■**Caution** In this example, showing an 85 percent overall improvement in performance could be mislead-
ing. If the query takes five seconds to execute from a user experience perspective you are basically covering
up the problem instead of solving it. (Eighty-five percent of the requests will execute fine, but 15 percent of
them will still be very slow.) If you find yourself in this situation, caching at the application level is indeed
important, but care must be given to identify the root inefficiencies of the underlying bottleneck.

Knowing Your Cache Effectiveness

Once you have identified a potentially cacheable operation, the next pitfall too many developers fall into is thankfully a relatively obvious one to understand and solve—bad cache-key generation. This is a critical calculation for your application, as it will determine the effectiveness of your caching mechanism when caching data based on variable input. Since there are a million ways to generate a cache key for any given cacheable piece of data, it behooves the developer not to focus first on the cache key itself but instead to focus on the cache hit/miss ratio—the number of times a request for data results in data being returned from the cache (a cache hit) vs. the number of times the data must be calculated because it was not found in the cache (a cache miss). Often represented as a percentage of cache hits vs. total attempts, in a high-performance application it is often in the 90th percentile. It is critical that you are aware of the effectiveness of your caches as much as it is important that you profile your applications to understand where a cache might be useful in the first place.

Note There are other reasons a cache can miss other than a poor cache key; for example, an expired cache item or the caching mechanism removing items because it has to make room for newly entered cached items due to an uncharacteristically high cache miss rate.

The Various Zend_Cache Back Ends

Now that we've discussed the general techniques used to implement successful caching mechanisms (presumably using one of the Zend_Cache front ends) we can now look at the various storage mediums available to your cached data through Zend Framework and the pros and cons of each. For this discussion we will group the various available back ends into three categories.

The following are file-based back ends:

- Zend_Cache_Backend_File

- Zend_Cache_Backend_Sqlite

The following are local memory back ends:

- Zend_Cache_Backend_Apc: An APC-based cache-storage engine

- Zend_Cache_Backend_Xcache: An Xcache-based cache-storage engine

- Zend_Cache_Backend_ZendPlatform: A Zend Platform based cache-storage engine

The following is a server-based back end:

- Zend_Cache_Backend_Memcached

File-Based Back Ends

The simplest of all cache-storage mediums is the local file system of the web server, and
it can be implemented using either the Zend_Cache_Backend_File or Zend_Cache_Backend_
Sqlite back-end cache engines. These back ends are useful for smaller setups but ultimately have scalability issues due to their reliance on the I/O abilities of the underlying
file system. Starting with Zend_Cache_Backend_File, this back end will store cached data as
a file (whose name maps to the cache key itself of the data) and store one cache record
per file. Let's take a look at some basic usage in Listing 4-1.

Listing 4-1. *A Simple Usage of the Zend_Cache File Back End to Cache a Function Call*

```php
<?php

require_once 'Zend/Cache.php';

function calculateFib($seq)
{
    $prev1stDigit = 0;
    $prev2ndDigit = 1;
    $retval = 0;

    if($seq == 0) return 0;
    if($seq == 1) return 1;

    for($i = 0; $i < ($seq-1); $i++)
    {
        $retval = bcadd($prev1stDigit, $prev2ndDigit);
        $prev1stDigit = $prev2ndDigit;
        $prev2ndDigit = $retval;
    }
```

```
        return $retval;
}

$cache = Zend_Cache::factory('Function', 'File',
                             array(),
                             array('cache_dir' => '/tmp/'));

$startTime = microtime(true);

$answer = $cache->call('calculateFib', array(50000));

$endTime = microtime(true);

print "Sequence took " . ($endTime - $startTime) . "s to calculate\n";

?>
```

In this simple example, we use the Zend_Cache component to cache the results of a function that calculates the value of a number in the Fibonacci sequence (in this case the 50,000th number in the sequence). In our test environment when we ran this program the first time it took roughly five seconds to calculate. However, since the result is cached, subsequent executions yielded an almost insignificant execution time as expected. In this example, we stored the cache data as multiple individual files in the local file system. Alternately, you could also make the management of your cache a little easier by replacing the call to Zend_Cache::factory() in Listing 4-1 with a back end of "Sqlite" instead of "File" and specifying the "cache_db_complete_path" configuration option to the full path and file name of the SQLite database to use (which doesn't have to exist) in place of the "cache_dir" configuration setting.

While the biggest benefit of a file-based caching back end is simplicity, as previously stated one of its downsides is that you are limited by the capabilities of your file system for performance. For the file-based back end, there are a few things you can do to improve the performance. Let's take a look at a few of them.

- *Disable file locking*: While you risk cache corruption, disabling the back-end locking of a cache file using the "file_locking" configuration setting can improve performance.

- *Use a RAM disk*: Creating a RAM disk to store your cache files can *significantly* improve its performance but at the cost of losing your cache entirely in the event of a power failure.

- *Disable or tweak read control*: By setting "read_control" to false you can disable the check to ensure that the data was read from the file system properly. Of course you run the risk of the data being read incorrectly, but it will increase performance. You can keep read control on and speed things up a little bit as well by changing the read control type using the "read_control_type" configuration parameter (see the Zend Framework documentation).

- *Create a hashed directory structure*: Using the "hashed_directory_level" configuration parameter, you can specify how many levels deep the engine will create directories to store cache files in. If you intend to have huge quantities of cached data (number of individual pieces, not size of the data itself) it is strongly recommended that you use this to distribute the resulting files into multiple directories.

If for whatever reason you cannot get the performance you want out of the file-caching mechanism (for example, if you are unable to create a RAM disk) or maybe just don't want to use files, an alternative is to consider using one of the local memory back ends such as that provided by Zend Platform. This solution, rather than being file-based, stores the data in shared memory, allowing the entire server to benefit. Of course, like a RAM disk, data stored in the cache is only as persistent as your power supply but is as easy to set up as a file-based back end with all performance benefits built in.

Regardless of the solution you use for your back end, be it file-based, SQLite, or local shared memory, there is a major performance problem with each of them—they are all local server solutions. Since there is no way to share data that is cached across physical servers, in all of the solutions mentioned so far, at best every server in the farm must calculate and store data in its cache locally. To solve this problem (and create the most powerful caching solution) we will need to introduce Memcached and the Memcached caching back end.

Caching with Memcached

One of the latest success stories in the space of scaling and performance is a technology called Memcached. Created originally for the massive blogging site http://www. livejournal.com, it is now used by the biggest web sites on the planet to improve performance on scales most of us will never have to worry about. So what is this miracle technology exactly and how does it work? Thankfully there is no magic. All Memcached does is provide a mechanism for storing a piece of data with a unique key and then retrieve that value later by providing the key, like any other cache. The key difference, however, is that Memcached is a network-based cache, meaning to store data within it you must open a network connection to the server to do so, and it is distributed, allowing you to run multiple instances and store data across them.

This may not seem like a huge deal, but it offers a wide range of possibilities that would otherwise not be possible. For starters, you can create massively large shared caches that normally would violate the maximum memory the system allows for a single program by running multiple instances on the same machine. Additionally, you can run multiple instances across multiple physical machines creating single-function caches that span incredibly large server farms.

Installing Memcached and Friends

All of this sounds great; so how do you get started? You'll be happy to know there aren't any configuration files to worry about. Simply download and install the Memcached server and run it from the command line. First, download the latest version of Memcached from the web site `http://danga.com/memcached/download.bml` and build it for your system:

```
$ ./configure
$ make
# make install
```

Note You may have to install libevent as well if you don't already have it on your system. You can find download and installation instructions on the libevent web site at `http://monkey.org/~provos/ libevent/`.

Once installed you can start it up by executing the `memcached` command as a daemon:

```
$ memcached -d
```

Of course, while functional, this is the most basic setup you can use, and it should be adjusted to your own needs (see tips later in the book). With the server up and running, next you must install the Memcache PECL extension and include it in PHP. This involves the following steps:

1. Download libmemcached (`http://tangent.org/552/libmemcached.html`).

2. Compile and install libmemcached.

3. Download the memcache PECL extension (`http://pecl.php.net/memcache`).

4. PHPize the extension by running the **phpize** command.

5. Compile and install the extension.

6. Enable the extension in your `php.ini` file.

Following is a listing of the commands you must execute to accomplish the previous steps. It is assumed that all necessary files have been downloaded.

```
$ tar -zxvf libmemcached-0.26.tar.gz
$ cd libmemcached-0.26
$ ./configure
$ make
# make install
$ cd ..
$ tar -zxvf memcache-3.0.3.tar.gz
$ cd memcached-3.0.3
$ phpize
$ ./configure
$ make
# make install
$ <add the memcache.so to your php.ini extension list>
```

To test your installation, call the phpinfo() function and look to see that the memcache extension is loaded into your PHP. Once completed, you're ready to start using it.

■**Naming** There are two memcached extensions available for PHP, one called "memcache" and a newer one called "memcached." At the time of this writing, in order to take advantage of memcache from within Zend Framework using the Zend_Cache component, only the more stable "memcache" extension can be used.

Using Memcached

Using Memcached ultimately is simple. You only need to specify the Memcached back end when creating a Zend_Cache object. Listing 4-2 demonstrates its use using the same fundamental example from Listing 4-1.

Listing 4-2. *Example of Using Memcached from Zend Framework*

```php
<?php

require_once 'Zend/Cache.php';

function calculateFib($seq)
{
```

```
    $prev1stDigit = 0;
    $prev2ndDigit = 1;
    $retval = 0;

    if($seq == 0) return 0;
    if($seq == 1) return 1;

    for($i = 0; $i < ($seq-1); $i++)
    {
        $retval = bcadd($prev1stDigit, $prev2ndDigit);
        $prev1stDigit = $prev2ndDigit;
        $prev2ndDigit = $retval;
    }

    return $retval;
}

$memcached_servers = array(array('host' => '127.0.0.1',
                                 'port' => 11211));

$cache = Zend_Cache::factory('Function', 'Memcached',
                             array(),
                             array('servers' => $memcached_servers,
                                   'compression' => false));

$startTime = microtime(true);

$answer = $cache->call('calculateFib', array(50000));

$endTime = microtime(true);

print "Sequence took " . ($endTime - $startTime) . "s to calculate\n";

?>
```

Note that in Listing 4-2 we specify an array of Memcached servers. This can be (as in our example) a single server or a collection of Memcached instances to use as part of the cache. These instances can run on a single machine (useful when you want to make a cache that is larger than the maximum process size allowed by the kernel) or span multiple machines. Optionally you can also enable cache compression, whereby Zend Framework will automatically compress the data being cached before sending it to Memcached, allowing you to store more data per instance.

Now that you have everything set up, here are a few tips and things you should be aware of before you start using it as your cache back end:

- There is no security in Memcached. Rather, it is expected that your network typography will prevent unauthorized clients from connecting to the cache (i.e., only accessible from a private network between the servers).

- There is a limit of one megabyte per cache entry (uncompressed).

- As its name implies, Memcached is a volatile caching mechanism and can lose data if there is a loss of power or the server is taken offline. Be careful to store data you need to retain in a persistent storage mechanism such as a database.

- At the time of this writing, Zend Framework support for Memcached does not allow you to specify different server weights. If you require support for these advanced features of Memcached, please refer to the new memcached extension mentioned previously.

Conclusion

In this chapter you were introduced to a wide range of caching techniques from full-page caching to powerful server-based solutions such as memcache. More important than the technology alone, you should have also acquired a better sense of *how* to cache data (even if it seems it can't be cached) to squeeze significant performance out of even out of applications that have operational requirements to function seemingly in real time.

We've covered a lot of material in this chapter, but all of it is incredibly important in the creation of high-performance web applications. Caching, in all of its forms, is without a doubt one of the most critical skills to master. Like many things in PHP, experience goes a long way, but if you can distinguish when to use full-page caches vs. dynamic caching, you're off to a good start. The most important thing to remember, though, is that just about *everything* can be cached and that even a cache that seems incredibly short-lived (like seven seconds) can save you *thousands* of cycles without having to give much up. In all, it comes down to knowing the behavior of your application under high-load environments, which is where the concepts introduced in Chapters 2 and 3 on using tools to determine your bottlenecks can go a long way in helping you. If you skipped over those chapters go back and at least read the latter portion of Chapter 2 on Zend Studio profiling tools, which often are the most useful to identify cacheable points in your application.

CHAPTER 5

Asynchronous Operations with PHP

The notion of asynchronous operations is not a new one to the web space; technologies like Java have employed it for years for their web development tooling. However, for PHP the notion of performing inline asynchronous operations is a new one—and a very powerful one at that. In this chapter we'll explore what and how to use asynchronous operations in your PHP applications to maximize performance with almost zero impact on your application's abilities.

In PHP, the only way to take advantage of asynchronous operations without a lot of pain is to use the various asynchronous technologies available as part of Zend Platform—specifically the Zend Job Queue. This technology allows you to, sometimes completely transparently, take a load off of your web servers by executing PHP logic or other tasks in an asynchronous fashion.

Before we get too much further into it, what exactly it means to be asynchronous in a web context is something worth discussing. An asynchronous operation is an operation that happens simultaneously alongside another one. The savvy developer may ask what the big deal is then, since obviously a web server allows you to execute multiple requests simultaneously and therefore must be asynchronous. This is true; however, we are not talking within the context of a single web request.

In a standard PHP application, the time between when a client connects to the server to perform a request (executing PHP code along the way) and when the client breaks the connection is considered a single web request. The number of these requests you can execute per unit of time is a significant measure of web application performance (requests per second) and in fact is an entirely synchronous set of operations. This is why performance materials around PHP should always be careful to avoid mentioning if possible the execution of "blocking" operations in a PHP request, as they can be fatal to even the largest web farms. However, let's be honest—if you really need to send that e-mail to the user, where else are you going to do it but from within PHP? This is where a technology like Zend Job Queue earns its stripes.

Note A "blocking" operation is an operation that prevents any other operations from moving forward until it is completed. Many PHP operations are blocking, especially ones dealing with database requests and all communication with servers (i.e., sending mail or web services). They can be fatal to a web server because a blocking operation not only ties up the PHP script but also the web process controlling it, preventing it from servicing any other requests.

So how does something like Job Queue work? Basically, the Zend Job Queue manages a completely different set of PHP processes for the execution of scripts outside of the web server. These PHP processes can be utilized by the PHP scripts executing within the web server to offload expensive or otherwise blocking operations to the Job Queue, allowing them to execute in a leisurely fashion while keeping the user experience (i.e., the web request) as fast as possible. A diagram demonstrating this difference can be found in Figure 5-1.

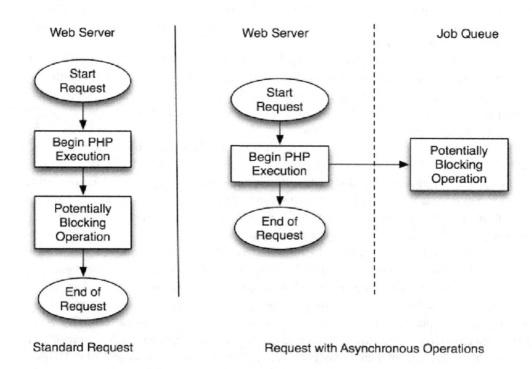

Figure 5-1. *The difference between a standard web request and one utilizing asynchronous operations*

As shown in Figure 5-1, in a standard web request, a potentially blocking and expensive operation has to be executed while the user is connected (and must wait to complete). However, in a web request utilizing the Job Queue, this operation can be executed in an entirely different PHP instance. This allows the web request and user experience to remain as fast as possible without sacrificing any functionality. Moreover, because the Job Queue is an entirely separate binary from the web server, you can run these PHP scripts on a completely separate machine and in fact run multiple Job Queue servers together to create an entire farm of asynchronous processing power.

Getting Started with Job Queue

So how do you take advantage of this functionality in your PHP applications? To begin, you need a version of Zend Platform installed with the Job Queue server enabled. This can be on the same machine as your web server, or you can install a new server specifically to handle Job Queue functionality (please refer to the Appendix for assistance in the installation of Zend Platform). Once installed, you can access the Job Queue web interface by logging into Zend Platform and clicking on the Job Queues tab shown in Figure 5-2.

Figure 5-2. *The Zend Platform web management console, Job Queues page*

While this interface does not provide complete access to all of the abilities of the Job Queue, all of the major aspects of the usage of a Job Queue server are covered, including

- An overview of all of the jobs in your various Job Queue servers

- The ability to review executed jobs and their output

- The ability to create new jobs manually on a scheduled or recurring basis

- Configuration of the Job Queue servers, including bringing them online or offline

In a fresh installation, before you can use the Job Queue you must configure it appropriately. To do this you need to click the Settings link, which brings up the Queue Settings page shown in Figure 5-3.

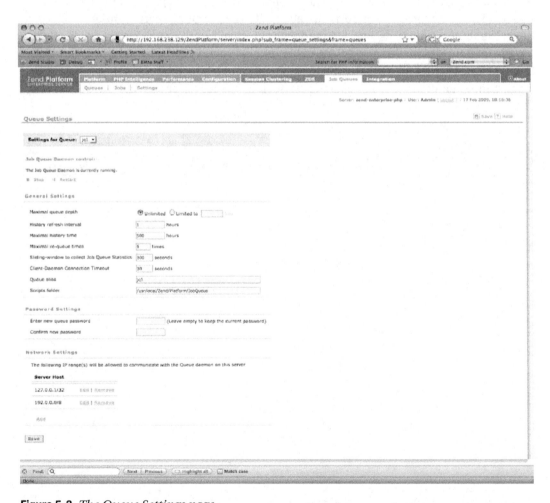

Figure 5-3. *The Queue Settings page*

When using the Job Queue, the Queue Settings page is an important place to start, as it identifies among other things the "Scripts folder," the location where you will store the PHP scripts that are executed in the Job Queue. By default, this directory is the `JobQueue` directory located under the root of your Zend Platform installation. If desired, this directory can be changed to anything you desire. Following is a brief listing of the rest of the settings available from within the Queue Settings page:

- *Maximal queue depth*: How many backlogged jobs to allow in the Job Queue before no more jobs will be accepted

- *History refresh interval*: The amount of time in hours between refreshes or removals of old historical data from the Job Queue

- *Maximal history time*: The amount of time in hours to keep historical Job Queue data before it is purged

- *Maximal re-queue times*: The number of times a failed job will be re-queued before the job will no longer be attempted

- *Sliding-window to collect Job Queue Statistics*: The window of time, in seconds, that is used to populate the statistics of the Job Queue statistics page in the Zend Platform queue

- *Client-Daemon Connection timeout*: The amount of time in seconds without activity before a connection between a Job Queue client and the server is broken

- *Queue alias*: The alias used to represent the Job Queue server

Advanced Job Queue Configuration

As previously mentioned, there are a number of different aspects of the Job Queue that cannot be configured from the web console. In the next few sections we will introduce each of these aspects through examples that will need to be followed in order to continue on with the rest of the examples in this chapter.

Replacing Job Queue's PHP with Your Own

In any serious Job Queue setup one of the first tasks that should be undertaken is the replacement of the PHP binary that ships with Job Queue with one of your own choosing. While this may seem like it should be unnecessary, it is strongly recommended if you require any extensions that are not immediately available in Job Queue. The reason for this is that, unlike the PHP binaries that ship with Zend Core, the Zend Platform PHP binaries do not come with the necessary tools (`phpize` and `php-config`) to build shared modules for them. While it is entirely possible to compile your own PHP binary for use with the Job Queue from scratch using a PHP distribution from http://www.php.net, it is much easier to simply adjust the Job Queue configuration to point to the binary provided by Zend Core that has the necessary tooling (and a lot more precompiled and supported extensions).

Note If you must compile your own PHP binary for Job Queue, you must match the major version of PHP exactly (the first two digits of the PHP version, e.g., 5.2.x) and compile a FastCGI-compatible version of the binary. Job Queue uses FastCGI for executing the PHP scripts managed by the queue.

To change the binary used by the Job Queue, open the etc/fastcgi-jobq.conf file (from the base of your Platform installation), an example of which is shown in Listing 5-1.

Listing 5-1. *The fastcgi-jobq.conf File of Zend Platform*

```
; Static PHP servers for default user
Server type="application/x-httpd-php" CommandLine="/usr/local/Zend/Platform/bin/php-➥
fastcgi5" ConnectionTimeout="60"➥
RequestTimeout="60" StartProcesses="4"➥
Impersonate="1"➥
SetEnv="PHP_FCGI_CHILDREN=1"➥
 SetEnv="PHP_FCGI_MAX_REQUESTS=100"➥
 ConnectionTimeout="30"➥
 SetEnv="PHPRC=/usr/local/Zend/Platform/etc/fastcgi"

; Minimum and Maximum of dynamic servers
MinDynamicServers 8
MaxDynamicServers 16

; Default parameters for other dynamic servers (Perl)
DynamicServer ConnectionTimeout="30"

; Where to place socket files
IpcDir /tmp
```

Note The fastcgi-jobq.conf file shown in Listing 5-1 is a standard FastCGI configuration file. If you are curious as to the meaning behind all of the other directives within it, please consult the FastCGI documentation for more information.

In this configuration file shown in Listing 5-1, we are currently interested in the CommandLine parameter with the default value of `/usr/local/Zend/Platform/bin/php-fastcgi5` (depending on your installation location, your path may vary). To make the PHP version used by Job Queue be the same as the one provided with Zend Core, you must modify this line to point to the `php-cgi` binary that can be found in the `bin/` directory of your Zend Core installation (i.e., `/usr/local/Zend/Core/bin/php-cgi`).

With this binary adjusted, you must now alter the configuration of the PHP itself to adjust the directory used to locate extensions to load in PHP. We will discuss this now.

Modifying the Configuration of Job Queue's PHP

If, for whatever reason, you ever need to modify the configuration settings of the PHP used by Job Queue itself (for instance, following from the previous section you have to modify the `extension_dir` configuration directive to point to the Zend Core PHP modules), you can find it in the `etc/fastcgi/php.ini` file (from the Zend Platform base installation directory). If you followed along with the previous section of replacing the PHP binary that ships with Zend Platform to the one provided by Zend Core, then you will need to open this file and change the `extension_dir` line to the location of your Zend Core PHP modules: `/usr/local/Zend/Core/lib/php/20060613` (assuming your base Zend Core installation is in `/usr/local/Zend/Core`).

To follow along with the examples in this text, you will need to at least add the bcmath extension to your Job Queue PHP. Assuming you have followed along with all of the exercises in this text, you should just have to add the following line to the `etc/fastcgi/php.ini` file to enable this extension:

```
extension=bcmath.so
```

Once added, restart the Job Queue. (Instructions on doing this from the command line follow in the next section.) In the next section you will learn how to create your first job (a simple PHPInfo script), and at that point you can test to make sure the extension was loaded properly by checking for it in the output of that script.

Controlling the Job Queue from the Command Line

At times, especially for system administrators, it is desirable to control various services that execute on a server from the command line. This can be done for the Job Queue as well by using the `jqd.sh` script found in the Platform `bin/` directory. This script functions in the same way as any other common management script and supports the options "start," "stop," "restart," and so on. If you have modified the binary used by Job Queue or changed the PHP configuration settings of the Job Queue PHP as was discussed in the previous two sections, you can restart the server and have the changes take effect by executing the following command as root or super user:

```
# /usr/local/Zend/Platform/bin/jqd.sh restart
```

Using the Job Queue to Execute PHP Scripts

Now that you have an introduction to the Job Queue web interface, let's create our first job—a simple PHPInfo script.

Creating Your First Job

Start by creating a `phpinfo.php` file in your Job Queue script directory (found in the Queue Settings page) with a single function call to `phpinfo()` within it. You can now create a new job by clicking the icon in the Add Job column near the end of the Queues Statistics table (Figure 5-2). This will bring up the Add New Job page shown in Figure 5-4.

The Add New Job page allows you to create an arbitrary job to run either once or on a recurring basis as desired. Following is a listing of the various fields in this form and their meaning:

- *Name*: The name of the job, a simple arbitrary human-readable identifier

- *Priority*: The priority of the job in the queue in relation to other jobs pending

- *Application*: The name of the application this job relates to; used for grouping purposes in the web interface and accessible from the API (to be discussed)

- *Script File*: The script file (within the Job Queue scripts directory) to execute for this job

- *Dependency*: A numeric job number indicating what job must complete successfully first before this job can be executed

- *Scheduling*: The time when, and how often, this job should execute

For the purposes of a PHPInfo script it's safe to fill out this form in any way you see fit; however be careful to ensure that the PHPInfo script you created (and stored in the Job Queue scripts directory) is properly identified. Once you have filled out the form, click Save, and you should be informed that the job has been created.

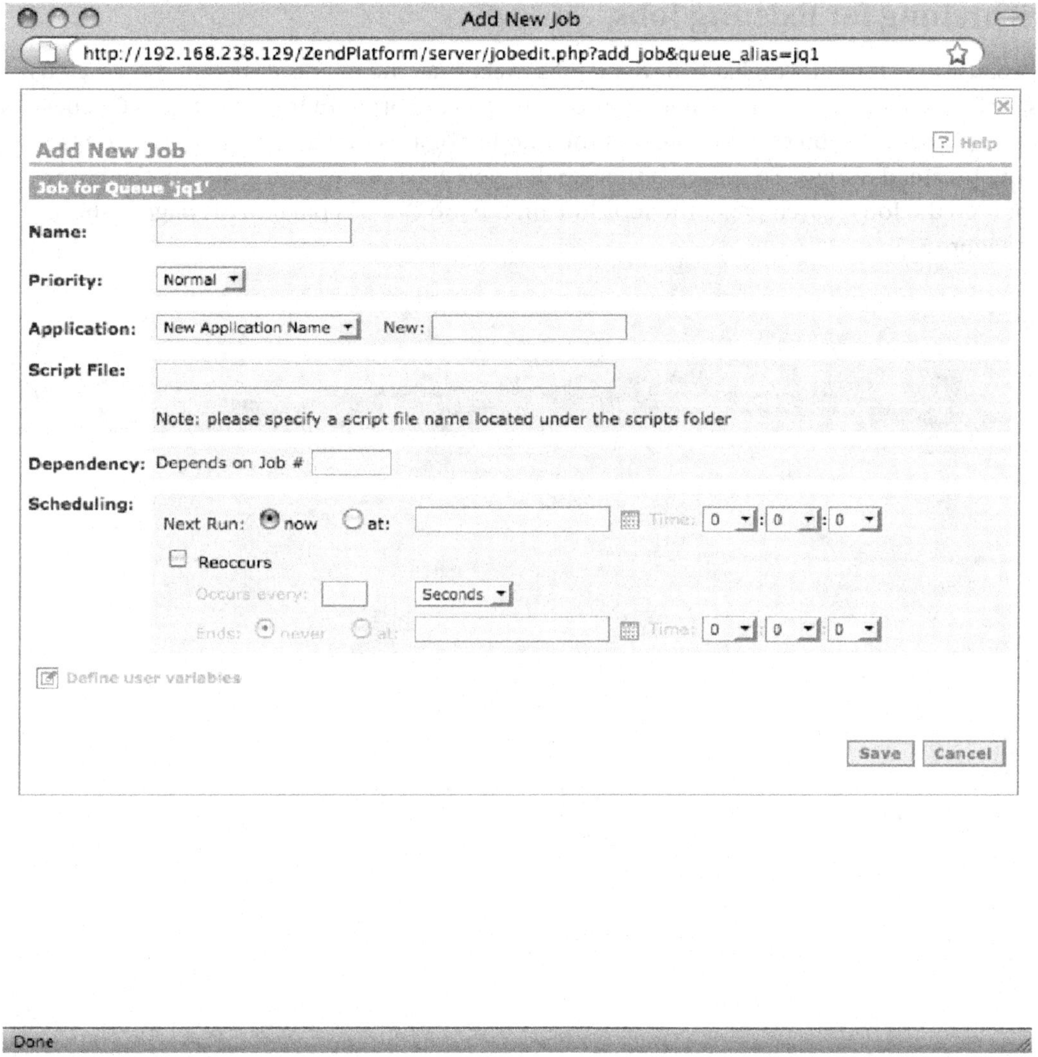

Figure 5-4. *The Add New Job page*

Searching for Existing Jobs

Because at this point you likely have no jobs executing, the job described in the previous section should execute immediately, and when you are brought back to the Job Queues page (Figure 5-2) you should note that the number of jobs in the Successful column is now 1 instead of zero. To see what this job did, you will need to find it first by searching for it on the Jobs search page (the Jobs link on the Job Queues page). This page is shown in Figure 5-5.

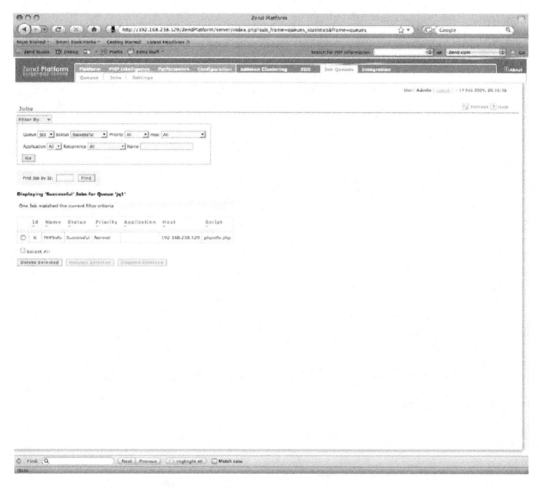

Figure 5-5. *The Job Queue search interface*

Note You can perform some typical searches for things such as "Successful Jobs" or "Failed Jobs" simply by clicking on the statistical number found in the Job Queues status page (Figure 5-2).

Using the Job Queue search interface, you can search for jobs that are known in the queue (successful, complete, pending, failed, or otherwise) using the filtering mechanism found at the top of the page. To examine the details about a job, click on the desired job—resulting in the Job Details pop-up window shown in Figure 5-6.

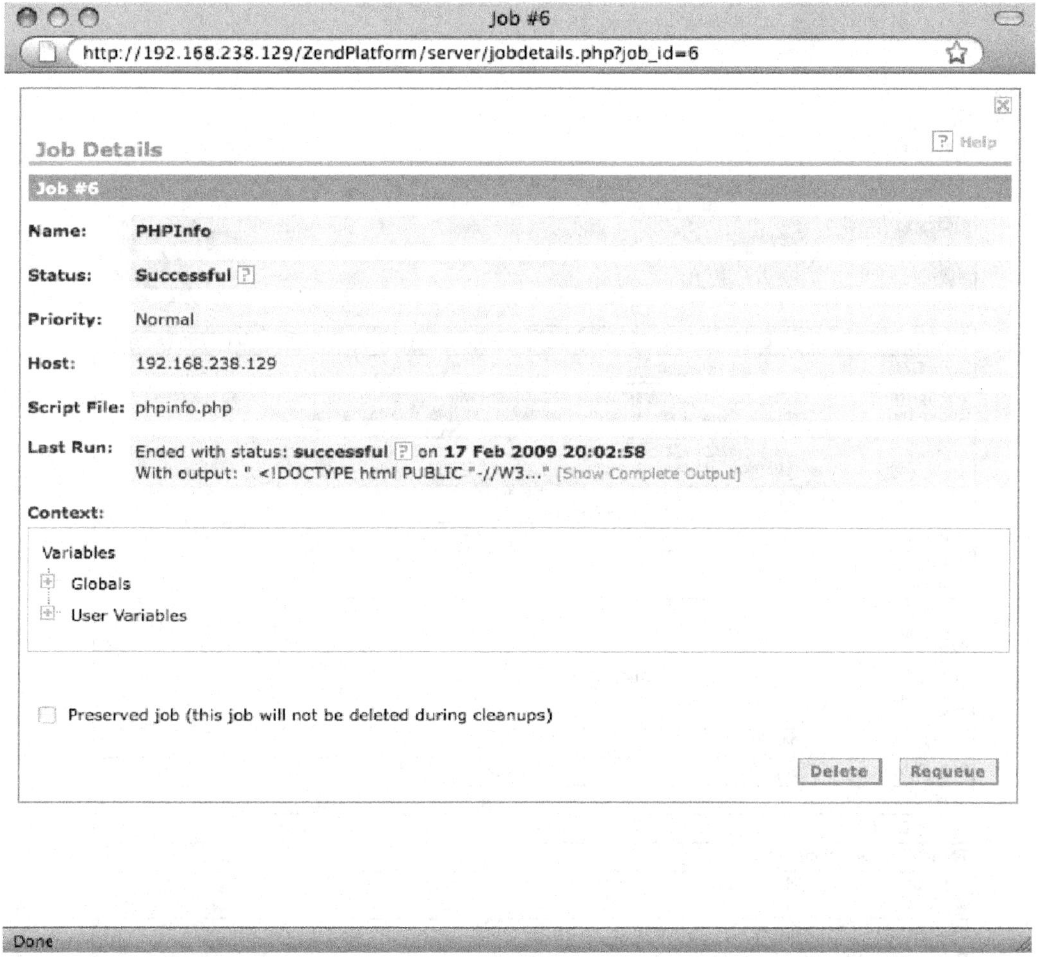

Figure 5-6. *The Job Details screen*

From the Job Details screen you can see everything that is known about the job in question including its status (did it succeed?), the output of the script after its last execution, and all of the variables that were defined at the time the job executed. If you have been following along in this book, then it is very likely that the job you look at will be your PHPInfo script job added from the previous section. If you would like to see the output of this script execution, click the Show Complete Output link in the Job Details screen to bring up the Job Output viewer shown in Figure 5-7.

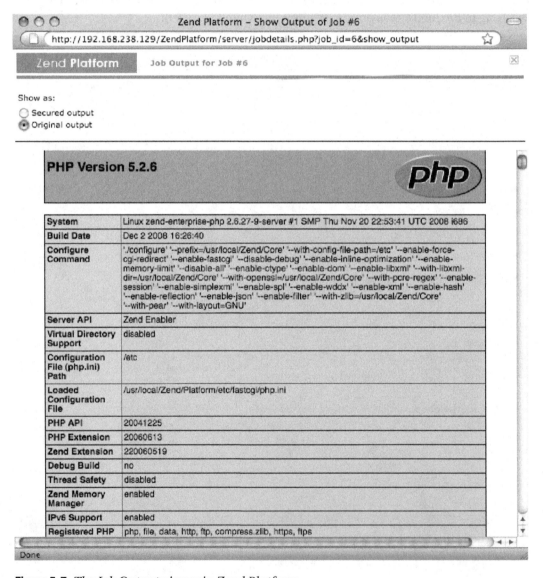

Figure 5-7. *The Job Output viewer in Zend Platform*

The Job Output viewer allows you to view any and all output produced by the PHP engine that executed the job through its entire life cycle. You can use this output for informational or debugging purposes, and it can be rendered in "Secured output" mode (meaning that all HTML will be escaped, the default), or "Original output" mode (shown in Figure 5-7, where all HTML is rendered). Being able to view the output of jobs (from a print statement or otherwise) and consequently their logs and other information through the console is a very powerful feature that should be leveraged in all of your Job Queue scripts.

Using Input Parameters in Job Queue Scripts

One of the more powerful features of the Job Queue server is that, when you create a job, you can specify variables to pass into it before it executes. These values can be any valid PHP variable and can be passed in from the API (discussed later) or created from the web interface. Once passed into a job, these variables are then available to your Job Queue PHP script by accessing them from the global scope. Let's examine such a script, shown in Listing 5-2.

Listing 5-2. *The fibonacci.php Job Queue Script*

```php
<?php

function calculateFib($seq)
{
    $prev1stDigit = 0;
    $prev2ndDigit = 1;
    $retval = 0;

    if($seq == 0) return 0;
    if($seq == 1) return 1;

    for($i = 0; $i < ($seq-1); $i++)
    {
        $retval = bcadd($prev1stDigit, $prev2ndDigit);
        $prev1stDigit = $prev2ndDigit;
        $prev2ndDigit = $retval;
    }

    return $retval;
}
```

```
if(!isset($sequenceNum))
{
    set_job_failed("Sequence Number not provided");
}

print "Running Job to calculate Fibonacci Sequence....<br/>";
print "Calculating for Sequence #: " . $sequenceNum . "<br/>";

print "<br/>Answer:<hr/>";
print calculateFib($sequenceNum);
```

In this simple script to calculate Fibonacci sequences, we have a single function calculateFib() that does the calculation, executed by the code in the global scope. As you can see, this by all accounts is a standard PHP script, but there is one significant difference—the $sequenceNum variable. This variable is not set anywhere in the script, because it is expected that this variable will be set by the Job Queue server when it executes this job. Thus we must confirm that it was indeed an input value and consequently we check to make sure it is defined before allowing the job to execute. Assuming it exists, we execute the remainder of the script and calculate the value for that particular number in the sequence.

Note You will also notice that our first Job Queue API function, set_job_failed(), is used in Listing 5-2. This function is used within a PHP script run from the Job Queue to trigger a logical "Job failed" to the Job Queue server. It takes a single parameter (a string error message) and causes the immediate exit of the PHP script. We will discuss this function and others in more detail later in the chapter.

To use this script, we simply need to put it into the path where all of the Job Queue scripts are stored (as specified in the configuration of the Job Queue) and create a job from the web interface to execute it just as we did with the PHPInfo script earlier in the chapter. However, for this particular script we need to go through the one extra step of defining the input parameter $sequenceNum for the job as well. To do this, when creating the job simply click the "Define user variables" link at the bottom of the Add New Job page (Figure 5-4), bringing up the interface shown in Figure 5-8. Simply add the variable names and values you need, and click Save.

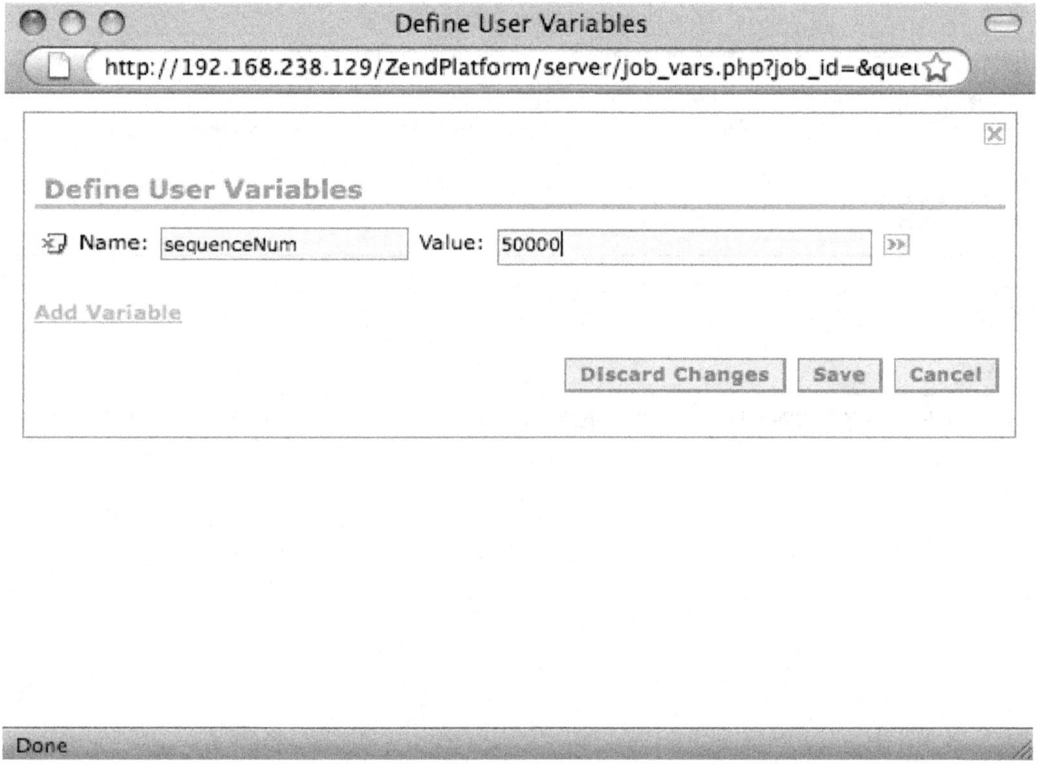

Figure 5-8. *The Define User Variables page for new jobs*

Note From the web interface, your ability to add values is limited to strings only. From the API interface, you can add much more complex values such as objects and more.

Once you have set up the input parameters of the job and saved it, the job will be executed per your scheduling specifications. Ultimately the job will execute and the sequence will be calculated and be available for viewing from the web interface. An example of this execution is shown in Figure 5-9.

Figure 5-9. *The output of the* fibonacci.php *script from the Job Queue console*

Creating Jobs Programmatically Using the Job Queue API

Thus far we have only used the web interface provided by Zend Platform to create and view the output of jobs, and hopefully you have done so with complete success. While useful, the real power of the Job Queue is creating jobs logically from your web application as necessary. In this section, we'll explore how this is done using the Job Queue API provided by Zend Platform to not only create jobs from your web applications but also retrieve the results of jobs after they have executed.

To demonstrate the usage of the Job Queue functionality from within a PHP script, we first must create an application. For this application we will of course use Zend Framework; for the sake of brevity we will not discuss every aspect but will focus only on the relevant logic to the Job Queue functionality. Note that in the code examples provided with this book you can find the complete application for your own inspection. That said, specifically we will be looking at three different scenarios of using the Job Queue that adequately exercise its API functionality:

- Adding a single job to the Job Queue for asynchronous execution

- Adding 25 asynchronous jobs to the queue from a single web request

- Creating a long-running real-time asynchronous job

For all of these demonstrations we will continue using the Fibonacci Job Queue script developed in previous examples.

■**Note** We will not be discussing every single API call available to the classes and functions of the Job Queue API, as these API calls are largely self-explanatory and are described in detail within the Zend Platform User's Guide, available on the Zend Technologies' web site: `http://www.zend.com/en/products/platform/resources`.

Adding a Single Job to the Queue

To begin our examination of the Job Queue we will first look at an example of adding a single asynchronous job to the queue through PHP API calls. This is done in the addAction() of the JobqueueController class, shown in Listing 5-3.

Listing 5-3. *The JobqueueController::addAction() Method for Adding a Job to the Queue*

```
public function addAction()
{
    $queue = new ZendAPI_Queue(self::QUEUE_HOST);

    $job = new ZendAPI_Job("fibonacci.php");
    $job->setJobName("Fibonacci Sequence Calc");
    $job->setUserVariables(array('sequenceNum' => 50000));
```

```
    if(!$queue->login(self::QUEUE_PASSWD))
    {
        throw new Exception("Could not login to Job Queue");
    }

    $job_id = $queue->addJob($job);

    if($job_id < 1)
    {
        throw new Exception("Could not add Job to Queue");
    }

    $this->view->job_id = $job_id;
}
```

Examining Listing 5-3 you can see a number of objects and methods called that are related to the Job Queue. The first is the ZendAPI_Queue object created—this class is an internal class available to PHP installations with Zend Platform job queuing enabled and takes a single parameter (the hostname and port number of the Job Queue you are connecting to). The second object created is an instance of the ZendAPI_Job class, which is again available to job-queued-enabled PHPs and represents a programmatic representation of a job within the queue. The ZendAPI_Job class is both accepted as a parameter to methods within the ZendAPI_Queue class (for instance, when adding a new job) and also returned as a value when requesting information (such as retrieving a job's details by job ID). In this case we are using it to add a new job to the queue, so we must first create an instance of it and pass it the name of the Job Queue PHP script to be executed (in this case fibonacci.php). Once we have created our job object, we can set numerous values such as scheduling, priorities, name of job, user variables to pass into the job, and so on. For our purposes we simply call two methods—first the setJobName() method (setting a human-readable name for the job in the web interface) and second the setUserVariables() method, which accepts an associative array of key/value pairs defining the variables and their values to pass into the job when executed.

■**Tip** When calling the setUserVariables() method from the API you may desire to send complex data types such as object instances to the Job Queue script instead of simple primitive values or arrays. If this behavior is desired, you must ensure that these classes are defined in advance in the Job Queue PHP instances by adding an auto-include file that resolves their class declarations. Failure to do this will result in the objects either deserializing incorrectly or causing a fatal error.

With our job object defined, we can begin the process of adding the job to the queue. The first step in this process is to establish a connection to the server by calling the ZendAPI_Queue::login() method, passing in the password you defined when the queue was set up, and ensuring that it returns true, indicating that a connection was made. With the web PHP successfully connected to the Job Queue server, you can add the job to the queue by calling the addJob() method and passing in the ZendAPI_Job object defined earlier in the script. Upon success, the addJob() method will return an integer representing the ID of the job within the queue for future reference if needed. As expected, when this script is executed a new Fibonacci sequence job calculating the Fibonacci sequence number 50,000 is triggered to execute as soon as possible. (The results of this execution can be seen in the Job Queue web interface.) For completeness' sake our provided demo application displays the resulting job ID, allowing you to quickly find it within the Zend Platform interface.

Adding Multiple Jobs in a Single Web Request

Just as prepared statements in databases allow you to reuse variables bound to the statement (just by changing their value and executing the statement again), Zend Platform's Job Queue API allows you to reuse your ZendAPI_Job objects to add multiple similar but independent jobs concurrently. An example of this is shown in Listing 5-4 in the Jobqueue Controller::add25Action() method, which adds 25 Fibonacci sequence calculations to the queue in a single web request.

Listing 5-4. *The JobqueueController::add25Action() Method for Adding 25 Jobs in a Single Request*

```php
public function add25Action()
{
    $queue = new ZendAPI_Queue(self::QUEUE_HOST);

    if(!$queue->login(self::QUEUE_PASSWD))
    {
        throw new Exception("Could not login to Job Queue Server");
    }

    $job_ids = array();

    for($i = 0; $i < 25; $i++)
    {
        $job = new ZendAPI_Job("fibonacci.php");
```

```
        $job->setJobName("Fibonacci Seq (" .
                             ($i+1). " of 25))");
        $job->setUserVariables(array(
                             'sequenceNum' => 50000 + $i));

        $job_id = $queue->addJob($job);

        if($job_id < 1)
        {
            throw new Exception("Could not add Job to Queue");
        }

        $job_ids[] = $job_id;
    }

    $this->view->job_ids = $job_ids;
}
```

While the example shown in Listing 5-3 is very similar to that found in Listing 5-4, the latter is interesting because it demonstrates how through the use of the job queuing functionality of Zend Platform you can schedule significant amounts of work to be done asynchronously from a single web request. The result upon executing this script (if looking in the Zend Platform web interface) would be the creation of 25 jobs, each being executed at the earliest moment until completed.

■**Note** The number of concurrent asynchronous jobs that can be executed at any given point in time is limited entirely by the number of FastCGI processes available to the Job Queue server and is thus limited by the number that can be kept in memory at once on the Job Queue server.

Using Job Queue for Long-Running Real-Time Operations

One of the most interesting applications of the Job Queue is using it to perform expensive real-time operations without preventing your web servers from serving other requests during that operation's execution. This process is described in Figure 5-10.

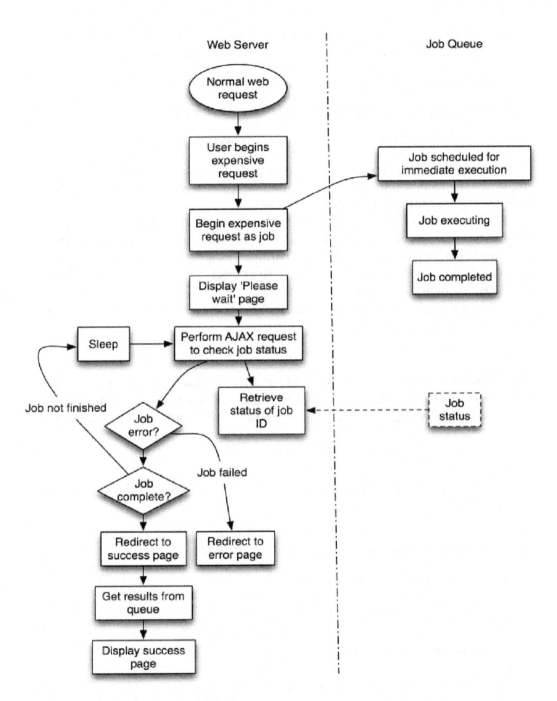

Figure 5-10. *The workflow of performing expensive real-time operations effectively using the Zend Platform Job Queue*

As shown in Figure 5-10, the secret to making expensive real-time operations feasible using the Job Queue is broken down into three fundamental components:

- Creating the expensive real-time operation as a job within the Job Queue

- Redirecting the user to a "Please wait" page while the job executes

- Use JavaScript to make periodic requests to check the status of the job

So why is this a better method of performing real-time expensive operations than simply running them within your PHP script residing on the web server? Because, despite the long-running nature of the operation in question, the burden of that execution is carried by your Job Queue while the web server itself is quickly freed to answer other requests. Of course, some of these requests will be from the JavaScript code checking the status of the job placed into the queue (hardly an expensive operation), but all of the others can be users taking advantage of that web process/thread to do other useful and completely unconnected things.

As you may expect, each of these three steps has some level of PHP code associated with it. Let's explore them now.

■**Tip** The workflow described in Figure 5-10 can be expanded. For example, instead of simply checking whether the job failed or succeeded, you can check the output of the job once it has succeeded to determine how the user currently waiting will continue in your application instead of simply checking for a fail/succeed condition.

To begin, let's take a look at the `JobqueueController::addbigAction()` method, shown in Listing 5-5.

Listing 5-5. *The JobqueueController::addbigAction() Method*

```
public function addbigAction()
{
    $queue = new ZendAPI_Queue(self::QUEUE_HOST);

    if(!$queue->login(self::QUEUE_PASSWD))
    {
        throw new Exception("Could not login to Job Queue");
    }
```

```php
$job = new ZendAPI_Job("fibonacci.php");
$job->setJobName("Fibonacci Sequence Calc");
$job->setUserVariables(array('sequenceNum' => 50000));

$job_id = $queue->addJob($job);

if($job_id < 1)
{
    throw new Exception("Could not add Job to Queue");
}

$this->view->job_id = $job_id;

}
```

Looking at Listing 5-5, you'll notice that it is basically identical to our earlier `JobqueueController::addAction()` shown in Listing 5-3. This is because we have not fundamentally changed anything about how we use the Job Queue. Rather, the magic of this process can be found in the view template for this action, shown in Listing 5-6.

Listing 5-6. *The addbig.phtml View Script*

```html
<h1>Job Processing</h1>
<hr/>
Please wait, we are processing your job.
<script language="JavaScript">
<!--
    function getXmlHttpRequest()
    {
        var xmlHttp;

        try
        {
            xmlHttp = new XMLHttpRequest();
        }
        catch(e)
        {
            try
            {
                xmlHttp = new ActiveXObject("Msxml2.XMLHTTP");
            }
```

```javascript
        catch(e)
        {
            try
            {
                xmlHttp = new
                        ActiveXObject("Microsoft.XMLHTTP");
            }
            catch(e)
            {
                alert("Your browser can't do AJAX!");
                return false;
            }
        }
    }

    return xmlHttp;
}


function checkJob(jobId)
{
    var xmlHttp = getXmlHttpRequest();

    xmlHttp.onreadystatechange = function()
    {
        if(xmlHttp.readyState == 4)
        {
            var response = eval(xmlHttp.responseText);

            switch(response)
            {
                case false:
                    alert("There was an error checking the status!");
                    break;
                case 1:
                    window.location="/JobQueue_Web/jobqueue/getanswer?➥
                        job_id=" + jobId;
                    break;
            }
            return;
        }
    }
```

```
        xmlHttp.open("GET", "/JobQueue_Web/jobqueue/checkjob?job_id=" + jobId);
        xmlHttp.send(null);

        setTimeout('checkJob('+jobId+')', 1000);
    }


    checkJob(<?php print $this->job_id;?>);
-->
</script>
```

Looking at Listing 5-6, you'll notice that there is a fair amount of JavaScript used. This JavaScript is used to create a Ajax request object under various browsers (the getXmlHttpRequest() function) and then perform an asynchronous browser request to our server, ultimately calling the JobqueueController::checkjobAction() method. Per Figure 5-10, the purpose of the request is to check the status of the job by providing its ID to the back end. Once a status has been established, the JavaScript then redirects the user to a result (or error) page. To see how this works, let's look at Listing 5-7, which is the JobqueueController::checkjobAction() method.

Listing 5-7. *The JobqueueController::checkjobAction() for Asynchronous Job Queue Status Requests*

```
public function checkjobAction()
{
    $this->_helper->viewRenderer->setNoRender();
    $this->_helper->layout->disableLayout();

    $job_id = $this->_getParam('job_id', 0);

    if($job_id <= 0)
    {
        print Zend_Json_Encoder::encode(false);
        return;
    }

    $queue = new ZendAPI_Queue(self::QUEUE_HOST);

    if(!$queue->login(self::QUEUE_PASSWD))
    {
        print Zend_Json_Encoder::encode(false);
        return;
    }
```

```
    $job = $queue->getJob($job_id);

    if(!($job instanceof ZendAPI_Job))
    {
        print Zend_Json_Encoder::encode(false);
        return;
    }

    print Zend_Json_Encoder::encode($job->getJobStatus());
}
```

While Listing 5-7 is a fairly decently sized code block, most of the logic contained within it exists for the purpose of error checking rather than anything of particular consequence to us in this discussion. Rather, it isn't until the latter half of the method where a call to the ZendAPI_Queue::getJob() method is made to retrieve the job details from the Job Queue server where things get interesting. This call accepts a single parameter (the job ID in question) and upon success will return an instance of ZendAPI_Job that contains all of the details of the requested job ID. Using this object, we can simply call the ZendAPI_Job::getJobStatus() method to return an integer status of the job back to the server. Since our request is being made through an Ajax request we use the Zend_Json_Encoder::encode() method in all cases to produce JavaScript Object Notation (JSON) output for any return value provided.

Note The integer status provided by the ZendAPI_Job::getJobStatus() method is a valued represented by one of the job status constants provided for by the Zend Platform Job Queue API. For a complete listing of these constants, values, and meanings please consult the Zend Platform User's Guide.

The final piece of our real-time example is to redirect the user to the success page and display the Fibonacci value for the requested sequence. Looking back at the JavaScript of Listing 5-6, this is handled by the JobqueueController::getanswerAction() whose job is, given the completed Job ID, to retrieve the output of the job and display the full calculated Fibonacci number. This code is shown in Listing 5-8.

Listing 5-8. *The JobqueueController::getanswerAction() Method*

```
public function getanswerAction()
{
    $job_id = $this->_getParam('job_id', 0);
```

```php
    if($job_id <= 0)
    {
        throw new Exception("No Job ID provided");
    }

    $queue = new ZendAPI_Queue(self::QUEUE_HOST);

    if(!$queue->login(self::QUEUE_PASSWD))
    {
        throw new Exception("Could not log into Job Queue");
    }

    $job = $queue->getJob($job_id);

    if(!($job instanceof ZendAPI_Job))
    {
        throw new Exception("Invalid Job ID");
    }

    $output = $job->getOutput();

    $answer = substr($output, strpos($output, "!!!!ANSWER_START!!!!") +
                            strlen("!!!!ANSWER_START!!!!"));

    $this->view->answer = $answer;
}
```

Looking at the Listing 5-8, again we are using the ZendAPI_Queue::getJob() method to retrieve an instance of ZendAPI_Job representing the job referenced by the provided job ID. However, instead of using the ZendAPI_Job::getJobStatus() action we call the ZendAPI_Job::getOutput() method to retrieve the output of the request.

This is where things get a bit interesting, because if you recall from the original jobs we created using the Job Queue earlier in the chapter, the output of our job (including the Fibonacci sequence answer) was meant to be read from the browser by a person, and it included some basic HTML for formatting. Since we are using the exact same script for this example, how exactly are we to retrieve the answer from the job without going through the hassle of parsing the HTML content? The answer is simple: we simply provide two versions of the output for each job. The first version is exactly as we have seen before (human-readable HTML) so that it can be examined from the web interface. However, the second version should be machine-readable so your web server PHP instances can retrieve the output and extract the output easily.

For these purposes we can simply add to the bottom of the output of the job a unique separator that can be used to identify the start of the machine-readable output and then follow that separator with the machine-readable data. In our case we are only interested in the actual Fibonacci sequence, so that is all we will provide, but more complex use cases can return serialized objects or any other serialized data. To put code to this discussion, let's look at Listing 5-9, a replication of the original Fibonacci sequence Job Queue code base shown in Listing 5-2 with the machine-readable additions described in this section.

Listing 5-9. *The Modified Fibonacci Job Queue Script to Allow It to Be Machine-Readable*

```php
<?php

function calculateFib($seq)
{
    $prev1stDigit = 0;
    $prev2ndDigit = 1;
    $retval = 0;

    if($seq == 0) return 0;
    if($seq == 1) return 1;

    for($i = 0; $i < ($seq-1); $i++)
    {
        $retval = bcadd($prev1stDigit, $prev2ndDigit);
        $prev1stDigit = $prev2ndDigit;
        $prev2ndDigit = $retval;
    }

    return $retval;
}

if(!isset($sequenceNum))
{
    set_job_failed("Sequence Number not provided");
}

print "Running Job to calculate Fibonacci Sequence....<br/>";
print "Calculating for Sequence #: " . $sequenceNum . "<br/>";
```

```
$result = calculateFib($sequenceNum);

print "<br/>Answer:<hr/>";
print $result . "<br/><br/>!!!!ANSWER_START!!!!$result";
```

Looking at Listing 5-9 and comparing it to Listing 5-2 you can see the slight modifications. Most notably, the sequence value itself is displayed twice—once in a human-readable HTML format and a second immediately following the unique identifier !!!!ANSWER_START!!!!. This unique identifier is searched for in Listing 5-8 when retrieving the output of the job to locate the sequence number and ultimately display it to the user.

With that, we've explained both in concept and code how expensive operations can be performed in real time without sacrificing your web server's ability to respond to requests! Obviously the concepts illustrated in this section can be refined and improved, but in principal the concepts shown here can be used in a very effective manner for important real-time transaction such as credit-card processing.

Conclusion

Thanks to Zend Platform's Job Queue functionality, PHP can now enjoy the same benefits of asynchronous operations that other languages such as Java have been utilizing for years, adding yet another tool to your arsenal as a developer. From simple reoccurring scheduled jobs to complex asynchronous image manipulation, as should be obvious after reading this chapter, the Job Queue functionality provided by Zend Platform is hands-down one of the most powerful performance features ever introduced into the PHP landscape. I hope through the guidance in this chapter you have learned enough to begin utilizing this exciting technology in your own applications to gain more performance from your applications and enhance the overall user experience.

## CHAPTER 6

Securing Your PHP Applications

As the Web has evolved over the years it has become a critical, nearly transparent part of our everyday lives as people. As developers, this evolution has meant an ever-growing risk of abuse from those with malicious intent to our applications—and more importantly our data. In this chapter we'll discuss these threats in both their tangible and abstract forms and help you prepare yourself to defend not only from the attacks we know of today but also the ones to emerge tomorrow.

Setting the Context

The first thing we believe it is important for you to understand is the lens through which we will be discussing security. That is to say, you could follow everything we say in this chapter word by word and implement every single thing we suggest and *still* find yourself the victim of a security breach. The reasons for this are numerous, but we think that the most important is that *security involves vastly more than your web application itself.* While abusing the logic of an application is clearly a possible way to attack you, it is by far not the only potential attack. In this chapter when discussing concrete security issues we'll be looking only through a PHP-colored lens and avoiding potential vulnerabilities that may exist elsewhere in your technology stack.

We have decided not to rehash in their entirety every detail of every type of attack you'll find out there in the vast Internet. To do so would be to repeat the message of others when they have done a magnificent job of speaking on the subject. Rather, the goal of this chapter is to create in you a security-aware mindset that will hopefully prepare you to identify and defend against attacks on any level—even if you tend to lean toward the PHP layer.

Note For those of you who are interested primarily in concrete security examples beyond those provided in this chapter we recommend that you supplement this book with *Essential PHP Security* (O'Reilly, 2005) by PHP security expert and friend Chris Shiflett. Chris has dedicated the majority of the past five or more years to studying the security implications of PHP applications, and we highly recommend his book.

Defining Security

Over the years John has spoken worldwide at various technical conferences on the subject of security, and one thing he has always found interesting is the fundamental lack of understanding most developers have when it comes to what *exactly* security is. Ask most developers about security and you often will find their responses to be entirely focused on specific attack vectors and the defenses against them. While having an in-depth knowledge of these things is indeed important, a postmortem discussion of the causality between a known attack and its defense will hardly protect your application.

We say this because chances are that if you are aware of a particular attack then so is your attacker, and they fully expect all of the previously exposed and used attacks to be ineffective against your application. Rather than studying attacks and countermeasures as if you were studying the game of two chess masters, study the attackers themselves. The more you understand about the attackers trying to compromise your system the more you will be able to target your defenses against them, and the more effective your overall security policy will be. After all, every time you read in the news or hear about a successful attack against an Internet application, typically you don't hear that the victim was negligent in their security practices, but you do hear how it was a new, unique attack that no one had seen before.

In short, realize that the practice of security is first to understand who your attacker is and second to find out what interests them in your application. Is your greatest threat an 18-year-old who wants to become the most popular kid on a social networking site, or is it a member of a dark criminal organization looking to steal the money and identities of your customers? It is an important question, because it not only tells you what is the most likely thing to be attacked but also helps you balance the annoyance of security defenses in an application with the ultimate business expectations your application serves.

Ultimately security is about one thing: information. Your job is to keep the private information of your application and that of your users away from attackers while attempting to collect as much information as possible about potential attackers to use against them. Ultimately that is the best you can do. Applications will always have bugs, and even if they don't, history has shown us that browsers, operating systems, and databases will. The best you can hope to do is be as proactive in identifying these threats as possible before they can be used against you.

With that said, let's discuss some more tangible aspects of security.

Common Threats and Defenses

When discussing security in a PHP application there is a common set of threats and defenses that you should be aware of. The vast majority of threats in web application security can be prevented with one simple rule: filter input, escape output.

You will see as we discuss the various attacks in this chapter that almost all of them can be prevented following this single simple rule. The problem is that while this rule is simple to understand, you will see that it applies in so many ways to so many different situations. It is often quite easy to overlook a particular aspect of it and in turn create security vulnerabilities.

A corollary to this rule of filtering input and escaping output is an even more valuable notion: defense in depth. This notion represents the idea that no single layer of security is suitable to defend you from an attack and that the only viable defense is one that consists of many defenses working together to ward off attackers. As we go through the following concrete examples of threats and their defenses, it is important to realize that they should be followed at all levels of your application. For example, just because you have sanitized a given piece of input at the beginning of your application does not mean you shouldn't sanitize it later. It may seem redundant, but it will help you prevent attacks that you may not realize exist!

Let's take a look at some practical examples of security attacks and their defenses.

Input Security

The best way to prevent an attack against your PHP application (assuming no one has literally coded in a back door) is to prevent an attacker from finding a way to trick the logic of your application into doing something the developer didn't intend. There are many subcategories to this topic, but they all break down to these basic concepts:

- Input sources

- Data filtering and validation

- White-list validation

- File uploads

- Round-tripping of data

Input Sources

The first thing all applications should do is be careful where they accept data from and accept data from the outside only under very specific and controlled circumstances. This is actually a bit of a problem for PHP applications because historically ease of development trumped any potential security implications. One great example is the `$_REQUEST` superglobal. This array contains all of the input (specifically GET, POST, and HTTP cookie data) received from the user and was originally created to simplify the transition from older PHP scripts that had the `register_globals` configuration directive enabled. The problem with this concept from a security perspective is that you still have absolutely no idea where exactly the data you are using has come from. Consider the code snippet in Listing 6-1.

Note Unlike many other authors, we will not again point out the utterly unacceptable security practices of writing an application that relies on the `register_globals` directive to be enabled in order to function. For those applications that do require this directive the only reasonable security practice is to remove this dependency as the first and highest priority before continuing on with the other threats discussed in this chapter.

Listing 6-1. *An Example E-mail Address Update Script*

```php
<?php

// Get the user's new e-mail address
$email = $_REQUEST['email'];

// Update the database

$query = "UPDATE accounts
            SET e-mail='" . mysqli_escape_string($email) .
        "' WHERE account_id = " $_SESSION['account_id'];

$db = get_db();
mysqli_query($db, $query);

?>
```

Listing 6-1 is intended to represent a very simple script that accepts a new e-mail address from one of the application's users. The intent of the developer is that this script would receive an HTML form submission from the user (that contains a text form element with an ID of "email") and in turn update the database. However, because the `$_REQUEST['email']` approach was used to access this user input, the developer has no way to be certain of the source of the data. In fact, it is possible that if an attacker was able to trick the user's browser into creating a cookie with a name of email (perhaps through another vulnerability on the site) they could trick the previous script into storing any e-mail address that the attacker saw fit. Why is this important? Well, how many web sites have a "Forgot password?" link on their login pages, many of which send a new password to the e-mail address on file for that account?

To prevent this sort of attack vector from being successful your application should always be very specific about where it expects its input to come from. For example, instead of using the $_REQUEST superglobal (that could mean it was a GET, POST, or cookie value), use the specific data source superglobals of $_GET, $_POST, or $_COOKIE as needed for the logic of your application.

Another common source of attack vectors comes from an unhealthy trust of the $_SERVER superglobal within PHP applications. While there are certain data elements of this array that you could argue are indeed worthy of trust, many of the more commonly used values are provided by the client during the request and are just as dangerous as any data found in $_GET. For example, while the $_SERVER['REMOTE_ADDR'] field is a safe value (the IP address that originated the request) the $_SERVER['HTTP_X_FORWARDED_FOR'] variable (used if the requesting client is behind a proxy) is not and must be validated to ensure that data was not interjected. Likewise, the $_SERVER['HTTP_REFERER'] variable (the URL of the previously requested page) is entirely determined by an HTTP header sent by the client and must be scrutinized before usage.

Of all of the $_SERVER variables, however, the ones that are the most dangerous are also the ones that are used by far the most in PHP applications: the $_SERVER['PHP_SELF'], $_SERVER['PATH_INFO'], $_SERVER['HTTP_HOST'], and $_SERVER['PATH TRANSLATED'] variables. These variables are dangerous because their value is actually determined in significant degree by the URL requested by the client to the web server and therefore are potential attack vectors. For example, the $_SERVER['PHP_SELF'] variable is widely used as the action attribute of an HTML form but is calculated based on the URL used to request the current page. Since a request to a URL such as http://www.example.com/index.php/foo/bar is a completely valid request (causing the index.php script to be requested with /foo/bar as the $_SERVER['PATH_INFO']), using this variable blindly allows an attacker to encode JavaScript into the path information and ultimately cause it to be executed in the application when the output is returned. That said, the bottom line is clear: just because it is data you are receiving from the underlying web server doesn't mean it is secure. There are a number of times the web server simply passes the data it receives from the requesting client along to PHP, and therefore all of it should be filtered and validated as any other data is.

Data Filtering and Validation

Once you have limited your input data sources to the specific ones expected by your application (and identified the untrustworthy data), next it is important that you filter the data from these sources and then validate that data to ensure that it meets your assumed criteria. For example, if you expect the variable $_GET['name'] to be an alphabetical string between 2 and 20 characters, you would first filter that variable to remove any non-alphabetical characters that may exist and then validate that the resulting string is between 2 and 20 characters in length.

This process of input filtering and validation can be a time-consuming process and often is a place where corners are cut in order to meet deadlines. Thankfully however,

Zend Framework provides numerous facilities to make this important security measure less painful to implement through the Zend_Filter and Zend_Validate family of classes and components, which we will now discuss.

The Zend_Filter family of components is nothing more than simple classes that each accept a value as input and return filtered against some criterion that the class represents. For example, the Zend_Filter_Alnum component, when given an input string, will return that string minus anything that is not an alphanumeric character. In contrast, the Zend_Validate family of components is used to validate a given input string after it has been filtered to ensure that it meets the assumed criteria such as the Zend_Validate_StringLength component, which validates that the input is within a specific length range.

Depending on your needs, both the Zend_Filter and Zend_Validate component classes can be used completely individually to filter and validate data. However, for the sake of simplicity Zend Framework also offers an optional framework for using these components to filter your input data through the Zend_Filter_Input class. We will be leveraging this component in our following discussions of data filtering.

When using the Zend_Filter_Input component you start by defining two associative arrays: one for the filters to apply to the input variables and a second to define the validation rules for those variables. These filtering and validation definitions are then passed into an instance of the Zend_Filter_Input class along with an associative array of the data you wish to validate. The result is an object instance that allows you to access the input data in a clean and sanitary way. Listing 6-2 demonstrates how this functionality works to validate that the input value $_GET['name'] contains only alphabetical characters and is between 2 and 20 characters in length.

Listing 6-2. *An Example of Using Zend_Filter_Input*

```php
<?php

$filters = array('name' => 'Alpha');
$validators = array('name' => array('StringLength', 2, 20));

$input = new Zend_Filter_Input($filters, $validators, $_GET);

print "This is the name you gave me: " . $input->name;
?>
```

As shown in Listing 6-2, we start off by creating two arrays, $filters and $validators, that contain input variable names as keys (in this case a single variable identified as name) and attaches those variables to a single filter (the Zend_Filter_Alpha filter identified by the string 'Alpha') and a single validator (the Zend_Validate_StringLength validator).

Note For a full explanation of the syntax accepted by the `Zend_Filter_Input` and supporting components, please consult the Zend Framework documentation at `http://framework.zend.com/`.

Once the individual filters and validators have been applied to the input variables, both these arrays plus the superglobal input source (i.e., `$_GET` for GET parameter input variables) are passed in to the constructor of the `Zend_Filter_Input` class. The resulting object can then be used to access all of the input parameters from the original source array in a safe and sanitized manner by referencing them as properties of the object (i.e., `$input->name` corresponds to a sanitized and filtered version of `$_GET['name']` in Listing 6-2).

White-List Validation

When working with input data that is based on a primitive (such as a string), the filtering and validation components provided by the `Zend_Filter_Input` component can work very effectively. However, for other common types of user input such as option boxes, check boxes, radio groups, and even hidden form elements, sometimes creating a simple white-list validation mechanism is a much faster and more secure approach to data input security. Listing 6-3 is an example of using a white-list validation routine to ensure that an attacker cannot compromise the logic of your application by manually submitting an HTTP request with different values for a radio button.

Listing 6-3. *An Example of White-List Validation of User Input*

```php
<?php

$months = array("Jan", "Feb", "Mar", "Apr",
                "May", "Jun", "Jul", "Aug",
                "Sep", "Oct", "Nov", "Dec");

if(!empty($_POST['month']) && in_array($_POST['month'], $months))
{
    print "Valid input";
}
else
{
    exit("Invalid input");
}
?>
```

As you can see, a white list is as simple as creating a list of known accepted values for a given input variable and disallowing any value that isn't explicitly defined in the list. Depending on the nature of the input data, this approach can be less cumbersome to implement than using `Zend_Filter_Input` and `Zend_Validate` or, alternately, can be used in conjunction with the `Zend_Filter_Input` component as necessary.

■**Note** Often developers attempt to use a blacklist approach to security. Instead of defining the acceptable values, they attempt to define the unaccepted values. This is always a bad idea, as by its very nature the majority of successful attacks are caused by attacks that haven't been identified yet and thus can't be predicted.

Securing File Uploads

For web applications, file uploading over HTTP can pose numerous security risks that need to be handled properly. To begin, unless your application has a need to accept file uploads, the best security practice is to disable them entirely by setting the `file_uploads` PHP configuration directive to "off." If your application does need to accept uploads, then there are a few different things you need to consider from a security perspective. For starters, you should limit the size of files being uploaded by making sure the `upload_max_filesize` and `post_max_size` configuration directives are set to values that are as conservative as is reasonable for the nature of the file being uploaded. Note that even if you elect to disable file uploads, the `post_max_size` directive should still be configured to a reasonable maximum value to prevent denial of service attacks caused by concurrent massive post requests.

Another important and often overlooked configuration directive when it comes to security is the `upload_tmp_dir` directive. This directive controls where PHP will store files it receives over an HTTP upload. By default it is set to the operating system's global temporary directory. This can be problematic from a security perspective, as in most every system this directory has the loosest permissions of anywhere in the system and may very well give anyone with any access to the machine access to any file uploaded from your application. To prevent this, it is recommended that a special directory (one per application) be created to handle file uploads with a permission setting more suitable to keep prying eyes at the shell or FTP level from accessing the data.

Once you have configured your file-uploading directives to their appropriate values, we are ready to start looking at how to handle file uploads in a secure fashion.

How PHP Accepts Uploaded Files

When a file is uploaded via a PHP script, a reference to the file is stored in the $_FILES superglobal under a key defined by the submitting POST request. Within this key you will find an associative array of values defining various details of the uploaded files. Listing 6-4 provides an example of the structure of this superglobal.

Listing 6-4. *An Example $_FILES Entry*

```
$_FILES['myfile'] => Array
{
    [name] => foobar.txt              // The original filename
    [type] => text/plain                  // The reported MIME type
    [tmp_name] => /tmp/phpojs4iw   // The file as stored locally on the server
    [error] => 0                           // The error code (if any)
    [size] => 382839                  // The file size in bytes
}
```

When looking at the previous set of associative keys within an entry of the $_FILES superglobal, the first thing to realize from a security perspective is that only the tmp_name, error, and size keys can be trusted, as all of the other values are provided to PHP from the request itself and therefore could be falsified by an attacker. Knowing this, the remaining array keys name and type should be considered as vulnerable to compromise as any other user input, and they should be filtered and validated appropriately. In the following section we will explain how this is done.

As described in Listing 6-4, the name key represents the file name as it was stored in the submitting client's local file system. Since this data is provided by the browser, it is best at the very least to filter and validate it to ensure that it does not contain unexpected content. For many purposes this can be as simple as filtering it using the basename() function (to remove any path information) and then filtering it to contain only alphanumeric content and the period character. However, obviously you can apply any filtering and validation rules needed to suit your application.

The MIME type, like the file name, is also provided by the client uploading the data during the POST request and therefore cannot be trusted. Unfortunately since you cannot trust this type you must go through a fair amount of extra effort to determine the exact MIME type of the file uploaded before you can filter or validate it. To do this you must have a PECL extension called "fileinfo" installed. This useful extension examines the actual content of a given file and determines the type of file it is based on its structure. Please refer to the PHP manual for PECL extensions (http://us.php.net/manual/en/install.pecl.php) for instructions on adding this extension to your PHP installation.

Note For certain file types (such as images) PHP provides alternative approaches to validating the nature of the file uploaded. If you are dealing with images being uploaded you can use the `getimagesize()` function to validate the file as a valid image instead of installing and using the fileinfo extension.

Once you have the fileinfo extension installed you can use it in a fashion similar to that shown in Listing 6-5 to validate the nature of the file (in this case, a white-list validation of the MIME type).

Listing 6-5. *An Example of Using White-List Validation and the fileinfo Extension to Validate an Uploaded File's MIME Type*

```php
<?php

    $finfo = finfo_open(FILEINFO_MIME);

    if(!$finfo)
    {
        die("Could not create fileinfo resource")
    }

    $mimetype = finfo_file($finfo, $_FILES['myfile']['tmp_name']);

    $valid_types = array("image/png", "image/gif");

    if(!$mimetype || !in_array($mimetype, $valid_types))
    {
        die("Invalid MIME type of uploaded file");
    }

?>
```

In Listing 6-5, we are accepting a file uploaded under the POST key of `myfile` and are validating to ensure that the uploaded file is either a valid PNG or GIF image based on the actual content of the file, not the reported MIME type from the user. This is the only secure way to validate the content of an uploaded file and should always be used.

Once you have filtered and validated the file, because of the way PHP works you now must process this file within the request it was uploaded in. (PHP will delete the originally uploaded file at the end of the request.) Under most circumstances this involves moving the file from its temporary storage location (identified by the `tmp_name` key in the uploaded file's `$_FILES` superglobal entry) to its final location. However, unlike a normal file operation, in PHP there are two important functions for dealing with uploaded files: move_uploaded_file() and is_uploaded_file(). These two functions will move a file uploaded over HTTP to another directory or tell you whether the given file is a file that was uploaded over HTTP, respectively. The reason the standard PHP file operations are not recommended is because HTTP uploads themselves are tracked internally within PHP, and when these specific functions are used, before any operations are performed a check against this internal list is performed to ensure the file being treated like an uploaded file was indeed uploaded and was not some sort of attack. Listing 6-6 demonstrates using both of these functions to move an uploaded file to a more long-term location safely.

Listing 6-6. *Using is_uploaded_file() and move_uploaded_file() to Deal with HTTP File Uploads*

```php
<?php

    if(is_uploaded_file($_FILES['myfile']['tmp_name']))
    {
        $result = move_uploaded_file($_FILES['myfile']['tmp_name'], "/path/to/move");

        if(!$result)
        {
            die("Error moving uploaded file");
        }
    }

?>
```

Securing Round Trips of Data

One common thing that is done in PHP applications is using hidden HTML form elements to effectively "round trip" complex data types between requests. That is to say, a complex array or object is serialized using the standard PHP serialize() function and then stored as the value of a hidden key or stored into a cookie. This value is then provided back to the server on the next request, and the data is unserialized and used as part of the application's logic. From a security perspective, it is critical to realize that once the data has left your server and been provided to the user, any subsequent time that data is returned to you it has to be treated as insecure as any other user input. For complex serialized objects, however, you have an advantage of knowing what the data should be before the user receives it and can validate that when that data is returned, it was done so unmolested by any potential attacker.

To do this is a matter of accompanying the serialized data with a hash fingerprint of it combined with a secret key known only to your server. When the data is returned, the hash can be recalculated using the user-supplied serialized data and validated before any attempt is made to use it. There are many different ways this can be accomplished. For the purposes of our example in Listing 6-7 we will use the SHA1 algorithm to generate a hash when creating our form and then validate that hash in Listing 6-8 before using the data.

Listing 6-7. *Generating a Hash for a Complex Serialized Value Used in a Form*

```php
<?php

define("SECRET_KEY", "EnterprisePHP");

$complex = array(1,2,3,4,5);

$serialized = serialize($complex);

$hash = sha1($serialized . SECRET_KEY);
?>

<form method="post">
   <input type="hidden" name="complex"➥
              value="<?php print urlencode($serialized); ?>">
   <input type="hidden" name="complex_hash"➥
              value="<?php print urlencode($hash); ?>">
   <input type="submit" value="Submit">
</form>
```

Listing 6-8. *Validating the Hash of a Form with a Complex Hidden Variable*

```php
<?php

   if(!isset($_POST['complex']) || !isset($_POST['complex_hash']))
   {
      die("Invalid submission");
   }

   $calc_hash = sha1($_POST['complex'] . SECRET_KEY);
```

```
if($calc_hash !== $_POST['complex_hash'])
{
    die("Hash validation failed");
}

$complex = unserialize($_POST['complex_hash']);

?>
```

Note In Listing 6-8 we used the constant SECRET_KEY, which is fine but does leave the possibility of an attacker figuring out what that key is and breaking our encryption. A more complex and more secure approach would be to randomly generate the key per session and use that value for our "secret key," effectively making it different for every user.

As shown in Listing 6-7 we use the sha1() function to create a hash value of the serialized data we are providing to the user, but we also append a secret value known only to the server in the hash calculation. Then, in Listing 6-8 when this submission is returned we recalculate the same hash using the complex data type provided by the user in the form submission (along with our secret key) and compare it to the hash also provided by the user. Since a potential hacker has no means to determine the secret key used in the original hash calculation they cannot modify the serialized data, thus protecting it from unwanted manipulation.

Output Security

When it comes to output security, the name of the game is simple: since the browser will automatically in 99 percent of the cases execute JavaScript code returned to it from a request, it is critical that your application never leave room for misinterpretation by properly encoding all output based on input from the user. Failure to ensure that the user's input is treated literally when displayed as part of the output can be leveraged by an attacker to perform a nearly unlimited number of severe attacks against your users, your application, or a third party.

As simple as it sounds, the notion of properly encoding the input of a user to prevent this sort of misinterpretation is an incredibly complex subject. With multiple different of encodings to consider and the fact that not all browsers (ahem, Internet Explorer in particular) interpret these encodings the same way, there is plenty of room for error.

For the sake of brevity we will not walk you through all of the nuances of this problem, as this alone could be an entire chapter in a security book. In fact, to read the various books

on the subject, they all say the same thing basically anyway—the htmlspecialchars() function, while useful at solving some of the problem, is not in any way suited for dealing with
encodings that are not ISO-8859-1. Since browsers like to honor other encodings regardless
of the stated encoding for the page (again, some versions of Internet Explorer), attackers
can effectively sidestep this function by pre-encoding the content before submission.

Properly Encoding Output with Non-ASCII Support

For example, take an input string of HTML from the user. To the browser,
this will be decoded to mean the string "HTML" and potentially could be abused by an
attacker. Of course you could pass that string through the htmlspecialchars() function,
but this will only replace the ampersand "&" character with its entity equivalent, &,
converting the string to &#72&amp#84;&#77;&#76. This may be acceptable to
ISO-8859-1 character sets (since there is no reason *not* to use the character itself to represent an ASCII character), but a legitimate user looking to display a non-ASCII character
would be unable to do so—not the most ideal solution.

   To solve this problem and make a truly acceptable encoding and escaping mechanism, you must couple the htmlspecialchars() function with regular expressions. The
concept is simple. Use the htmlspecialchars() function to escape the output, but then use
regular expressions to clean up double-encoded entities when they represent non-ASCII
characters (and thus run no danger of being misinterpreted as code by the browser).
Thankfully there are very intelligent people in the world who have already looked at this
problem, one of whom is Ilia Alshanetsky, who wrote *php|architect's Guide to PHP Security*
(Marco Tabini & Associates, 2005). In his chapter on output escaping he proposes the use
of the preg_replace_callback() function to perform the necessary encoding. His solution is
presented in Listing 6-9.

Listing 6-9. *An Example of Properly Encoding for Multiple Character Sets for Display As
Output*

```php
<?php

function decode($matches)
{
    if(!is_int($matches[1]{0}))
    {
        $val = '0' . $matches[1] + 0;
    }
    else
    {
        $val = (int)$matches[1];
    }
```

```
    if($val > 255) // Non-ASCII
    {
        return "&#{$matches[1]};";
    }

    if(($val >= 65 && $val <= 90) || // A-Z
       ($val >= 97 && $val <= 122) || // a-z
       ($val >= 48 && $val <= 57)) // 0-9
    {
        return chr($val);
    }

    return $matches[0];
}

$input = htmlspecialchars("&#72;&#84;&#77;&#76;");

$output = preg_replace_callback('!&#((?:[0-9]+)|(?:x(?:[0-9A-F]+)));?!i',➥
                                'decode', $input);

print $output;

?>
```

Along with handling our example user input of HTML cleanly,
Listing 6-9 also handles &#0x48;&#0x54;&#0x4D;&#0x4C;—the same "HTML" encoded string
value except using hexadecimal values instead of decimals when representing each character (yet another encoding circumstance to be aware of). Not quite as simple as just
calling the htmlspecialchars() function but not too cumbersome either once the problem
is correctly understood. It is important to note that these solutions are quite useful when
the goal is to prevent an attacker's malicious input from compromising the integrity of
your output to a degree that allows the execution of unauthorized JavaScript through
property encoding of data, but at what cost?

Allowing User-Provided Markup

There are many times in the development of certain types of web applications (forum
systems come to mind) where it is desirable to allow user input to contain some degree of
markup such as a harmless set of <b></b> tags. For situations where this is the case, how
do we filter and validate the input?

The short answer, unfortunately, is basically you can't.

If you read the various PHP security books we have mentioned throughout this chapter, you will find a few perfectly valid (and at times *very* complex) solutions that seek to allow you to manage the HTML a user can use to a subset that is considered safe and secure. While all of them are valid (and most written by people we consider personal friends), in our opinion they all contain a fatal flaw from a security perspective: they are all ultimately blacklist approaches.

We mentioned the notion of why blacklist approaches to security are a bad idea earlier in the chapter when we discussed using a white list to validate and filter combo boxes, radio buttons, and so on during a form submission, and the same holds true here. Regardless of the complexity of the logic you use to filter and validate the data, you are ultimately trying to predict how an attacker will attempt to compromise your system out of potentially limitless possibilities, and you are bound to miss one.

■**Note** MySpace learned the hard way how difficult it is to prevent security breaches in a web application using a blacklist approach. The JS.Spacehero worm (also known as the Samy worm) was developed by taking advantage of bugs in specific browsers that previously were entirely unknown. It became literally overnight one of the most successful Internet worms of all time. The lesson from that experience is clear—since you have absolutely no control over bugs in a browser, you can't possibly predict what is safe and what is not.

So how do you still allow users creative freedom within your web application but maintain security? The only surefire way is to create your own markup-style language that the server can translate into HTML when rendered. While this is most certainly the most difficult approach (not to mention most expensive approach in terms of time and processing resources), any attempt to allow users to provide you with HTML that your application will then present to other users to render will most certainly expose it to a potential JavaScript-based attack. Not to say our recommended approach doesn't have that same potential, but at least with a custom approach you have the benefit of actively generating the HTML yourself, and you never give an attacker a previously known means of sneaking a JavaScript attack past your filters and validation routines.

Conclusion

In this chapter we discussed many of the fundamental concepts behind security as it applies to a PHP application. We discussed input filtering, using the `Zend_Filter_Input` component, output escaping, and some of the more common problems faced by developers such as round-tripping data, allowing HTML input, and uploading files.

We will be the first to admit that in this chapter we have barely grazed the surface of web application security, but we hope you have learned enough to realize one very important fact: there are no magic bullets. For every new attack that emerges in the Web there is quickly devised a countermeasure to defeat it, but the next attack will *always* happen again. Don't underestimate these attackers. Security (both creating and breaching) is a very difficult skill to master and cannot be done by memorizing patterns of past attacks alone. How you apply those patterns in your application's defense (remember defense in depth!) and how much you understand about those trying to attack you are your primary weapons, so use them wisely. We assure you, the attackers trying to get in your application are doing the same thing and working hard to come up with creative new ways to fool your application into doing their bidding.

CHAPTER 7

■■■

Monitoring Your Applications

Any professional PHP application needs to have effective facilities for monitoring its status and health in both development and production. Unfortunately many application developers do not take the time to plan how their monitoring facilities will function when they begin their development. This not only makes the entire process more painful during development but also increases long-term upkeep costs. In this chapter, we will explore some enterprise-class monitoring tools and technologies available to PHP applications and how they can be effectively used.

We will begin the chapter by introducing the tools available in Zend Framework for monitoring your applications. We'll begin with the Zend_Log component and then discuss how to use it effectively in a Zend Framework MVC application. We will then move on to the more powerful commercial solutions provided by Zend Platform by detailing the use and customization of the PHP Intelligence functionality.

Effective Logging Through Zend_Log

Application logging is a critical aspect of any large-scale PHP development application. As a general rule of thumb, your application should perform enough logging so that given only your logs, you can determine what if anything has gone wrong in your application. Thus a few simple rules should apply:

- Logging should be done early and done very, very often.

- Logging should be done under different filterable categories.

- Logging facilities should be consistent throughout the application.

Thankfully, Zend Framework provides some wonderful tools that help you adhere to these rules through its Zend_Log component. In this section we'll look at this component in detail and show you how it can be used to manage all of your logging needs.

Getting Started with Zend_Log

The Zend_Log component is designed from the ground up to serve as a general-purpose logging tool. Among its many features, Zend_Log supports logging to multiple different backends using multiple formats along with filtering messages to appear in different logs nicely. The component is broken down into three aspects that we will discuss in this section:

- *Log writers*: These subcomponents write the log data to a storage medium (such as a log file).

- *Log filters*: These subcomponents prevent a given piece of log data from reaching a writer based on the business logic contained within it (such as ignoring log messages flagged as debugging messages).

- *Log formatters*: These subcomponents format the content of a log message before it is given to the writer.

These three aspects and their relationship with each other is shown in Figure 7-1.

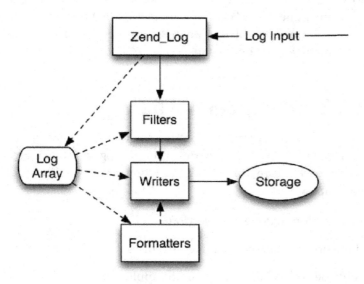

Figure 7-1. *The relationship between the various Zend_Log subcomponents*

Using the Zend_Log component is quite simple. You create and assign a writer to store the log messages and then use the component to send log messages to it. A simple example of this can be found in Listing 7-1 using the Zend_Log_Writer_Stream writer class.

Listing 7-1. *A Simple Example of Using Zend_Log*

```php
<?php
$writer = new Zend_Log_Writer_Stream("/tmp/mylog.txt");

$logger = new Zend_Log($writer);

$logger->log("My first log message", Zend_Log::INFO);
?>
```

In the first line we create an object $writer from the Zend_Log_Writer_Stream class. This class requires at least one constructor parameter (the stream to open for the log), for which we provide the file name /tmp/mylog.txt. This writer is passed into the constructor of the Zend_Log class to create the instance of our logger, which is used by calling the Zend_Log::log() method to log a message with an "information" priority using the Zend_Log::INFO constant.

■**Note** The second parameter to the Zend_Log::log() method is called the "priority identifier" and serves to classify the nature of the log message to be used later in filtering. By default Zend_Log defines eight priorities available as constants in the Zend_Log class: ALERT, CRIT, DEBUG, EMERG, ERR, INFO, NOTICE, and WARN. These priorities are assigned a numeric value (between 0 and 8) and use that value to determine their ranking within the logging process. Please consult the Zend Framework manual for a detailed definition of these logging priorities.

As expected, when this code is executed the result will be the creation of the /tmp/mylog.txt file with a single line item representing our log entry formatted using the standard format provided by the component.

BEHIND THE SCENES OF ZEND_LOG

As represented in Figure 7-1, when a log action occurs by a call to the Zend_Log::log() method, the Zend_Log component creates a data structure (array) that contains all of the relevant information for that log entry. This includes the log message you provided, priority, the timestamp, and so on. From this point forward your log data is represented in this format until the last step, where it is converted into something else (and immediately written to the storage medium). This is an important point later in the chapter when we discuss creating custom logging facilities, but for now just keep it in the back of your mind.

By default you can write logs to many different storage mediums by creating a different writer instance and providing it to the Zend_Log class. This can be a custom writer component written by you (by extending the Zend_Log_Writer_Abstract class), or it can be one of the out-of-box writers provided by Zend Framework shown here:

- Zend_Log_Writer_Stream: A stream-based writer that can write to any PHP-supported stream (such as a file, standard out, and so on)

- Zend_Log_Writer_Db: A database-based writer that can write to any database that has an adapter in Zend Framework

- Zend_Log_Writer_Firebug: A unique writer that can be used to write log data to the Firebug Firefox plug-in FirePHP

- Zend_Log_Writer_Mock: A simple log writer wrapper around an array that can be used to capture log messages within the application without writing them anywhere

- Zend_Log_Writer_Null: A black-hole log writer used in testing to simulate logging without actually logging anything

Now, under some circumstances all of these writers and all of this functionality would be enough for an application—but in many applications more is required. For example, if your application would like to write your logs to multiple destinations at the same time, you can use the Zend_Log component to add multiple writers to the Zend_Log class as shown in Listing 7-2.

Listing 7-2. *Writing to Multiple Log Destinations Using Zend_Log*

```php
<?php
$log_one = new Zend_Log_Writer_Stream("/tmp/mylog.txt");
$log_two = new Zend_Log_Writer_Stream("/tmp/anotherlog.txt");

$logger = new Zend_Log($log_one);
$logger->addWriter($log_two);

$logger->log("This message is written to two places", Zend_Log::INFO);
?>
```

In the case of Listing 7-2 the purpose of such a use case may not be very useful as there aren't very many reasons you would like to write the exact same log content to two separate log files. However, being able to log debugging messages in a separate file from all other log messages could indeed be useful. To do this we must introduce filters.

Using Zend_Log Filters

Filters in the Zend_Log component are used to prevent certain log messages from being written to certain writers. These filters can be applied to all log writers (by attaching them to the instance of Zend_Log being used) or applied to specific writers by attaching them to those writers.

What determines when a particular log message is rejected by a filter is entirely up to the business logic of the filter itself. Architecturally the only requirement for a filter is that it conform to the Zend_Log_Filter_Interface interface defined by Zend Framework. As a matter of convenience Zend Framework does provide a few useful filters out of the box:

- Zend_Log_Filter_Priority: Filters log messages based on their priority

- Zend_Log_Filter_Message: Filters log messages based on whether the message matches a regular expression

Looking back at our multiwriter example of Listing 7-2, we could make the act of writing two separate log files much more useful by logging debugging messages to one file and everything else for another. To do this we will need to use the Zend_Log_Filter_Priority filter class as shown in Listing 7-3.

Listing 7-3. *Using Zend_Log with Zend_Log_Filter_Priority to Filter Log Entries to Writers*

```php
<?php
$log_one = new Zend_Log_Writer_Stream("/tmp/mylog.txt");

$log_two = new Zend_Log_Writer_Stream("/tmp/anotherlog.txt");

$filter = new Zend_Log_Filter_Priority(Zend_Log::DEBUG, '==');

$log_two->addFilter($filter);

$logger = new Zend_Log($log_one);
$logger->addWriter($log_two);

$logger->log("This message is written to log_one only", Zend_Log::INFO);

$logger->log("This is written to both logs", Zend_Log::DEBUG)
?>
```

In Listing 7-3 we create two stream writers as we did in Listing 7-2, but we also create a priority filter. This filter accepts two parameters in its construction. The first is the log level to filter against, and the second is a string representing the operator to use in the comparison. This operator is identical to that used in the PHP version_compare() function and allows you to filter on an open-ended range of log messages. (Please consult the Zend Framework reference manual for default priority rankings.)

Another example of using filtering is shown in Listing 7-4, where we use the same technique on the base Zend_Log class to exclude entirely any debugging messages from the logs.

Listing 7-4. *Using Zend_Log Filters to Filter an Entire Log Instance*

```php
<?php
$log = new Zend_Log_Writer_Stream("/tmp/mylog.txt");

$filter = new Zend_Log_Filter_Priority(Zend_Log::DEBUG, '!=');

$logger = new Zend_Log($log_one);
$logger->addFilter($filter);

$logger->log("This is ignored", Zend_Log::DEBUG);
$logger->log("This is written", Zend_Log::INFO);

?>
```

Formatting Logs with Zend_Log

The last concept we will discuss in our introduction to Zend_Log is its ability to format logs using a series of formatting plug-ins. While similar from an API perspective, there are a few notable differences between the formatter components and filters previously discussed. For starters, formatters are applied only to writers directly and cannot be applied globally to all writers by assigning them to the Zend_Log instance directly (as was the case with filters). Second, only writers that write the log data as textual lines of data may have formatters applied to them (i.e., a database writer cannot have a formatter as it writes to columns, not lines of text).

Out of box the Zend_Log component comes with two formatters: the Zend_Log_Formatter_Simple component and the Zend_Log_Formatter_Xml component. We will examine both of these formatters in the examples that follow.

■**Note** If you attempt to use a formatter with a writer that does not support formatting, the writer in question will throw an exception when you attempt to do so.

Let's start with the `Zend_Log_Formatter_Simple` formatter. This formatter is used to perform simple formatting of a log line item and supports a basic variable-replace syntax to represent various keys in the event data structure (i.e., `%message%`). This can be useful to make basic formatting changes to a standard log file. For example, if no formatter is explicitly specified, the `Zend_Log` component uses the following format for its log messages using this component:

```
%timestamp% %priorityName% (%priority%): %message%
```

If you wanted to alter this line item format (for instance, remove the `%priority%` value), you could do so for your writer as shown in the example in Listing 7-5.

Listing 7-5. *An Example of Using* `Zend_Log_Formatter_Simple` *to Format Log Line Items*

```php
<?php
$log = new Zend_Log_Writer_Stream("/tmp/mylog.txt");

$format = "%timestamp% %priorityName%: %message%" . PHP_EOL;
$formatter = new Zend_Log_Formatter_Simple($format);

$log->setFormatter($formatter);

$logger = new Zend_Log($log_one);

$logger->log("This is custom formatted", Zend_Log::INFO);

?>
```

Note In Listing 7-5 we make use of the `PHP_EOL` constant. This is a PHP constant that represents the correct end-of-line string for the particular operating system you are running the code on. If you plan to create cross-platform PHP applications this is the correct way to terminate a line in a text file instead of writing code to distinguish between the string `"\r\n"` and `"\n"` yourself.

Another useful formatting component available to the `Zend_Log` component out of the box is the `Zend_Log_Formatter_Xml` component. This component allows you to render your log files as XML documents for the purpose of easy processing by other programs or monitoring systems. To use this component you simply create an instance of it and assign it to a writer as the formatter in a fashion identical to that shown in Listing 7-5. Unlike `Zend_Log_Formatter_Simple`, however, the `Zend_Log_Formatter_Xml` constructor takes an optional configuration array as a parameter that allows you to define the specific tags used in the XML output. Before I discuss that, the following XML snippet shown in Listing 7-6 demonstrates the default XML output of the component.

Listing 7-6. *The Default Format of the Zend_Log_Formatter_Xml Subcomponent*

```
<logEntry>
  <timestamp>2009-04-06T10:24:37-03:00</timestamp>
  <message>xml log message</message>
  <priority>6</priority>
  <priorityName>INFO</priorityName>
</logEntry>
```

If you would prefer to change the tags used to represent a log entry within the application, including removing some data points from the log, you can do so by passing your preferences in as the class constructor. This is done by setting the root tag name as the first parameter and by passing an array of key-value pairs mapping XML tag names to the key values found in the event data. An example of this is shown in Listing 7-7 by creating an XML log that only logs the timestamp and message from each log item.

Listing 7-7. *An Example of Custom XML Log Formatting Using the Zend_Log Component*

```php
<?php
$log = new Zend_Log_Writer_Stream("/tmp/mylog.txt");

$tagMap = array('eventTime' => 'timestamp',
                'msg' => 'message');

$xmlFormatter = new Zend_Log_Formatter_Xml('logData', $tagMap);

$log->setFormatter($xmlFormatter);

$logger = new Zend_Log($log_one);

$logger->log("This is custom XML formatted", Zend_Log::INFO);

?>
```

If you were to execute the code in Listing 7-7 you would find that it outputs an XML structure shown in Listing 7-8.

Listing 7-8. *The Output of Listing 7-7*

```
<logData>
    <eventTime>2009-04-06T10:24:37-03:00</eventTime>
    <msg>This is custom XML formatted</msg>
</logData>
```

Advanced Monitoring

Using the Zend_Log component provided by Zend Framework alone can make your applications much easier to manage, debug, and keep secure—but only if you both implement it and monitor your logs regularly! While surely a best practice, it would be extremely helpful if there were a way to call out particular key problems with your application and perhaps even notify someone in your organization.

Consider this situation: your application is running beautifully, but at 3 a.m. local time for some reason the MySQL database stops functioning correctly, and queries from the PHP application begin to fail and your logs begin filling with errors. To make matters worse, the MySQL server still appears online to your simple ping monitoring scripts, and no one notices the problem until the next morning, potentially costing you thousands of dollars in downtime.

Unfortunately, no matter how good your logging practices were in the situation described it wouldn't have helped you notice the problem when it occurred (although likely it would be very valuable in fixing it). Preventing these sorts of situations requires something more, and thankfully that something more is provided by Zend Platform in the form of PHP Intelligence.

What Is PHP Intelligence?

PHP Intelligence is a key feature of the Zend Platform package and provides white-box monitoring of PHP and the application code it executes. Following is a brief list of the types of things PHP Intelligence can monitor on your behalf:

- Slow queries

- Failed queries

- Slow script execution times

- Odd result output sizes (i.e., too small, too big HTML responses)

- Server load

- PHP errors, warnings, and so on

All of these monitoring facilities are extremely easy to set up and can be attached to actions such as sending e-mails, SNMP pings, or completely custom logic.

Getting Started with PHP Intelligence

Setting up PHP Intelligence is as simple as installing Zend Platform and configuring it. To get started you need to log into Zend Platform and select the PHP Intelligence tab, bringing up the interface shown in Figure 7-2.

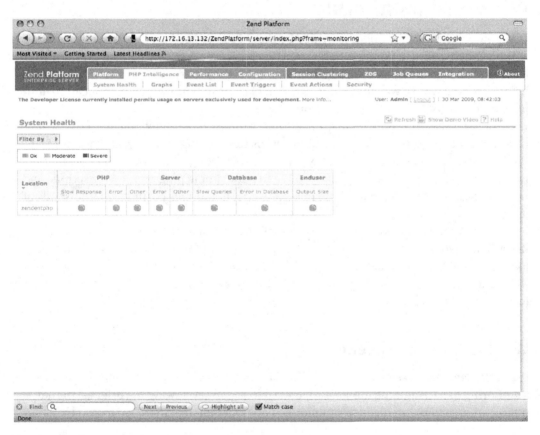

Figure 7-2. *The PHP Intelligence dashboard*

The page shown in Figure 7-2 is the System Health page of the PHP Intelligence system and is designed to give you a quick overview of the overall health of not just the server you are currently logged in to but also the entire cluster of web servers. If you would like further analytics, the Graphs submenu item can provide them, or to get very specific you can view and search for events by selecting the Event List submenu item. For

now, however, we are interested in learning how PHP Intelligence is set up, and for that
we need the Event Triggers submenu, which brings up the interface shown in Figure 7-3.

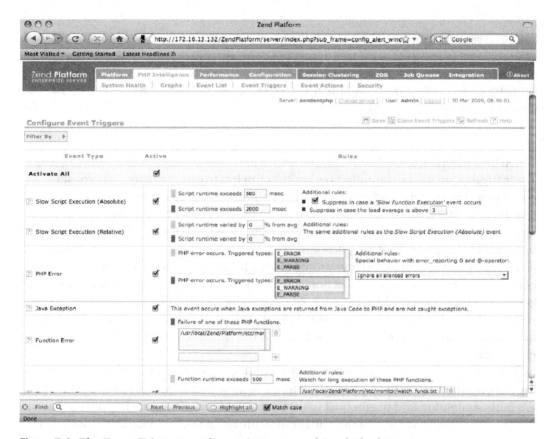

Figure 7-3. *The Event Triggers configuration screen of Zend Platform*

From this interface you can define the monitoring rules used by Zend Platform to
watch your various PHP servers and create notifications (events) for anything that falls
within the defined parameters. There are two types of events in the PHP Intelligence system (warnings and errors), and the thresholds for each event type can be identified by the
color. Yellow is a moderate warning or error, and red is a severe error. Let's take a look at
the various metrics the PHP Intelligence system can monitor.

PHP Intelligence Event Triggers

We will walk through each of the possible event triggers, describe their purposes, and make
recommendations as to what these values might look like under ideal circumstances. Note

that some self-explanatory triggers are omitted from discussion; please consult the Zend Platform User's Guide if you require more explanation on those items.

Note In this section we will make some blind recommendations as to how event trigger values should be set up. These values should be validated against your own needs and adjusted accordingly. From a performance perspective, PHP Intelligence can cause significant problems if it is constantly creating events (instead of when there is really a problem), so it is important that you give realistic values instead of the ideal ones used in this text.

At the beginning of the Event Triggers list we have two Slow Script Execution triggers. These triggers are used to monitor how long a script has to execute before it is considered a problem by Zend Platform, expressed in both absolute (real time) and relative (a threshold deviation from statistical expectations) values. Typically in an enterprise PHP application you shouldn't expect a PHP script to execute for more than 100–200 milliseconds, with many powerhouse applications responding even faster. In relative terms we feel that 25 percent in any direction should at least be a warning, with 40 percent or higher being a clear sign of error. In this section you also have the ability to suppress these triggers if server load gets too high (which is recommended). Unfortunately because of the highly variable circumstances behind load numbers in connection to performance, it is impossible to provide recommendations on how this number should be set in your specific situation.

The PHP Error event monitors any PHP error (i.e., E_ERROR, E_WARNING) that occurs during the execution of a script and reports it as an event within Zend Platform. Because this is a fairly straightforward trigger (just select which error codes trigger which event types), we will simply say that the default configuration provided by Zend Platform is sufficient for most needs.

The Function Error trigger is used to identify PHP functions by name (either internal or user-defined) that should trigger an event within Zend Platform if an error occurs during their execution. A default list of functions and methods that behave this way is provided by Zend Platform in the etc/monitor/watch_funcs.txt file (from the base of the Platform install). The format of this file is one function per line. In the case of methods, you can specify a method by using the class::method syntax, or you can specify an entire set of methods under a class using the class::* syntax. This particular event trigger allows you to specify multiple definition files to parse on startup, so it is recommended that you create your own list rather than modify the one provided by Zend Platform.

The Slow Function Execution trigger is a combination of the Slow Script Execution and Function Error triggers. It allows you to monitor the performance of specific functions within PHP (internal or user-defined functions) and create an event if one of these functions exceeds a threshold of real execution time. Typically (based on our general experience), no single function should execute for more than a handful of milliseconds, making 10–15 milliseconds a potential warning and about 50 milliseconds a likely indication of something gone awry.

The Slow Content Download trigger monitors the `fpassthru()` function in PHP in the same way as the Slow Function Execution trigger does. It only exists because of the special purpose of the `fpassthru()` function in PHP scripts. Because typically this function is used to send significant amounts of data to the client, it isn't uncommon for this function's runtime to be much higher than that of other functions in PHP. An appropriate value is directly connected to the size of the data you are sending, making it impossible to make a blind recommendation.

The Maximum Apache Processes Exceeded trigger is specifically for Zend Platform/PHP installations running on an Apache web server and is used to monitor the number of Apache HTTP processes currently active and report an error or warning if that number exceeds a maximum threshold. While each server is different, typically the defaults provided by Zend Platform of 200 for a warning and 250 for an error are a good place to start. That said, it is important that this value be adjusted if you increase the maximum number of process configuration directives in the Apache `httpd.conf` file to prevent unnecessary error and warning reporting.

The Excess Memory Usage triggers, expressed in both absolute and relative terms, monitor memory usage of every PHP script and allow you to be notified if the memory needs of any given script exceed the defined thresholds. As with other triggers in PHP Intelligence, it is impossible to make an accurate blind recommendation as to the memory requirements of your PHP scripts. We will point out, however, that these values should always be less than the maximum values for memory usage set in the `php.ini` file, as an out-of-memory error will take precedence over this trigger, causing memory errors to show up as `E_ERROR` errors instead of being properly reported.

The Inconsistent Output Size trigger is useful for monitoring the behavior of your PHP applications in a passive manner by keeping track of the average size (in bytes) of the output you respond to the user with. For any given script, if the amount of data returned to the user is 40 percent smaller or larger than normal, that may be a good indication that something isn't right, and an 80 percent difference is likely to be proof that something is very wrong. Typically this trigger is most useful when your responses are fairly large to begin with (in terms of byte count), as small responses have a greater chance of fluctuating over a broad range, making it harder to set thresholds.

Note The Inconsistent Output Size trigger is often useful in identifying problems, because when something does go wrong, often it has a measurable impact on the output of the script. For instance, a fatal PHP error would cause the output to stop and in all likelihood result in a much smaller output than that of a normal function. It is important to realize, however, that by no means is the output size designed to be a surefire monitoring technique but only one spoke in the wheel of a more complex set of monitoring rules.

Viewing Events

Once an event has been recorded into Zend Platform, you have various means to view the event from the web interface such as from the Platform dashboard or the Event List submenu item under PHP Intelligence. Regardless of how you arrive there, you can open up the details of the event by clicking on it, bringing up an interface similar to that shown in Figure 7-4.

Figure 7-4. *Viewing the details of an event in Zend Platform*

From the detailed view of an event you are presented with a wealth of information about the event that allows you to completely understand and diagnose the problem that triggered the event, including the entire context of the event. The context can be invaluable to a developer trying to diagnose an issue, as it provides all of the data passed into the function (if the event was caused by a function) as well as any superglobals or variables that were passed into the script.

You are also provided with a number of tools to help you debug and diagnose the issue. Assuming you have properly set up debugging of your application through Zend Studio for Eclipse, you can debug and profile the event (reproducing the circumstances that caused it) with a simple click, or at the very least review the offending lines of source code that caused the event.

Creating Advanced Monitoring Facilities

Some of the event triggers that were omitted from the discussion in the previous section were the Custom Event and HTTP Error triggers. These triggers are tied to a set of PHP functions only available in versions of PHP with Zend Platform installed that allow you to tie your application logic directly into Zend Platform's PHP Intelligence facilities. In the text to come we will explain how these functions can be used by connecting them directly to some custom Zend_Log components to create a truly integrated error-handling and monitoring solution. But first, let's look at some of the more advanced features available.

Attaching Actions to Events

One of the most powerful features of the PHP Intelligence tool in Zend Platform is not just the ability to trigger events but also the ability to have those events trigger actions. In this section we'll introduce how event actions work. These actions are found under the Event Actions submenu item of the PHP Intelligence interface (shown in Figure 7-5).

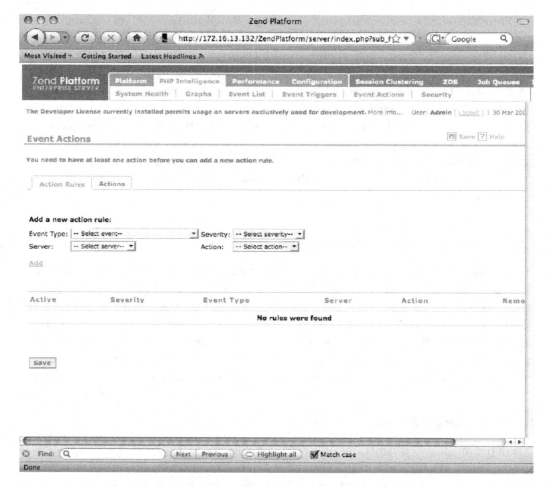

Figure 7-5. *The Event Actions interface in Zend Platform*

Attaching an action to an event is a two-step process. The first step is to create the various actions to execute, and the second step is to create rules to define which types of events should execute which actions. Actions take three different forms:

- *Send an e-mail*: Sends a report of the event to an e-mail address

- *Send SNMP trap*: Sends a report of the event via SNMP trap to the target machine (very useful for integrating with other enterprise monitoring systems)

- *Send an HTTP POST*: Sends a report of the event in XML form to a URL by doing an HTTP POST (sent as the event_data variable)

The format of the XML document sent via URL is represented as follows (taken from the Zend Platform User's Guide):

```
# Each attribute exists if it exists in the Event Details screen
<?xml version="1.0" ?>
<event type event_id timestamp time severity>
#if there is an error:
    <error type>error text</error>
    <stats triggered_value avg load_average/>
#if there is a source file:
    <source file line/>
    <script name host uri>
        <vardata type name value/>
    </script>
#if there is a function:
    <function name>
        <args>
            <arg num value/>
        </args>
    </function>
#if there are included files:
    <included_files>
        <file name\>
    </included_files>
#if there is a backtrace for this event:
    <backtrace>
        <call depth function file line/>
    </backtrace>
</event>
```

Once you have defined one or more actions, you can attach those actions to events or groups of events by creating an action rule using the following criteria:

- The event type

- The severity of the event

- The specific server or server group where the event occurred

You can create extremely complex rule and action sets that allow you to monitor your PHP applications in the most effective way possible. In the next section we will take this one step further by introducing the PHP APIs provided by Zend Platform that allow you to create custom events based on the logic of your application.

The PHP Intelligence API

In addition to the web interface provided by Zend Platform's PHP Intelligence, an extensive PHP-based API is provided that allows you to integrate it with your web applications on a much more fundamental level. In this section we'll introduce the various API calls and their usage.

The most useful of the API calls related to PHP Intelligence provided by Zend Platform is the `monitor_custom_event()` function, which has the following prototype:

```
void monitor_custom_event($str_identifier, $str_event_msg, [$int_severity,➥
    $user_data]);
```

This method is used to create events within Zend Platform as if PHP Intelligence had detected them as any other event. These events can then be tied to actions to cause a multitude of actions to take place. The first parameter of this method, `$str_identifier`, is a string identifier of the developer's choosing (used to create multiple different types of custom events), followed by the actual event message itself, `$str_event_msg`. The last two parameters are optional, the first being the severity of the event (an integer value of 1 means it is a severe event, a value of 0 means it is a warning event) and the last variable being user data. This user data variable is to provide context information you would like to accompany the event, which will be made available as part of the event details.

■**Note** See the "Customizing `Zend_Log` Behavior and Integrating with Zend Platform" section of this chapter for an example of the `monitor_custom_event()` function.

Supporting the `monitor_custom_event()` function are two additional functions, the `monitor_set_aggregation_hint()` and `monitor_pass_error()` functions. The first of these functions is used to provide some context for a custom event when dealing with a consolidated error-reporting architecture. The purpose of this function is to identify what logical part of the application you are currently executing in when an error occurred so when you trigger an event using the `monitor_custom_event()` function, it will be identified in such a way to help you understand the origin of the error better. Its prototype is as follows:

```
void monitor_set_aggregation_hint($str_hint);
```

where `$str_hint` is a "hint" string that will be attached to every event created through a call to `monitor_custom_event()`. This function can be called as many times as necessary within an application. This can be useful, for example, in an MVC model, where the aggregation hint can be the controller and action being executed, or in any other place where there is a primary script that is consistently executed in front of the real logic (potentially causing Zend Platform to report all errors occurring in that script).

The second function, `monitor_pass_error()`, is a special-case version of the `monitor_custom_event()` function used specifically within a custom PHP error handler implemented through a call to the `set_error_handler()` function. The prototype of this function is as follows:

```
void monitor_pass_error($int_errno, $int_errstr, $str_errfile, $int_errline);
```

For this function, these parameters match exactly those of the callback set by `set_error_handler()`. The purpose of this function speaks to a behavior of PHP Intelligence as, by default, setting a custom error handler will prevent PHP Intelligence from logging any PHP errors as events. To restore this behavior this function must be called from the custom error handler callback.

Another function related to custom events is the `monitor_httperror_event()` used to create an event related to an HTTP error (such as the 404 File Not Found HTTP error). The prototype is as follows:

```
void monitor_httperror_event($int_httperrorcode, $str_url [, $int_severity]);
```

The first parameter of this function is the HTTP error code (i.e., 404); the second parameter is the offending URL that caused the error; and the third optional parameter is the severity. (In the third parameter, just as in `monitor_custom_event()`, a value of 1 indicates a severe error, and 0 indicates a non-severe error.) The primary use of this function would be in a circumstance where HTTP errors are being handled by PHP directly (i.e., a Zend Framework MVC application) to ensure that these events are still recorded within Zend Platform.

■**Note** There are additional API functions provided by Zend Platform that are primarily for internal uses: the `register_event_handler()` and `unregister_event_handler()` functions. While documented to some extent, they should not be used by the general public as they are not stable.

Customizing Zend_Log Behavior and Integrating with Zend Platform

Thus far in this chapter we have only discussed how the `Zend_Log` component is used out of the box. Often this can be sufficient, but there are many circumstances (especially in enterprise systems) where the built-in behavior of any component isn't enough. Thankfully, like all Zend Framework components the `Zend_Log` component architecture allows you to create custom behaviors quickly and easily for your application.

From the beginning of the chapter (and Figure 7-1), you will recall that the time between the call to Zend_Log::log() from your application and when that data is actually stored in a medium by a writer is represented as an associative array of key/value pairs that is passed into the various writers, formatters, and filters and acted upon. One thing we have not mentioned yet is that this data structure can be augmented to include data not natively available. This is a key bit of knowledge if you are interested in creating application-specific filters, formatters, and writers. To add data to this data structure (and have it available to every log message data structure internally), you call the Zend_Log::setEventItem() method and pass it two parameters: the key used to retrieve the item from the data structure and its value. Listing 7-9 provides an example of using this method by combining it with the Zend_Log_Formatter_Simple formatter to add custom data to the log file.

Listing 7-9. *Using the Zend_Log::setEventItem() Method to Set Custom Event Data in a Log Message*

```php
<?php
$log = new Zend_Log_Writer_Stream("/tmp/mylog.txt");

$format = "%timestamp% %priorityName%: %message (%random%)" . PHP_EOL;

$formatter = new Zend_Log_Formatter_Simple($format);

$log->setFormatter($formatter);

$logger = new Zend_Log($log_one);

$logger->setEventItem('random', rand(1, 10));

$logger->log("Message #1", Zend_Log::INFO);
$logger->log("Message #2", Zend_log::INFO);
?>
```

In Listing 7-9 we use the Zend_Log::setEventItem() method to set a custom piece of data random that has a random number between 1 and 10. This value random is then referenced in the format of the Zend_Log_Formatter_Simple formatter for every subsequent log message. Because the value of this random key is only set once before any log messages occur, you can expect the same value to be displayed in both log lines.

In addition to setting custom log data points for log items, the Zend_Log component also allows you to create custom priorities through the use of the Zend_Log::addPriority() method. This method can only be used to add new priorities (the ones provided by Zend_Log by default are unchangeable), but it can be useful depending on the needs of

your application. Listing 7-10 demonstrates the use of this by extending the Zend_Log class
to add a new priority and then using it in a logging action.

Listing 7-10. *Extending Zend_Log to Add Custom Priorities*

```php
<?php

class My_Logger extends Zend_Log
{
    const CUSTOM = 9;

    function __construct(Zend_Log_Writer_Abstract $writer = null)
    {
        parent::__construct($writer);

        $this->addPriority("CUSTOM", self::CUSTOM);
    }
}

$log = new Zend_Log_Writer_Stream("/tmp/mylog.txt");

$logger = new My_Logger($log);

$logger->log("Message #1", My_Logger::CUSTOM);
?>
```

■Tip Depending on the nature of what you are trying to do, it may make sense to extend the Zend_Log
(or any framework component) to do setup of custom behavior instead of building logic around the default
component to do so. In the case of Listing 7-10, since all of the constants for the priorities existed in the
Zend_Log class, it made sense to extend the class to add a new one instead of calling the Zend_Log::
addPriority() method from an external logic.

Building Custom Writers

In order to really customize the behavior of Zend_Log you will have to write some custom
components. If you'd like to create a log that stores to a custom storage location (to perhaps store log data in a medium not provided for out of the box), you will have to create a
custom writer. As previously discussed in this chapter, one great example of a facility not

provided directly by Zend Framework that is of value to enterprise users is a writer that allows you to record log messages into the Zend Platform PHP Intelligence system.

To build such a writer subcomponent for Zend_Log, you have to extend the Zend_Log_ Writer_Abstract class and implement the abstract method Zend_Log_Writer_Abstract:: _write() within it. This has been done for you (along with some logic to check to make sure Zend Platform is enabled) in Listing 7-11.

Listing 7-11. *A Custom Zend_Log Writer Component for Zend Platform PHP Intelligence*

```php
<?php
require_once 'Zend/Log/Writer/Abstract.php';
require_once 'Zend/Exception.php';

class ZEnt_Log_Writer_ZendPlatform extends Zend_Log_Writer_Abstract
{
    function __construct()
    {
        if(!function_exists("monitor_custom_event") ||➡
            !function_exists("monitor_license_info"))
        {
            throw new Zend_Exception("Zend Platform must be available with PHP " .
                                                "Intelligence enabled");
        }

        $licenseInfo = monitor_license_info();

        if(!isset($licenseInfo['license_ok']) ||
            !isset($licenseInfo['startup_ok']) ||
            !$licenseInfo['license_ok'] ||
            !$licenseInfo['startup_ok'])
        {
            throw new Zend_Exception("PHP Intelligence module not properly" .
                                                " loaded in Zend Platform");
        }
    }

    public function _write($event)
    {
        if(isset($event['aggregation_hint']))
        {
            monitor_set_aggregation_hint((string)$event['aggregation_hint']);
        }
```

```
    $severity = 0;

    switch($event['priority'])
    {
        case Zend_Log::ALERT:
        case Zend_Log::CRIT:
        case Zend_Log::EMERG:
        case Zend_Log::ERR:
            $severity = 1;
            break;
    }

    monitor_custom_event($event['priorityName'], $event['message'],➥
                                    $severity, $event);
    }
}
?>
```

In Listing 7-11 we create a writer that takes advantage of the PHP Intelligence APIs described earlier in the chapter to create a log destination that displays within Zend Platform. In this writer we use two of the Zend Platform APIs: monitor_set_aggregation_hint() to allow a hint to be set in the event through a call to Zend_Log::setEventItem() and of course the monitor_custom_event() method to actually write the log data to Zend Platform.

Note This writer, while useful, should be used only in conjunction with the proper filters to ensure that only log entries that truly are warnings or errors are funneled into Zend Platform. From a performance perspective the volume of events logged into Zend Platform per request has a direct impact on the speed and response times of your application. Thus it should only log real problems.

Building Custom Filters

To complement our custom writer using the Zend Platform APIs, let's create a custom filter that will ensure that only those events that truly deserve to be logged into Zend Platform are logged. To do this, we must create a class that implements the Zend_Log_Filter_Interface that (at the time of this writing) was nothing more than a single method accept() that returns a Boolean true if the message was accepted. An example of this sort of custom filter is provided in Listing 7-12.

Listing 7-12. *A Custom Zend_Log Filter Component*

```php
<?php

require_once 'Zend/Log/Filter/Interface.php';

class ZEnt_Log_Filter_SevereOnly implements Zend_Log_Filter_Interface
{
    public function accept($event)
    {
        switch($event['priority'])
        {
            case Zend_Log::CRIT:
            case Zend_Log::EMERG:
            case Zend_Log::ERR:
            case Zend_Log::ALERT:
                return true;
        }

        return false;
    }
}
?>
```

■ Note If the purpose of Listing 7-12 weren't to demonstrate how to create a Zend_Log filter component with custom logic, it wouldn't be a proper implementation. The Zend_Log_Filter_Priority() built-in filter was more than sufficient to perform the necessary behavior.

Building Custom Formatters

To complete our discussion of customizing the Zend_Log component, we will look at creating a custom formatter. To recall the discussion earlier in the chapter, a formatter is applied to a writer and provides a means to change the format of the event before it is written to the log. While there is no clear-cut use case for this functionality in the same thread as our integration of Zend_Log with Zend Platform, we'll still provide a simple example. In this example (Listing 7-13), we will create a formatter that takes the log data and represents it in a comma-separated format. This is done (as with filters) by creating a class that implements the Zend_Log_Formatter_Interface interface. As was also true with filters, this basically means implementing the Zend_Log_Formatter_Interface::format() method as shown in Listing 7-13.

Listing 7-13. *An Example of a Custom Zend_Log Formatter*

```php
<?php

require_once 'Zend/Log/Formatter/Interface.php';

class ZEnt_Log_Formatter_Csv implements Zend_Log_Formatter_Interface
{
    public function format($event)
    {
        return implode(",", $event);
    }
}
?>
```

As the note pointed out for filters, if it wasn't for the need for an example, the code in Listing 7-13 would be considered a waste, as the Zend_Log_Formatter_Simple out-of-the-box formatter is more than suitable for displaying a log in CSV format.

Logging and Performance

With all of our discussion of the importance of logging, one thing you should be aware of is that there is always a performance cost to logging. Every logging operation means that more data is being passed through the script (increasing memory requirements) and is being written to a storage medium (increasing I/O activity). Thankfully you can use solutions we present in this chapter, if implemented correctly, with a minimal impact on performance. For using Zend_Log, the most important consideration is to take advantage of the various logging levels available to you and use them to distinguish between logging data that is informational vs. logging data that is critical. By making sure these are distinguished in your code, you can create filtering mechanisms as discussed in this chapter to ignore log messages that lack the necessary severity in a production environment without sacrificing the power of detailed logs in development and testing.

When it comes to a technology like PHP Intelligence, the name of the game is entirely setting your rules up to minimize your logging traffic in production in the same way logging levels minimize logging in your application. Being a low-level technology, PHP Intelligence is very fast, however, it was never designed to be a debugging tool and should only be used to monitor and react to log messages of a severity that warrants action on behalf of the development team in production. Failure to do this can cause significant performance problems and should always be considered.

Conclusion

In this chapter we discussed two very powerful tools to monitor the health of your applications both during their development and as they operate in production—Zend Platform's PHP Intelligence and Zend Framework's logging components. PHP Intelligence provides engine-level monitoring of your application's health using a variety of predetermined metrics, while the Zend_Log component allows you to implement application-level logging of your business logic.

That concludes our discussion on monitoring and logging in PHP applications. As was mentioned at the beginning of the chapter, an enterprise-class PHP application *must* have well-designed and frequently used logging facilities in order to make it maintainable long term without excess cost and a lot of frustration. We hope that by reading this chapter you have begun to formulate how the combination of Zend_Log and the PHP Intelligence of Zend Platform can be used to accomplish this critical task. You should always err on the side of overlogging than underlogging, and more importantly you should take advantage of the various priority levels provided in the Zend_Log component! Doing so will allow you to adjust your logging for the circumstances without being intrusive.

CHAPTER 8

Web Services and Zend Framework

Over the past few years web services in the fabric of Internet application development have grown from a useful technology to a cornerstone of enterprise development. A wide range of technologies and protocols has emerged. From heavier (complex) technologies such as Simple Object Access Protocol (SOAP) to lightweight protocols such as JavaScript Object Notation (JSON), no clear winner has emerged, resulting in a great deal of confusion as to how best to execute a plan to develop a service-oriented architecture. History tells us that as with all technologies, it may be quite a while before a clear winner takes the throne. Thankfully however, with a little preplanning and Zend Framework it is more than possible to create an architecture that can service all of them.

In this chapter we'll discuss a framework for creating web services that supports three different protocol formats: SOAP, JSON, and a standard XML serialization format while only writing the business logic behind the fundamental service once. This is of key importance in our future of uncertain services standards. We will also look at what it takes to consume these web services from within PHP using the tools provided by Zend Framework.

The Multi-Transport Services Architecture Using ZF

Let's start our discussion by creating the architecture to support multiple web services methods. This architecture is the standard MVC application built on top of Zend Framework (meaning it can serve normal web pages as well), except we will construct a special controller named the `ServiceController` that can handle the execution of service requests by clients. A key requirement of any such architecture is that duplication of business logic code is minimized as much as possible. (You don't want to have to write the same business logic for two different protocols, right?) We will start by introducing the command pattern.

The Command Pattern

The command pattern is a design pattern in object-oriented programming useful for abstracting business logic into discrete actions we know as commands. The command pattern in implementation can be broken down into the following concepts: a *client*, an *invoker*, and a *receiver*. We will discuss each in detail as it relates to the architecture.

Why are we introducing the command pattern in a web services discussion? The command pattern is an incredibly valuable object-oriented technique for abstracting the business logic of a web service from the way that web service is invoked. It allows us to write web services that are based on JSON, SOAP, XML, and so on without having any duplicate logic for how that service behaves.

The first two concepts of the command pattern we will discuss are client and invoker. The client's job is to determine the appropriate command to execute based on input and to create an instance of that command to be executed at a later point in time. The invoker's job is (as its name implies) to invoke the command itself that was created. This may sound familiar to you, and it should, as the command pattern shares many common traits with the model-view-controller pattern found in modern web applications. To us, the interesting piece regarding the command pattern is that both input and output to and from the receiver is abstracted, an important concept when we are trying to abstract the method by which commands (services) are executed.

Looking at how this pattern could be used more specifically in our particular services architecture, there won't be much of a distinction between the client and invoker since there will be little need to delay the execution of a command once it has been determined during the web request. For us, it is the receiver that is most important—the class that actually contains the business logic of our server request. These receivers are implemented as objects extending the abstract class ZEnt_Command_Abstract shown in Listing 8-1.

Listing 8-1. *The ZEnt_Command_Abstract Class*

```php
<?php

require_once 'Zend/Filter/Input.php';
require_once 'Zend/Controller/Action.php';

require_once 'ZEnt/Command/Response/Values.php';

abstract class ZEnt_Command_Abstract
{

    protected $_controller;
```

```php
protected $_requestParameterFilters = array();
protected $_requestParameterFilterOptions = array();

protected $_requestParameterValidators = array();
protected $_requestParameterUsed = array();

protected $_responseObj;

protected $_parameters = array();

final public function __construct()
{
    $this->_responseObj = new ZEnt_Command_Response_Values();

    $this->_initialize();
}

public function execute()
{
    $this->_scrubRequestParameters();

    if($this->_responseObj->isFailure())
    {
        return $this;
    }

    return $this->_execute();
}

public function getController()
{
    return $this->_controller;
}

public function setController(Zend_Controller_Action $ctl)
{
    $this->_controller = $ctl;
    return $this;
}
```

```php
public function getResponse()
{
    return $this->_responseObj;
}

protected function _scrubRequestParameters()
{
    $this->_requestParameterUsed = array_intersect_key(
        $this->getController()->getRequest()->getParams(),
        $this->_requestParameterValidators
    );

    $zfi = new Zend_Filter_Input(
        $this->_requestParameterFilters,
        $this->_requestParameterValidators,
        $this->_requestParameterUsed,
        $this->_requestParameterFilterOptions
    );

    if(!$zfi->isValid())
    {
        $msg = "Input Valiation Failed:\n";

        foreach($zfi->getMessages() as $pName => $failMsgs)
        {
            $msg .= "$pName:\n";
            foreach($failMsgs as $failMsg)
            {
                $msg .= "\t$failMsg\n";
            }
        }

        $this->_responseObj->setFailure($msg);
    }

    $this->_parameters = $zfi->getUnescaped();

    return $this;
}
```

```
    protected function _initialize()
    {
        return $this;
    }

    abstract protected function _execute();
}
?>
```

The purpose of the abstract command class shown in Listing 8-1 is to provide the first piece of framework needed to create our services architecture. The ZEnt_Command_Abstract class is responsible for the following tasks:

- Providing a mechanism for storing the output of a service call

- Accepting input from the holistic MVC and ensuring its security and integrity

- Housing the logic for the actual business logic of the service

Shown in Listing 8-1, the abstract implementation of our command pattern is provided a reference to the Zend Framework MVC by being given the instance of Zend_Controller_Action, which executed the command. This technique accomplishes two goals. It provides us a common means to access the request data for the service call, and it provides us with the necessary context data to take advantage of the Zend Framework MVC architecture from within our commands.

In order to encourage data filtering and validation, our ZEnt_Command_Abstract class also implements facilities for identifying, filtering, and validating those pieces of input that are relevant to the particular command being implemented through the use of a series of predefined protected arrays ($_requestParameterFilters, $_requestParameter-FilterOptions, $_requestParameterValidators, and $_requestParameterUsed). The class defines the relevant input parameters, their corresponding filters and validators, and the _scrubRequestParameters() protected method that processes these arrays. From a logical workflow perspective, as a developer extending the ZEnt_Command_Abstract class you would populate the arrays with the necessary information (examples provided later in the chapter), and the services framework itself would call the _scrubRequestParameters() method, ultimately populating the final array $_parameters with the relevant input prefiltered and validated for the command.

Along with the various input validation logic functions provided by this class is a mechanism for capturing the output of any service command executed through the ZEnt_Command_Response_Values object found in the $_responseObj property. Just as the ZEnt_Command_Abstract class provides a framework for the construction of a command and its input and output, the ZEnt_Command_Response_Values object is used to provide a consistent means of returning output from a command back to its invoker, shown in Listing 8-2.

Listing 8-2. *The ZEnt_Command_Response_Values Class*

```php
<?php

class ZEnt_Command_Response_Values
{

    const STATUS_REQ_SUCCESS = 'success';
    const STATUS_REQ_FAILURE = 'failure';

    public $reqStatus;

    public function __construct()
    {
        $this->status = new stdClass();
        $this->status->result = self::STATUS_REQ_SUCCESS;
        $this->status->messages = array();
    }

    public function isFailure()
    {
        return ($this->status->result === self::STATUS_REQ_FAILURE);
    }

    public function getFailureStr()
    {
        return implode("\n", $this->status->messages);
    }

    public function setFailure($msg)
    {
        $this->status->messages[] = $msg;
        $this->status->result = self::STATUS_REQ_FAILURE;
        return $this;
    }

    public function toStdObject()
    {
        $result = new stdClass();
```

```
        foreach($this as $prop => $value)
        {
            if($prop == "reqStatus")
            {
                continue;
            }

            $result->$prop = $value;
        }

        return $result;
    }
}
?>
```

A relatively simple class, the ZEnt_Command_Response_Values class is designed more to distinguish between server and logical errors than it is to enforce rules around an acceptable successful response. To these ends, this class has a single property defined, $reqStatus, which contains one of the string constants defined (STATUS_REQ_SUCCESS or STATUS_REQ_FAILURE) respectively. These two status values are then used in conjunction with the provided methods setFailure(), getFailureStr(), and isFailure() to notify the invoker if there is a server-related error that caused the service to fail. Assuming no such server error exists, arbitrary public properties may be added to the response object at runtime by a concrete implementation of the ZEnt_Command_Abstract class to return values back to the invoker.

■Note It is important to again state that the failure properties and methods of the ZEnt_Command_Response_Values are *not* for logical business errors encountered during the execution of a command but rather for server errors. For example, if you create a service command to update a record in the database, the response object should be set to failure if a connection to the database cannot be made but should return success if a connection was made but the record to update was not found. For the latter circumstance, the service call happened correctly, so the response object should instead set its own error properties or message as public member variables to be returned to the invoker.

Now that we have discussed both the ZEnt_Command_Abstract and ZEnt_Command_Response_Values classes, let us now look at the logic that encapsulates the client aspects of the pattern. In this implementation we use the factory pattern to locate and return instances of concrete command implementations and serve the needs of the client through a class called ZEnt_Command_Factory shown in Listing 8-3.

Listing 8-3. *The ZEnt_Command_Factory Class*

```php
<?php

require_once 'Zend/Exception.php';
require_once 'Zend/Filter/HtmlEntities.php';
require_once 'Zend/Loader/PluginLoader.php';

class ZEnt_Command_Factory
{
    const COMMAND_PATTERN = '/^[a-z]+(\.[a-z]+)+$/i';

    const COMMAND_CLASS_PREFIX - 'ZEnt_Command';
    const COMMAND_CLASS_PATH   = 'ZEnt/Command';

    public static function getCommand($command,
                       $prefix = self::COMMAND_CLASS_PREFIX,
                       $path = self::COMMAND_CLASS_PATH)
    {
        if(($match = @preg_match(self::COMMAND_PATTERN,
                                 $command)) === false)
        {
            throw new Zend_Exception("Invalid regular expression: " .
                                                self::COMMAND_PATTERN);
        }

        if(!$match)
        {
            $filter = new Zend_Filter_HtmlEntities();
            throw new Zend_Exception("Command '" . $filter->filter($command) .
                            "' does not follow pattern '" .
                            self::COMMAND_PATTERN . "'");
        }

        $commandName = str_replace(' ', '_',
                ucwords(str_replace('.', ' ', $command)));

        $pluginLoader = new Zend_Loader_PluginLoader(array($prefix => $path));

        $commandClass = $pluginLoader->load($commandName);

        $obj = new $commandClass();
```

```
        if($obj instanceof ZEnt_Command_Abstract)
        {
            return new $obj;
        }

        throw new Zend_Exception("Requested class does not have " .
                                "ZEnt_Command_Abstract as a parent");
    }
}
?>
```

■Note In Listing 8-3 we make use of the `Zend_Loader_PluginLoader` component to load the correct command class. This component is useful because it will automatically handle the mapping between a standard Zend Framework object (i.e., `ZEnt_Command_Account_Login`) to the correct path on the file system based on the Zend Framework naming convention (in our case, the `ZEnt/Command/Account/Login.php` file).

The purpose of the `ZEnt_Command_Factory` class is to take a string representation of a command name following the syntax `'<namespace>.<command>'` and return a concrete command class object to be executed by the invoker. To facilitate this, the `ZEnt_Command_Factory` class has a single static method, `getCommand()`, which requires at least one parameter (the command string) and accepts up to two additional parameters (used to define the command class location on the file system).

Using a combination of regular expressions and string manipulation, the goal of this class is to convert a string such as `'auth.login'` into a concrete class name—in this case `'ZEnt_Command_Auth_Login'`. This class name is then resolved into a concrete class through the use of the `Zend_Loader_PluginLoader()` class and an instance of the class returned to the caller.

This code allows you to create a Zend Framework style library of commands that are executed as service calls. Assuming you have the library path of your Zend Framework project as part of your include path, creating a new service (`auth.login`) should be as simple in most cases as creating the `ZEnt/Command/Auth/Login.php` script and implementing the `ZEnt_Command_Auth_Login` class within it.

■Note The path and class name `ZEnt_Command_Auth_Login` assumes you have not passed different prefixes to the `ZEnt_Command_Factory` class or otherwise modified the constants representing these prefixes within it. If you prefer different prefixes, of course these can be modified. Also note that the `ZEnt_Command_Auth_Login` class must extend the `ZEnt_Command_Abstract` class to be considered valid!

With the `ZEnt_Command_Factory` class we have implemented the majority of the command pattern used in our service architecture through the implementation of the client and receiver concepts. Now let's move on to the next level of the implementation handled by a specialized Zend Framework controller class, the invoker.

The ServiceController Action Controller

With the command pattern introduced in the previous section, it is now time to move into the MVC aspect of the service architecture and introduce the specialized `ServiceController`. In this controller, the goal is to use the service command class architecture introduced in the previous section along with some additional code to accept a service request in one of three distinct formats, execute the relevant command class for the request, and return the response in the desired format. For this we will be combining the standard `Zend_Controller_Action` class with the `ContextSwitch` controller helper (also a standard in Zend Framework) to implement a calculator service that can be accessed via a service call in SOAP, or GET/POST with XML, or JSON responses. In addition we will also introduce a rough notion of service API versioning, allowing you to create multiple versions of the same service without necessarily having them conflict with one another.

To get started we will create a standard MVC Zend Framework controller called `ServiceController` and use the `init()` callback to set up our environment as shown in Listing 8-4.

Listing 8-4. *The Beginning of the* `ServiceController` *Web Services Controller*

```php
<?php

require_once 'Zend/Controller/Action.php';
require_once 'XML/Serializer.php';

class ServiceController extends Zend_Controller_Action {

    const FORMAT_REST = "rest";
    const FORMAT_SOAP = "soap";
    const FORMAT_JSON = "json";

    const SOAP_PROXY_PREFIX = "ZEnt_Soap_Proxy";
    const SOAP_PROXY_PATH   = "ZEnt/Soap/Proxy";

    protected $_requestFormat = self::FORMAT_JSON;
```

```php
protected $_soapServer = null;

public function indexAction() {
    $this->_forward("index", "index");
    return;
}

public function getSoapServer()
{
    if($this->_soapServer === null)
    {
        $this->_soapServer = new Zend_Soap_Server(null,
                                array('uri' => Zend_Uri::factory(
                                    'http://' . $_SERVER['HTTP_HOST'] .
                                    $_SERVER['SCRIPT_NAME']
                                    )->__toString()
                                )
                            );
    }

    return $this->_soapServer;
}

public function init()
{
    $formatRequest = $this->getRequest()->getParam("format", self::FORMAT_JSON);

    switch(strtolower($formatRequest))
    {
        case self::FORMAT_JSON:
        case self::FORMAT_XML:
        case self::FORMAT_SOAP:
            $this->_requestFormat = $formatRequest;
            break;
        default:
            $this->_requestFormat = self::FORMAT_JSON;
    }

    $this->_helper->viewRenderer->setNoRender(true);
```

```
        $soapContext = array(
            'headers' => array(
                'Content-Type' => 'text/xml'
            )
        );

        $xmlContext = array(
            'headers' => array(
                'Content-Type' => 'text/xml'
            )
        );

        $contextSwitch = $this->_helper->contextSwitch();

        $contextSwitch->addContext(self::FORMAT_SOAP, $soapContext)
                      ->addContext(self::FORMAT_XML, $restContext)
                      ->addActionContext('v1',
                            array(self::FORMAT_JSON,
                                  self::FORMAT_XML,
                                  self::FORMAT_SOAP));

    }
}
```

Looking at Listing 8-4, you can see that it is indeed a standard Zend Framework Controller that contains one action, indexAction(). Since this is a special controller, we simply redirect the requestor to the IndexController::indexAction for this action (we will discuss the service-specific actions a little later). For now, we are interested primarily in the init() method, which sets up the various contexts for the service requests being made.

The first step in our init() method is to determine the response format the requesting client is looking to retrieve by looking in the Zend_Controller_Request_Http::getParam() method for the format variable. (By default we assume it will be a JSON response.) Next we validate that the format received was indeed one we expected through the creative use of a switch() statement to assign the $_requestFormat property of the controller. With both of these completed we are now ready to start setting up the various contexts available in this controller by using the ContextSwitch() Zend Framework Controller Helper.

The Zend Framework ContextSwitch Action Helper

The purpose of the ContextSwitch Action Helper is to facilitate the return of different response formats other than HTML from within a Zend Framework application. To use this helper, we must define the contexts available to the controller and then provide a mapping of which contexts are available to which actions within that controller. When a context is activated for a particular action, a number of things take place internally within the MVC architecture:

- Layouts provided through Zend_Layout are disabled if previously enabled.

- Any response headers that are required for the context are returned when the response is sent.

- An alternative user-defined view script suffix (other than .phtml) is used, allowing the developer to create a different view script for the context.

- If provided, callbacks for pre- and post-processing of the context are also provided.

Zend Framework's MVC out of the box supports the automatic encoding of JSON as a context, but for the other two contexts we wish to create (the XML response and a SOAP context) we must first add those as available contexts for the ServiceController class. To these ends we create two context arrays, $xmlContext and $soapContext, which contain the configuration values used by the ContextSwitch helper to determine how the contexts should be handled. While in our particular example these contexts basically have the same context configuration, if desired details between the two could be changed. (Please consult the Zend Framework manual for a full list of ContextSwitch options.) Once we have defined each context's configuration we can call the addContext() method of the ContextSwitch helper to add that context (identified by a string key). We are ready to map that context as an available context for an action.

Within the same chained statement as the addContext() call, we proceed to map a yet-to-be-defined action v1Action as accepting the three contexts we would like to make available for our service calls. This action will be the sole action used in our ServiceController to make use of the command pattern defined earlier to execute Service classes, and we named it v1 to indicate that it is "version 1" of these service calls. Listing 8-5 shows the implementation of this v1Action() method.

Listing 8-5. *The ServiceController::v1Action() Method*

```
public function v1Action()
    {
        $cmdParam = $this->getRequest()->getParam('command');

        if(($cmdParam === null) || empty($cmdParam))
        {
            throw new Zend_Exception("No Command Specified");
        }

        $this->_helper->contextSwitch()->initContext($this->_requestFormat);
```

```php
if($this->_requestFormat == self::FORMAT_SOAP)
{
    $soapProxyName = str_replace(' ', '_', ucwords(➥
                str_replace('.', ' ', $cmdParam)));
    $pluginLoader = new Zend_Loader_PluginLoader(➥
                array(self::SOAP_PROXY_PREFIX => self::SOAP_PROXY_PATH));

    $soapProxyClass = $pluginLoader->load($soapProxyName);

    $showWsdl = $this->getRequest()->getQuery('wsdl', false);

    if($showWsdl === false)
    {
        $server = $this->getSoapServer();
        $server->setObject(new $soapProxyClass($this));
    }
    else
    {
        $server = new Zend_Soap_AutoDiscover();
        $server->setClass($soapProxyClass);
    }


    $server->handle();

    return;
}

$cmdObject = ZEnt_Command_Factory::getCommand($cmdParam);
$cmdObject->setController($this);
$cmdObject->execute();

switch($this->_requestFormat)
{
    case self::FORMAT_JSON:
        $this->view->response = $cmdObject->getResponse()->toStdObject();
        break;
    case self::FORMAT_XML:
        $xmlSerializerOptions = array(
            'rootName' => 'response',
            'encoding' => 'UTF-8'
        );
```

```
          $xmlSerializer = @new XML_Serializer($xmlSerializerOptions);
          if(@$xmlSerializer->serialize($cmdObject->getResponse()➥
               ->toStdObject()))
          {
               print $xmlSerializer->getSerializedData();
          }
          else
          {
               throw new Zend_Exception("Failed to serialize result to XML");
          }
          break;
     default:
          throw new Zend_Exception("Unknown Request Format");
     }
}
```

Examining the v1Action() method in Listing 8-5, you can see that the first step in our controller is to determine the ultimate command or service call that is being made by the client by looking for the command parameter in the request object. Assuming this parameter exists, we move forward by using the ContextSwitch helper's initContext() method to switch the response context to the one previously determined in the controller's init() method. The next part, however, is where things become a little more complicated and will require a bit of explanation.

If we were to create a ServiceController class that simply accepted parameters using the standard input methods of Zend Framework (GET, POST, PATH_INFO, and so on) and were only concerned with ensuring that the response format was correct, this controller actually would be rather easy as the problem could be solved entirely by the ContextSwitch helper. However, since we have also included the SOAP protocol in the mix (a protocol that exclusively uses POST to send XML documents that contain the request information), we have to treat it separately from the other two protocols. Moreover, SOAP is also special in the sense that the services for it are largely defined by popular consensus through Web Services Description Language (WSDL) documents which should be retrievable from the service by passing wsdl as a GET parameter for the request. Thus, we will return to the special case of SOAP later in the chapter. For now, assume we are working strictly in JSON or XML response formats.

Assuming the response format is JSON or XML, you can see how it is the ServiceController::v1Action() that acts as the invoker in our original command pattern discussion. As you may expect, once we have initialized the context of the request through the ContextHelper, we then proceed to locate and execute the service command being requested, thus executing the service business logic. In order to provide the input data needed to perform this action, we provide the entire controller class to the command prior to execution. While in these examples surely passing just the Zend_Controller_Request_Http object would have sufficed, there is little reason not to provide the controller itself and thus ensure that future possible enhancements to the Zend_Controller_Action or MVC models can be taken advantage of from within the command architecture being implemented.

Once the command has executed, we can expect the response to have been stored within the same Command object itself and to be available through the getResponse() method call. The only thing left to do is, based on the response format requested, serialize this response object into that format. For JSON-encoded responses, this is very trivial as Zend Framework will automatically serialize all view variables in JSON format if the action has been set to the JSON context. For XML it is nearly as easy, as we should be able to simply print an XML document as output containing the response. However, there is a snag—there is no XML serializer currently available in Zend Framework. To overcome this hurdle we fall back on the trusty PEAR component library (http://pear.php.net/) and the XML_Serializer class to take our response object and convert it into XML on our behalf.

At this point, discounting the SOAP protocol, we have discussed everything you need to take advantage of the command pattern to create web services that work in both JSON and XML response formats. Unfortunately we're still not ready to bring SOAP into this picture just yet. Instead we will briefly walk through a concrete implementation of this service architecture by creating a simple calculator web service.

Creating a Simple Web Service

Now that we have explained the majority of the code behind the web services architecture built on top of Zend Framework, we are ready to start implementing a simple web service for us to play with: a simple four-function calculator. Thanks to our architecture this should be an extremely easy thing to accomplish as it simply involves creating four Command classes that accept two operands as input and produce a single result as output. However, since all of these services are so simple, we have gone the extra step and produced a fifth abstract class to consolidate the filtering and validation logic of the four operations. Two of these five classes are listed in Listing 8-6.

Listing 8-6. *The ZEnt_Command_Calculator_Abstract and ZEnt_Comamnd_Calculator_Add Classes*

`-- library/ZEnt/Command/Calculator/Abstract.php --`

```php
<?php

abstract class ZEnt_Command_Calculator_Abstract extends ZEnt_Command_Abstract
{
    protected function _initialize()
    {
```

```php
        $this->_requestParameterValidators = array(
            'op1'    => array(
                new Zend_Validate_Digits()
            ),
            'op2'    => array(
                new Zend_Validate_Digits()
            )
        );

        $this->_requestParameterFilterOptions = array(
            'breakChainOnFailure'    => true,
            'presence'               => 'required'
        );

        return $this;
    }
}
?>
```

-- **library/ZEnt/Command/Calculator/Add.php** --

```php
<?php

require_once 'ZEnt/Command/Calculator/Abstract.php';

class ZEnt_Command_Calculator_Add extends ZEnt_Command_Calculator_Abstract
{
    protected function _execute()
    {
        $op1 = (int)$this->_parameters['op1'];
        $op2 = (int)$this->_parameters['op2'];
        $this->_responseObj->answer = $op1 + $op2;

        return $this;
    }

}
?>
```

For any intermediate PHP developer with object-oriented experience, these classes should be fairly straightforward. As previously explained, we start with an abstract ZEnt_Command_Calculator_Abstract class, which implements the _initialize() method previously discussed to set up any filter and validation rules needed. This class is then extended by the ZEnt_Command_Calculator_Add class, which completes the service by implementing the _execute() method and performing our calculation. This answer is then stored into the _responseObj variable (a ZEnt_Command_Response_Values instance), and the method returns. When placed into the include path, you can give this service a quick test by going to the following URL:

```
http://<servername>/service/v1/command/calculator.add/?op1=2&op2=4&format=xml
```

Assuming you have everything set up correctly, you should get an output similar to the following:

```
<?xml version="1.0" encoding="utf-8"?>
<response>
    <answer>6</answer>
</response>
```

For your reference, the sample code that comes with this book includes all four services (Add, Sub, Div and Mul) as a fully functioning example.

Dealing with SOAP in Zend Framework MVC

Thus far in this chapter we have intentionally ignored how the SOAP part of our web services architecture works, and it was previously mentioned this was because it functioned fundamentally different than other architectures. Specifically, the issue that you find implementing SOAP services within the MVC is the fact that the SOAP server provided by Zend Framework wasn't necessarily designed to function within the MVC. Thus, when we expect to be dealing in terms of the SOAP protocol, we must treat this differently (and thus the special if conditional block in Listing 8-5 earlier in the chapter). Listing 8-7 highlights the specific code block within the ServiceController class relating to dealing with SOAP requests.

Listing 8-7. *The SOAP-Specific Routines Within the ServiceController Class*

```
$soapProxyName = str_replace(' ', '_',➥
                    ucwords(str_replace('.', ' ', $cmdParam)));
 $pluginLoader = new Zend_Loader_PluginLoader(
                    array(self::SOAP_PROXY_PREFIX => self::SOAP_PROXY_PATH));

$soapProxyClass = $pluginLoader->load($soapProxyName);
$showWsdl = $this->getRequest()->getQuery('wsdl', false);
```

```php
if($showWsdl === false)
{
    $server = $this->getSoapServer();
     $server->setObject(new $soapProxyClass($this));
}
else
{
    $server = new Zend_Soap_AutoDiscover();
    $server->setClass($soapProxyClass);
}

$server->handle();
```

Examining the previous code block (a subsection of Listing 8-5), you can see that we do some of the same general things we did for JSON and XML to convert the command name (i.e., auth.login) into a class, which is then used in conjunction with the Zend Framework Zend_Soap_Server component. However, SOAP is unique in not only the way data is transmitted to the server but also in the way SOAP is implemented, which requires special care. The issue boils down to the fact that SOAP as a web service implementation is designed to be introspective, meaning that any PHP class should be able to be exposed as a web service by making the Zend_Soap_Server component aware of it. To accomplish this feat the Zend_Soap_Server component (and helper class Zend_Soap_Autodiscover) rely on PHPDoc comments preceding each method within a given class being used as a web service end point to determine the typing and so on of information used. Unfortunately, that doesn't make as much sense when our services are implemented using the command pattern, as each Command only has one method _execute(), and that method takes no parameters.

To solve this problem, an extra step must be taken to enable SOAP services in our command pattern by introducing yet another object-oriented pattern called the proxy pattern. The proxy pattern is quite simple. We create another class that represents the service in the way we would like it represented, and rather than duplicating the business logic of our commands, proxy each method into a valid command to be executed. In this way, we can also include the necessary PHPDoc comments to autogenerate the WSDL document and execute the service request previously discussed. As was true with the concrete command classes, we start our implementation with an abstract SOAP proxy class shown in Listing 8-8.

Listing 8-8. *The ZEnt_Soap_Proxy_Abstract Class*

```php
<?php

abstract class ZEnt_Soap_Proxy_Abstract
{
```

```php
    protected $_controller;

    /**
     *
     * @return Zend_Controller_Action
     */
    protected function getController()
    {
        return $this->_controller;
    }

    function __construct(Zend_Controller_Action $controller)
    {
        if(is_null($controller))
        {
            throw new Zend_Exception➥
                        ("Must provide the controller to the Proxy class");
        }

        $this->_controller = $controller;
    }

    protected function callCommand($cmd, $params)
    {
        $cmdObject = ZEnt_Command_Factory::getCommand($cmd);

        $this->getController()->getRequest()->setParams($params);

        $cmdObject->setController($this->getController());

        $cmdObject->execute();

        $response = $cmdObject->getResponse();

        if($response->isFailure())
        {
            throw new Zend_Exception($response->getFailureStr());
        }

        return $response->toStdObject()->answer;
    }
}
?>
```

As shown in Listing 8-8, there is only one major method in the ZEnt_Soap_Proxy_ Abstract class worth discussing: the callCommand() method. This method accepts two parameters. The first is the command to execute (auth.login), and the second is an array of key/value pairs representing the parameters the command needs to execute. Given this data, the callCommand() method then proceeds to construct the correct Command object (as the client in the command pattern), set the parameters for the command, and then execute the command as the invoker. Upon completion the response is processed and converted into an exception if necessary; otherwise it is returned as a standard object.

■**Note** In this context an exception is handled automatically by the Zend_Soap_Server component and translated transparently into a SOAP "Fault" object and returned to the requesting client. Always make sure then that you throw exceptions for errors when using SOAP, as this is the correct behavior.

The purpose of the callCommand() method in our abstract class is to make the actual proxy classes we create for the SOAP server easy to implement (or even automatically generate potentially), as each "method" within the Proxy translates its parameters into a call to the callCommand() method of its parent. For the Calculator class, this is shown in Listing 8-9.

Listing 8-9. *The ZEnt_Soap_Proxy_Calculator Class*

```php
<?php

require_once 'ZEnt/Soap/Proxy/Abstract.php';

class ZEnt_Soap_Proxy_Calculator extends ZEnt_Soap_Proxy_Abstract
{
    /**
     * This method adds two numbers togther
     *
     * @param integer $op1 The first operand
     * @param integer $op2 The second operand
     * @return integer The addition of op1 and op2
     */
    public function add($op1, $op2)
    {
        return $this->callCommand('calculator.add', array('op1' => $op1,➥
                   'op2' => $op2));
    }
```

```php
    /**
     * This method subtracts two numbers
     *
     * @param integer $op1 The first operand
     * @param integer $op2 The second operand
     * @return integer The subtraction of op1 and op2
     */
    public function sub($op1, $op2)
    {
        return $this->callCommand('calculator.sub', array('op1' => $op1,➥
                    'op2' => $op2));
    }


    /**
     * This method multiplies two numbers
     *
     * @param integer $op1 The first operand
     * @param integer $op2 The second operand
     * @return integer The multiplication of op1 and op2
     */
    public function mul($op1, $op2)
    {
        return $this->callCommand('calculator.mul', array('op1' => $op1,➥
                    'op2' => $op2));
    }


    /**
     * This method divides two provided numbers
     *
     * @param integer $op1 The first operand
     * @param integer $op2 The second operand
     * @return float The divides of op1 and op2
     */
    public function div($op1, $op2)
    {
        return $this->callCommand('calculator.div', array('op1' => $op1,➥
                    'op2' => $op2));
    }
}
?>
```

As shown in Listing 8-9, the ZEnt_Soap_Proxy_Calculator is an extremely simple class, but it implements some very important details necessary when using the SOAP protocol.

First, it encapsulates all of our individual Commands (implemented as individual classes) under a single unifying class. Second, it provides a different API to access those methods that is completely documented using PHPDoc, making the auto-generation of WSDL documents possible. Note, of all the web service implementations we have discussed, this extra step of producing a Proxy class is only relevant for the SOAP implementation. If you plan on using JSON or XML for your transport mechanism, you can simply use the implementation discussed in this chapter significantly to those ends.

Consuming Web Services Using Zend Framework

Now that we have discussed in detail the production of web services using Zend Framework in a modular and robust fashion, let us turn our attention to consuming them. Web services are a major aspect of Zend Framework in ways no other framework for PHP (or for that matter, really any language) can claim. At the time of this writing Zend Framework version 1.8 provides direct APIs for 23 web services providers including Yahoo!, Twitter, Google, and even the Amazon EC and S3 technologies. These APIs will not be discussed in this book in detail as they are well documented within the Zend Framework manual. They are designed to make using these technology services as streamlined and easy as possible. For those services not directly supported by Zend Framework as components, Zend Framework provides an extremely robust set of generic web-service clients for processing the entire range of service requests that make up the fabric of Web 2.0 including REST, JSON, SOAP, RSS/ATOM, and XML-RPC. In this section we will explore how these components can be used to bring the power of web services into your application.

Note It is worthwhile to note that, like most Zend Framework technologies, the service components provided by Zend Framework are "use at will" and are not limited to applications written on top of the Zend Framework MVC but rather can be used in any architecture.

Consume REST-Style Services

The first set of services we will explore are what have been deemed REST-style services. That is, these services typically use the standard methods of GET, POST, PUT, and DELETE to transfer input into the web service (much like the services we created earlier in the chapter) but then often return their response in some sort of serialized data format such as XML or JSON. For these services Zend Framework does not provide any sort of specialized component per se but rather expects you to use the standard HTTP client to perform the request and to use a serialization component like Zend_Json to convert the response into a meaningful object usable in PHP.

To demonstrate how this technology might work, let's say for example there is a web service at the following URL that is used for geocoding:

```
http://www.example.com/service/geocode
```

This service expects a single parameter address (a qualified street address) as a GET parameter and will return a set of latitude and longitude coordinates representing where that address might be found on a map in JSON format. Thus, a possible query might be

```
http://www.example.com/service/geocode?address=<some address>
```

which may result in the following response:

```
{"result":{"lat":43.54323,"long":-82.84834}}
```

To take advantage of this service from within PHP using Zend Framework, it is as simple as creating an instance of the HTTP Client Zend_Http_Client, configuring it for the request at hand and then parsing the response as JSON using the Zend_Json component. This process is shown in Listing 8-10.

Listing 8-10. *Using Zend_Http_Client and Zend_Json to Perform Web Service Calls in JSON Format*

```php
$httpConfig = array(
    'maxredirects'   => 5,
    'strictredirects' => false,
    'useragent'      => 'My Http Client',
    'timeout'        => 10,
    'adapter'        => 'Zend_Http_Client_Adapter_Socket',
    'httpversion'    => Zend_Http_Client::HTTP_1,
    'keepalive'      => false,
    'storeresponse'  => true,
    'strict'         => true
    );

$client = new Zend_Http_Client();
$client->setConfig($httpConfig);
$client->setUri(new Zend_Uri_Http("http://www.example.com/service/geocode"));
$client->setParameterGet('address', '1234 somewhere, new york, ny 12345');

$response = $client->request(Zend_Http_Client::GET);

if($response->isSuccessful())
{
```

```
$resultRaw = $response->getBody();
$resultObj = Zend_Json::decode($resultRaw, Zend_Json::TYPE_OBJECT);

print "Lat: {$resultObj->lat}, Long: {$resultObj->long}";
}
```

As you can see, Listing 8-10 is quite straightforward. We start by creating an instance of the Zend_Http_Client class, configure it, provide it an endpoint URL and our GET parameter, and call its request() method to execute the request. The response, if successful, is then used in conjunction with the Zend_Json component to translate the JSON-formatted body into a standard PHP object.

Tip In the previous example we assumed the service would respond in JSON format. If the service responds in another format such as XML, you would use a different solution to deserialize it. Specifically for XML we recommend the use of the standard XML processing technologies (i.e., SimpleXML or DOM).

Consuming SOAP Services

Often the service format that must be consumed, especially in enterprise environments, is SOAP in order to interact with web services. Thankfully, Zend Framework provides the Zend_Soap component, which is useful for not only creating SOAP-based web services but consuming them as well. When using the SOAP client in Zend Framework it can operate in one of two modes: using a WSDL or manually. It is *strongly* recommended that the SOAP client only be used in WSDL mode, as it is extremely rare in today's Internet to find SOAP-based services that do not provide a WSDL document describing them—and it is an extremely tedious process to consume these services without it.

Assuming you have a WSDL document for your service (which is often attainable by simply appending a GET parameter of wsdl to the end of your endpoint URI), the process for consuming these services is very straightforward:

- Configure the Zend_Soap_Client component as necessary.

- Provide the client a copy of the WSDL document.

- Call the methods as if they were native methods of the Zend_Soap_Client object!

For example, if you were to use the Zend_Soap_Client to communicate with the calculator service described in the previous chapter, you could do so as simply as using the code in Listing 8-11.

Listing 8-11. *Using Zend_Soap_Client with a WSDL to Perform Service Requests*

```php
<?php

$wsdlUrl = "http://www.example.com/service/v1/command=calculator?wsdl";
$soapClient = new Zend_Soap_Client($wsdlUrl);
try {
    $result = $soapClient->add(1, 2);
} catch(SoapFault $e) {
    print "Service Fault: " . $e->getMessage();
}

print "Service call result: $result";

?>
```

One thing you may notice in Listing 8-11 is the usage of the try … catch block around our service call to the add() method. The reason we add this try … catch block is because Zend Framework will automatically convert any error returned from the server (known as a "soap fault") into an exception class of type SoapFault and throw it. Thus, to prevent this exception from bubbling out of scope we must catch it to determine whether an error indeed did occur.

Conclusion

In this chapter we have covered a great deal regarding the architecture and usage of PHP-powered web services through Zend Framework. Using this architecture, it is possible to not only make development of web services easy but also abstract away the challenges of providing a single service in multiple output formats. Combined with the obvious ease of consuming web services through Zend Framework, you have an extremely powerful tool for building and using service-oriented architectures across the Web. As always there is more to learn, and we strongly recommend the excellent documentation in the Zend Framework manual for the complete details of taking advantage of these exciting technologies.

CHAPTER 9

Production Farms for PHP

Once an application has been built, you have to get it onto at least one production server so that its intended audience can use it. The needs of your applications can vary wildly, and in this chapter we will explore some of the common options and discuss some of the common pitfalls that development teams run into when it comes to the server needs of your application. We'll discuss the general concepts behind production server farm architecture, some things about the Apache HTTP server, and challenges commonly faced in developing PHP applications.

Before we begin this discussion, it is worth stating (as we have often throughout the book) that during the architecture and development phases of your application's life cycle, a little forethought to your production needs can go a long way toward making the entire process less painful later. PHP has a specific, unique approach to web development and deployment, and understanding it (discussed later in this chapter) is important in avoiding many of the common pitfalls.

General Server Farm Architecture

One of the biggest perceived problems that server farm architecture is designed to solve is that of *scalability*, which unfortunately is often mistaken with performance. This could not be farther from the truth, and development teams who have made this mistake often find themselves in a position where it simply doesn't matter what their server farm architecture looks like. A scalable application can handle more users, processes, and so on with the introduction of new hardware resources (more servers); a high-performance application makes better use of the hardware it has. Thus it is critical that your application has the ability to *scale* its architecture first and foremost. That means it has to work on a single server and still be able to run on 20, 200, or 2,000 more servers without drastic application changes.

Why is this important in talking about server farm architecture? Well, it's because a standard LAMP stack application has a few unique traits to it that can affect whether, and how, your server farm should be built. Understanding these traits is the key to scalability, and they include the following:

- PHP is a "share-nothing" architecture, meaning that individual PHP scripts executing on the server are isolated from one another in pretty much every way.

- As will be discussed in the next chapter, MySQL has a number of traits that can drastically affect server architecture, such as the ability to function as a master or slave, clustering, full-text searching, and so on.

Figure 9-1 outlines a classic LAMP stack server architecture on which most common architecture is based.

The architecture shown in Figure 9-1 uses a total of six servers, three web servers and three MySQL servers. In this configuration all three web servers are managed by a single load balancer that interfaces with the public Internet to direct traffic to the web servers. In turn, the PHP application running on these web servers connects to either a MySQL master or MySQL slave farm to write or read data from the database respectively. (Slave machines are placed behind a load balancer as well, which the PHP application would connect to.)

Note If you aren't familiar with MySQL master/slave configurations, don't worry. They are discussed in more detail in Chapter 10. For now what you should take from this diagram is that the PHP application is going to the database load balancer when it wishes to *read* data from the database, but connects to the "master" database when it needs to *write* data to the database.

There are many assumptions made in the diagram shown in Figure 9-1 and many possible pitfalls to consider. The biggest assumption is that there will be no need for one web server to ever communicate with another one other than through the sharing of a common database back end. This makes sense, but from a performance or scalability perspective does it make sense for everything? It certainly makes sense for data that doesn't need to be updated every single request, such as a customer record, but what about something that is likely to be updated every request, such as session data? This brings up an incredibly important point regarding production farm architectures: more often than not for PHP, it isn't the web servers themselves that pose the biggest problems scaling but rather everything (such as session data) used by the PHP application. As we continue in this chapter we will address many of the common scalability problems and how they might impact your server architecture.

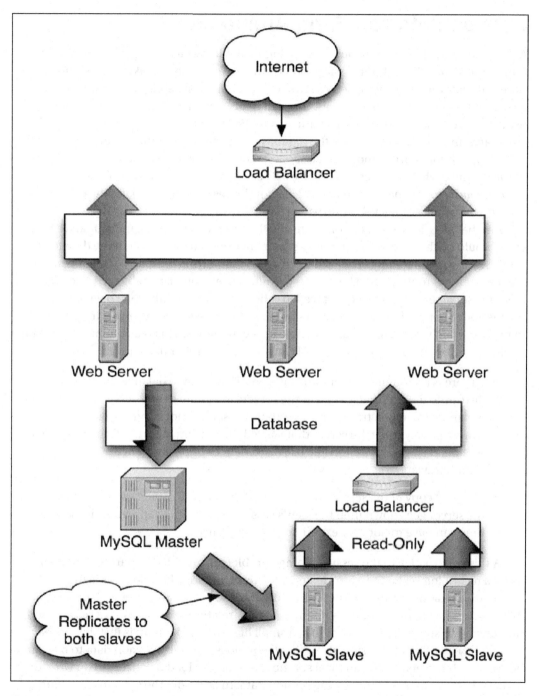

Figure 9-1. *A classic LAMP stack production farm architecture*

Session Data and Farm Architecture

As was mentioned in the previous section, Figure 9-1 leaves a lot of questions, among other things, questions about session management. You have to make a decision and a trade-off that will impact your server farm. On one hand it is relatively trivial to develop a custom session-management script that can read and write each user's session data using the database as a storage mechanism. On the other hand, this puts a potentially costly and unnecessary burden on the database that could affect the performance of the entire application. Furthermore, since session data is likely to be updated every single request, unlike what is depicted in Figure 9-1, each web server would probably have to *read and write* to the master server—at least for the session data, making the complications on the application level more expensive.

Another alternative is to continue storing the session data on the individual web servers as would be the case in a single-web-server environment. However, if the data for a user's session is stored only on a local web server, that means the load balancer determining how traffic is routed has to be certain to route a user who has established a session to the same server every single request (called "sticky" sessions). If the load balancer doesn't do this, then it's possible that your users will lose their session occasionally from request to request, which would make for a horrible user experience. This is a common choice for applications, but it's far from a foolproof solution, as a number of things can go wrong:

- If there is a sudden spike in traffic, it's possible the load balancer may not evenly distribute the traffic across all of the servers, resulting in one server attempting to handle too much traffic and the other two servers not handling enough traffic. Unfortunately since the server that started the session must continue to serve that session, it can result in horrible user experiences or performance even with sufficient hardware.

- The only copy of the session data is stored on the web server, which means that if the server goes down then the user's session is lost. This happening at the wrong time can have major user experience consequences.

A third alternative to the session storage problem is provided as part of Zend Platform using a technology called session clustering. This technology functions, as is the case with sticky sessions, by storing the session data on the local web server with one major difference: the load balancer does not manage any relationships between a session and the server that started it. Instead of this, a small lightweight daemon is installed on each web server as part of the session clustering technology, allowing session data to be shared between web servers. This is an ideal solution, as it allows load balancers to do what they do best (balance load) without losing session data. In addition, the session clustering technology can also function in what is known as high-availability mode, where multiple copies of the session data can be kept on multiple machines transparently and thus solve the problem of losing session data if the originating server crashes for any reason.

Note In extremely high-performance situations it is possible to sidestep the session storage problem entirely. If you are storing less than 1,024 bytes of data, you can store the data you would have stored in the session inside of a cookie and effectively "store" it on the client machine. Of course if you were to do this it is paramount to take appropriate security measures as well. Specifically, if you aren't concerned with the *contents* of the cookie (but don't want the values changed) you can sign the values using a combination of the cookie value and a secret server-side salt. If it is important for security that the data in the cookie be unreadable, you should use a strong encryption algorithm such as AES. Remember (as was discussed in the Chapter 6), any data you send to the client makes it untrustworthy, and it should be handled carefully.

Database Concerns in Farm Architecture

Another concern in our generic server architecture is the database layer. In Figure 9-1 we show only a single "master" MySQL server responsible for accepting database writes from the web servers, which poses a number of architectural problems to consider:

- A single master has a limited write capacity, meaning that while the generic architecture can scale from the web server/MySQL slave side of things, we will ultimately be limited in our ability to write to the MySQL master fast enough.

- A single master is a major danger from an availability standpoint, as it is a major single point of failure in our architecture. If the MySQL master database were to crash or otherwise become incapacitated, the web application would cease to function.

Note High availability in MySQL database systems can be an incredibly complex problem to solve and is largely out of the scope of this book. For an excellent resource for this subject, we recommend *High Performance MySQL* by Jeremy Zawodny and Derek J. Balling (O'Reilly, 2004).

Scaling the MySQL aspect of your architecture can take many forms. If you were to start with the generic architecture shown in Figure 9-1, there are two aspects to scaling out the database: the "master" MySQL server, which accepts writes, and one or more MySQL "slave" servers, which handle reads from the web application. For slaves the architecture can look a number of ways depending on the needs of your application described in the next section.

MySQL Slave Farm Architecture

In the most generic sense, scaling out the slave side of the MySQL layer of your stack architecture depends significantly on the needs of the application itself. Generally speaking, the concept is simple: MySQL can feed database updates to one or more slave servers. These slave servers are read-only, and the application running on the web servers typically will connect to one of these servers through a load balancer as shown in Figure 9-1. One thing to consider is that there is really no limit to how slaves can be scaled. While the master server is responsible for replicating its data to a slave, slaves can replicate from other slaves, making the architectures shown in Figure 9-2 possible.

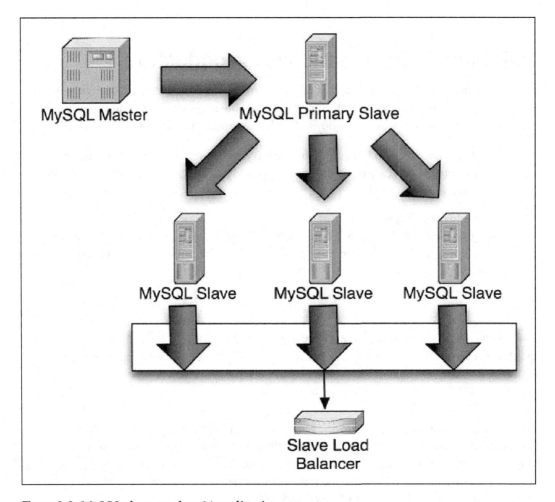

Figure 9-2. *MySQL slave-to-slave(s) replication*

In Figure 9-2, we have a single MySQL master that replicates to a slave we have designated the primary slave. From there, this primary slave can replicate its data to a pool of slaves it controls, and it can be scaled indefinitely. This is an important technique for reducing the load on the MySQL master because of the overhead associated with replicating from the master to a large number of MySQL slaves directly, and it can be quite useful without any outward application code changes.

Tip For intermediate replication slaves, such as in an architecture shown in Figure 9-2, it may prove useful to use the BLACKHOLE storage engine for all of the tables. For those who may not be aware, this storage engine doesn't actually store any data and would be equivalent to sending data to /dev/null on a Linux machine. The reason this is useful is because a table's storage engine does not have any impact on the binlogs on which replication functions, thus while you could never query the primary slave for data directly, using BLACKHOLE as the storage engine will increase its performance while still allowing it to serve as a replication intermediary.

This technique can also be used when your application has special needs where read queries can function better using different table-storage engines. One such example would be using the full-text functionality of MySQL. Consider the following hypothetical situation.

Your application stores recipes for its users and is incredibly popular. Users of the system have two methods of searching for a given recipe: by known ingredients or by a simple full-text search of all of the text fields of the application. Ingredient searches are done off of simple database keys and are very fast using the InnoDB database engine. As the application increases in popularity, however, the techniques used to perform a full-text search against an InnoDB table are starting to slow the entire database down. Your developers tell you that if you use the MyISAM database engine you could take advantage of MySQL full-text searching and significantly increase performance. But unfortunately, you'd lose performance everywhere else and key features such as transactions.

How does one solve a catch-22 problem such as this? If you were carefully reading you might have already realized the answer. Simply put, MySQL replication places no restrictions on consistency between database engines from one slave to another. This means you can have one instance that uses InnoDB as its storage engine that replicates to another instance using the MyISAM engine. This allows you to create custom pools for the web application to perform specific queries under their best possible circumstances, as shown in Figure 9-3.

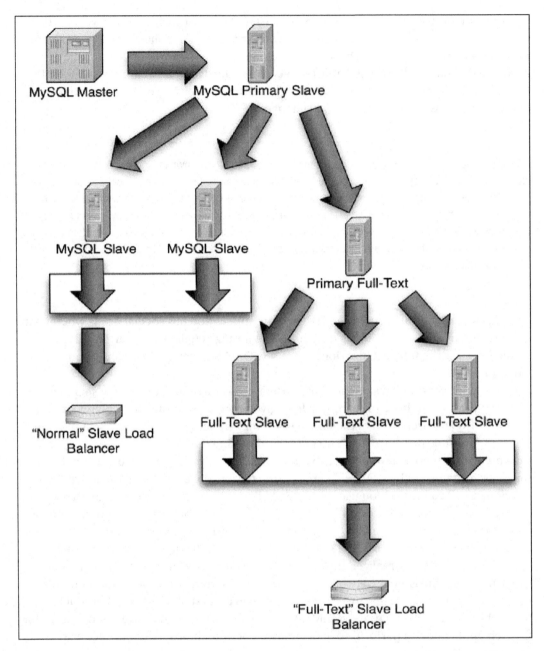

Figure 9-3. *Using MySQL replication to create slave farms with different storage engines and performance needs*

As shown in Figure 9-3, we have created two separate pools of servers used for read-only queries—the first from our original generic LAMP stack shown in Figure 9-1 and a second used specifically for full-text queries only.

MySQL Master Farm Architecture

Earlier in this chapter we were quick to mention that we cannot cover all aspects of MySQL farm architecture due to scope restrictions of this book. However, it is worthwhile to discuss how the master server in our MySQL configuration may ultimately look in a highly scalable system. As was previously mentioned, the generic LAMP stack shown in Figure 9-1 has a significant flaw in its scalability design—writing to the database is limited by a single machine. Some techniques for overcoming this will be discussed in Chapter 10 as we discuss MySQL in more detail, but in this chapter we will introduce some of that material by discussing the concept of data federation.

Data federation is a huge piece of building an application that can scale to meet the needs of millions of concurrent users in the LAMP stack. Data federation means that you create independent clusters of servers that each contains a different independent data set, each having its own master MySQL. The data set for each cluster is determined by a primary slave using the following generic technique:

- Split the data of a large unscalable table into multiple smaller copies based on a top-level key. For example, perhaps different application users may be organized into different tables.

- Ensure that all data related to that top-level key resides in the same cluster as the top-level key.

- Create a separate "lookup" server that, given the known top-level key, can instruct your web application as to which cluster to use for its requests for that data.

How you determine which top-level key belongs to which cluster can be a complex subject. It's very important to ensure that whatever the method, the distribution between clusters is as even as possible. The end result however is always the same, demonstrated in Figure 9-4.

Note This subject of data federation is discussed again in Chapter 10 when we discuss MySQL in more detail. For the sake of understanding, however, consider the notion of using the first character of the user's last name as the top-level key to determine which cluster the user belongs to. This could be a very costly decision financially because this requires 26 individual clusters for each alphabet character. The bigger problem, however, is that there are many more last names that start with the letter *M* than the letter *Z*, resulting in an uneven distribution that impacts the scalability of the solution.

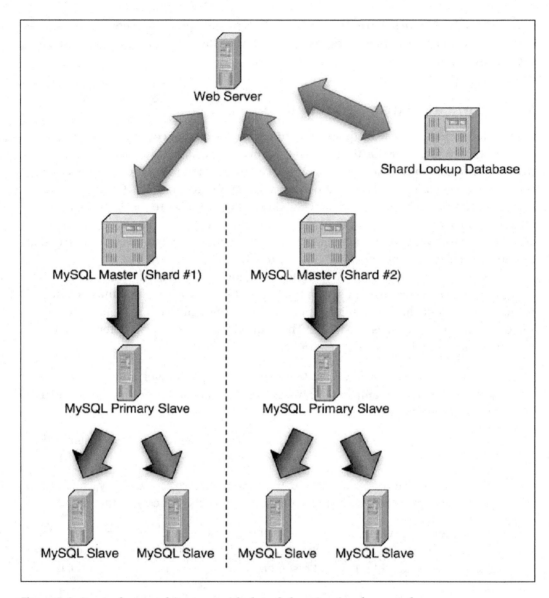

Figure 9-4. *Server farm architecture with data federation implemented*

Dealing with Serving of Files

Somewhat ironically, the simple act of serving static files in your web application can often be overlooked in the architecture of both the application and its production farm. Often developers make static resources such as images, JavaScript files, style sheets, Flash files, and so on an afterthought of their architecture needs. As it turns out, however, in a high-performance application these resources need to be considered more carefully and should always be handled through a separate web server dedicated to serving only static content. Compared to the dynamic nature of executing a PHP script, serving static content is much simpler but also potentially more time-consuming than executing the scripts. Thus, to improve performance you want to separate the requests that execute business logic (which have one set of performance needs) from those that simply shuffle data to the client.

Typically this is done by creating separate web servers that are only capable of serving static content to the user and storing all static content used by the web application on those servers. This makes the most efficient use of your PHP servers as they never deal with a request that doesn't execute a PHP script, and it naturally spreads the multiple secondary requests for resources by the end-user client across multiple servers, improving scalability. Consider the following example HTML output of a hypothetical PHP script in Listing 9-1.

Listing 9-1. *An Example HTML Output of a Hypothetical PHP Script*

```
<html>
    <head>
        <title>Example</title>
    <style src="http://www.example.com/styles/mystyle.css"/>
    </head>
    <body>
    My Image:<br/>
    <img src="http://www.example.com/images/myimage.png"/>
    </body>
</html>
```

In Listing 9-1, when processed by a browser, a total of three requests must be made to the web application in order for the request to be finished. The first is to execute the PHP script that generates the output in Listing 9-1, the second is to retrieve the style sheet resource, and the third is to retrieve the PNG image resource. If we assume that the same server that executed the PHP script to generate this output is the same server where the resources are located, this means that out of three requests, only one of them was actually spent executing business logic. From a performance perspective, this is less than ideal. Instead, these static resources should be moved to a server best suited to serve them, and the output of our hypothetical script should reflect this as shown in Listing 9-2.

Listing 9-2. *A Modified Example HTML Output of a Hypothetical PHP Script*

```
<html>
    <head>
        <title>Example</title>
    <style src="http://static.example.com/styles/mystyle.css"/>
    </head>
    <body>
    My Image:<br/>
    <img src="http://static.example.com/images/myimage.png"/>
    </body>
</html>
```

Taking this change into account, a more reasonable architecture for our generic LAMP stack shown in Figure 9-1 is found in Figure 9-5 showing the static servers.

Another common concern when designing a production farm is dealing with what we like to call runtime files. These are files that are created in the application as part of its normal operation. One example is accepting files from the end user (uploading files to the web application) that need to be immediately available. Because PHP applications have a share-nothing architecture, this is another variation of the session management problem discussed earlier in the chapter. The file is uploaded to a single web server yet must somehow be made available to the full set of users in a reasonable amount of time.

Depending on the size and characteristics of your application, there are many different approaches you could use to solve this problem, including (but not limited to) the following:

- Using some sort of network file share that stores these files and that is shared across the web servers

- Storing these files in a centralized source accessible from each web server, such as the database

- Implementing a reverse proxy for these files using a technology such as Apache's mod_proxy, squid, or other techniques

For the purposes of a discussion on production farm architecture we will focus on the third option, the implementation of reverse proxies.

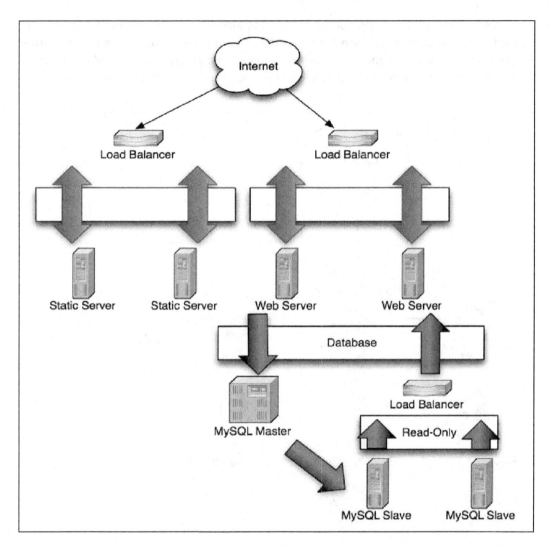

Figure 9-5. *A generic LAMP production farm with static servers included*

The concept behind a reverse proxy is the creation of an intermediate collection of caching servers between the source of the content (which maybe a single server) and the requesting client. Typically the content being served is held in memory of the cache server and allows for the scalability of runtime-created resources quite effectively.

Take for example the notion of accepting uploaded files at runtime and having them immediately available on a massive scale. In this situation, you could upload the resource to a single server and then place 100 reverse proxy servers managed by a load balancer as intermediate servers between it and the end user, as described in Figure 9-6.

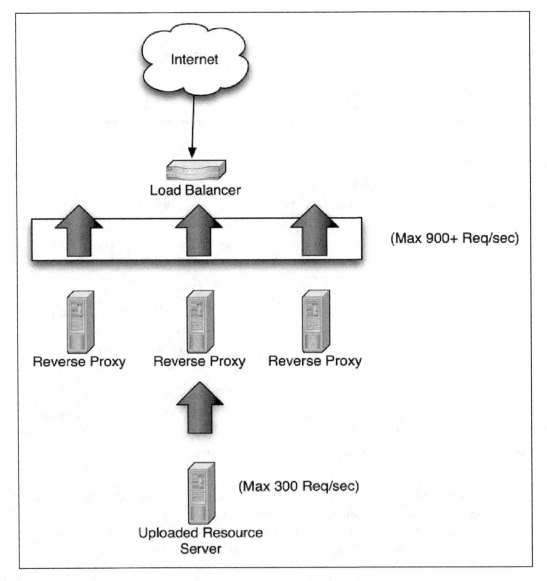

Figure 9-6. *Using a reverse proxy to increase the availability of a single resource*

As shown in Figure 9-6, when a resource is uploaded to a single server, the web application's ability to serve that resource to the end users is limited by the capabilities of that single server (we'll assume around 300 requests per second). This is clearly unacceptable for a large-scale application development and why a reverse proxy can be such a powerful tool. Rather than attempting to have end users request the resource off of the single server directly, or even attempting (at least immediately) to make multiple copies of the resource across a farm of static resources, we can use a reverse proxy to proxy the request on behalf of the end user. In this scenario, when the user makes a request for this uploaded resource, the request is made ultimately to a proxy server, which then does one of two things:

- If the proxy server doesn't know about the resource, it has logic and rules to make the request for the resource from its origin server and return it to the user. Once a resource has been retrieved the server will cache it locally for future requests (either in memory or on disk).

- If the proxy server is aware of the resource it will return it from memory or disk and never contact the origin server.

This is an incredibly powerful tool, as it allows you to take a single server that can serve an assumed maximum of 300 copies of a given resource at the same time and with three reverse proxy servers increase that to likely over 900 copies. (It is likely faster than a simple 3:1 ratio because the file will be stored in much faster RAM on the reverse proxy.)

Note Reverse proxy systems can get very complex if you are concerned with the idea that there should be more than one origin server that contains a runtime file resource, as you will have to not only have to figure out how to copy that resource between a farm of servers (we recommend that you use asynchronous operations described earlier in the book) but also intelligently spread the load of requests from the reverse proxy servers to only those origin servers that have received the resources in question. Unfortunately, this is outside of the scope of this discussion.

When using a reverse proxy server, it is strongly recommended that you use the URL of the file in the origin server (through some sort of regular expressions or business logic) to manage invalidation of data on the reverse proxies. This is to say, rather than attempting to flush a file from potentially hundreds of reverse proxy servers, it is much more effective to change the origin URL of the resource that requires updating and to allow each individual reverse proxy to naturally expire the original file from cache.

Asynchronous Operations and the Farm

The final aspect of a production farm we are going to examine in this chapter is the servers dedicated to asynchronous aspects of the web application (See Chapter 5 for a detailed discussion of the job queue). For the purposes of this discussion we will assume you are using the job queue technology provided by Zend Platform introduced earlier in the book.

Compared to other aspects of the stack (such as the MySQL database), factoring in asynchronous operation servers into the farm is a fairly straightforward concept. Each job queue server is completely independent from the next, and since by its very nature a queue has a nearly unlimited capacity, you could plan on having one server dedicated to the task. Of course, what kind of performance you need out of your asynchronous operations is a direct function of how much time between when a job is entered into the queue and its execution or completion. If you are using asynchronous job queues to improve performance of operations that must be completed in real time from a user perspective, it is an entirely different game from sending out welcome e-mails to new users as they sign up asynchronously.

If you are never interested in the web servers checking the status of the jobs it places into a job queue, then the job queue servers can be scaled out horizontally by purchasing more machines and placing them all behind a load balancer to be used by the web servers. However, if you have jobs that need to be "checked up" on by the web application (such as a credit card transaction), this solution doesn't work, as you cannot communicate directly with the server executing the job and the job ID numbers are not unique across servers. For these situations unfortunately you are limited by the power of a job queue server to process jobs and communicate with that server directly from your web servers.

While real-time asynchronous jobs require you to be able to communicate directly with the job queue server (making a load-balancer infeasible), there is nothing stopping you from having multiple independent job queue servers in use by your web application and defining rules as to which servers are used to process which real-time jobs. For instance, if you have twelve web servers you can provide one dedicated job queue server per four web servers, giving you a total of three job queue servers. An example of both configurations is shown in Figure 9-7.

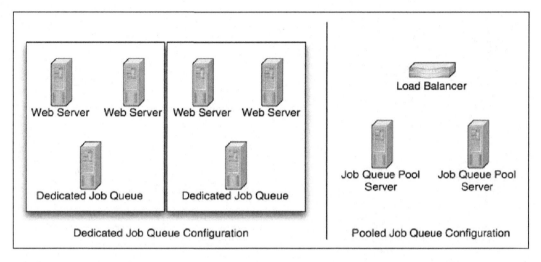

Figure 9-7. *Examples of server farm configurations focused on dedicated job queue servers (for real-time asynchronous operations) and job queue server pools*

Conclusion

In this chapter we have discussed many of the common questions and circumstances PHP-based web applications face trying to architect their applications to scale with their user bases. We introduced the classical server farm for the LAMP stack and discussed how to handle static files, uploaded files, and session management as your application's needs evolve. We also introduced how MySQL looks from a server farm perspective and what you might need to plan for. Finally, we discussed how asynchronous operation servers may factor into your designs.

When designing both your application and your server farm, the key to success is horizontal scalability. As much as possible your design should allow you to solve your performance and power requirements by adding more hardware systematically as requirements grow. That said, if you do find yourself in a position where horizontal scaling is not an option because of technical limitations, scaling vertically (more powerful hardware) is always at least a solid stopgap measure. Obviously we have only touched on some of the issues when dealing with production farms in this chapter, but you will find that we have discussed enough of the common circumstances that you should be able to apply the concepts to other technologies as needed.

## CHAPTER 10

The MySQL Database

In this chapter we look at the MySQL database server and how to tune it. There are three basic strategies we can employ to improve a database: adding hardware, tweaking settings within MySQL, and tweaking the queries that we send to MySQL or adding indexes so they will execute faster.

While it might seem easy to just throw hardware at the problem, it is very difficult to improve execution time by orders of magnitude from this approach. By contrast, the improvements that we can get from indexes or tweaking settings often can lead to performance that is better by orders of 10, 100, or even 1,000.

The Storage Engine Concept

One distinct feature in MySQL when we compare it to other database management systems is how it handles data storage. While more traditionally there may be one database storage format, MySQL elects to separate SQL from storage and to allow a series of storage engines to plug into the server.

Each of these storage engines will have an entirely internal storage format, and as a result each engine's features and performance characteristics are entirely different from that of others. From the developer's perspective, all storage engines appear the same, and you are to mix and match storage engines on a table-by-table basis (see Table 10-1).

Table 10-1. *Comparing Storage Engines Available with MySQL*

	MyISAM	**InnoDB**	**Archive**	**Memory**	**Cluster**
Transactional	No	Yes	No	No	Yes
ACID-compliant	No	Yes	N/A	No	Yes
Crash recovery	No	Yes	No	No	Yes
Full-text indexes	Yes	No	No	No	No
Tree indexes	Yes	Yes	No	Yes	Yes
Hash indexes	No	No	No	Yes	Internal hash only
Online backup	No	Yes	No	No	Yes
Supported statements	All	All	INSERT, SELECT	All	All
Foreign keys	No	Yes	No	No	No
Page checksums	No	Yes	No	No	No
Maximum individual table size	256 TB, but limited by crash recovery	64 TB	Information not available	Limited by memory	Limited by memory
Maximum full database size	No limit	64 TB	No limit	Limited by memory	Limited by memory
Locking level	Table	Row	N/A	Table	Row
Isolation levels	None	All Four	None	None	Read-committed

Although newer engines are under development (both by MySQL/Sun Microsystems and third parties), the most popular general-purpose storage engines today are MyISAM and InnoDB. While MyISAM is more lightweight, it also has a number of drawbacks as illustrated in Table 10-1. The biggest deal breaker using MyISAM is usually the inconsistency and unpredictable nature of crash recovery. To understand this point, try the following example in Listing 10-1 in MyISAM and then again in InnoDB.

Listing 10-1. *SQL Commands to Test Crash Recovery in the MyISAM Storage Engine*

```
-- Step 1 - Create a MyISAM table

CREATE TABLE my_big_myisam_table➡
    (id INT NOT NULL auto_increment PRIMARY KEY➡
    a char(255) NOT NULL) ENGINE=MyISAM;

-- Step 2 - Fill the table with dummy data
```

```
INSERT INTO my_big_myisam_table VALUES (NULL, REPEAT('a', 255));
-- Repeat the following line approximately 20-25 times.
INSERT INTO my_big_myisam_table➥
    SELECT NULL,  REPEAT('a', 255) FROM my_big_myisam_table;

-- Step 3 - Run a very long running update on the table.
-- Wait for the update to start, and then simulate a failure
-- (either pull the plug, or kill the mysqld process)

UPDATE my_big_myisam_table SET a=repeat('b', 255);
```

Note If you were to run `REPAIR TABLE my_big_myisam_table` and then `SELECT * FROM my_big_myisam_table`, you would discover that repairing the table and keeping all of the values consistent is not the same thing. Half the rows will have a value of "bbbbb…" and the other half will have all "aaaaa…." There is also the theoretical chance that one row might be half "a" and half "b". To add to this pain, it is worth noting that the crash recovery process in MyISAM is entirely dictated by the size of the table. If you have a single table that spans into hundreds of gigabytes, it may take several days before it is repaired and ready to use again.

Optimizing Queries with EXPLAIN

By far the best way to improve application performance is to improve the performance of individual queries. Sometimes this can be a case of just adding a simple index, but other times it will require some additional input to be able to rewrite a query. MySQL exposes a way for us to be able to see the internal path that it uses to execute a query via the `EXPLAIN` command. This internal path is often referred to as the execution plan, and in Listing 10-2 we can see by the type of ALL that the plan is to read through every row in the table one at a time in order to return our result—certainly not an ideal situation.

Listing 10-2. *The Execution Plan of the Query with MySQL's* EXPLAIN *Command*

```
mysql> EXPLAIN SELECT Name FROM Country WHERE Continent = 'Asia'➥
    AND population > 5000000 ORDER BY Name\G
*************************** 1. row ***************************
           id: 1
  select_type: SIMPLE
        table: Country
         type: ALL
possible_keys: NULL
```

```
          key: NULL
      key_len: NULL
          ref: NULL
         rows: 239
        Extra: Using where; Using filesort
1 row in set (0.00 sec)
```

Note The world database can be downloaded from the MySQL Manual at http://dev.mysql.com/doc.

Tip Not familiar with the \G statement terminator? It's used to return the results in vertical mode, instead of the default ; horizontal mode. With longer rows, it's much easier to read.

To improve the execution of the query in Listing 10-2, we need to add an index. But there are actually many different candidates to choose from. Here are just a few examples:

- We could add an *index on Name* to scan the index and then find the rows we need. Since the index would automatically be sorted, this could remove the expense of Using filesort.

- We could add an *index on Population* to first filter the countries that have a population greater than five million and then apply additional filtering on the row level to determine which countries are in Asia.

- We could add an *index on Continent* to find only those countries in Asia and then check to see that they have a population greater than five million at the row level.

- We could add a *composite index on Population and Continent* and then for the rows that match, just return the name column.

- Similar to the previous item, we could also add a *composite index on Continent and Population*.

- We can also add a special type of composite index, a *covering index on Continent, Population, and Name*. This index is special because Name is not specified as part of the where clause but is the only column we are requesting to retrieve. A covering index is sometimes referred to as an index-only fetch since we do not need to consult the data rows to be able to return the result.

Let's look at what happens when we add the index on just Population and repeat the same EXPLAIN command (see Listing 10-3). We can see that under possible_keys our newly added index appears, but under key (the key that ended up being used) the value is NULL.

What MySQL is doing is actually very smart. It detects that you are looking for population *greater than* 5 million, but it also knows that very few countries in the world have populations *less than* 5 million. MySQL ignores indexes that offer very little selectivity, so as a result, it chooses to ignore the index and continue table scanning.

■**Tip** In many texts you may see a reference to words such as "cardinality" and "selectivity" used in describing this index selection process. Cardinality is the unique number of rows in a table, and selectivity is the cardinality divided by the total number of records. For example, a primary key index on a table with 9,328 rows: 9,328/9,328 = 1.0.

This brings us to an important point—it is critical to revisit EXPLAIN immediately after adding indexes. The danger of adding unused indexes is that performance may suffer during INSERT, UPDATE, and DELETE statements.

Listing 10-3. *Adding an Index to Try to Improve the Performance of the Query*

```
mysql> ALTER TABLE Country ADD INDEX p (Population);
Query OK, 239 rows affected (0.01 sec)
Records: 239  Duplicates: 0  Warnings: 0

mysql> EXPLAIN SELECT Name FROM Country WHERE Continent = 'Asia'
AND population > 5000000 ORDER BY Name\G
*************************** 1. row ***************************
           id: 1
  select_type: SIMPLE
        table: Country
         type: ALL
possible_keys: p
          key: NULL
      key_len: NULL
          ref: NULL
         rows: 239
        Extra: Using where; Using filesort
1 row in set (0.00 sec)
```

■**Note** In Listing 10-3, MySQL is favoring the sequential read of a table over the random IO that would be required to keep switching between reading the index and then reading the data. The trade-off is that the index has to filter on about 75 percent of the rows or it will not be considered for use.

If we were to modify our query to search for countries of population greater than 50 million as in Listing 10-4, we can see that the index is now used.

Listing 10-4. *Searching for Countries Whose Population Is Greater Than 50 Million*

```
mysql> EXPLAIN SELECT Name FROM Country WHERE Continent = 'Asia'➥
    AND population > 50000000 ORDER BY Name\G
*************************** 1. row ***************************
           id: 1
  select_type: SIMPLE
        table: Country
         type: range
possible_keys: p
          key: p
      key_len: 4
          ref: NULL
         rows: 54
        Extra: Using where; Using filesort
1 row in set (0.00 sec)
```

In Listing 10-5, we can see that if both indexes on Continent and Population are present, the Continent index is preferred. If we look at the difference between the execution plans (the EXPLAIN output) we can speculate that MySQL made this choice because of the following reasons:

- The type has changed from range to ref. Comparison to a fixed string (Continent = 'Asia') is cheaper than comparison to a range (population > 5000000).

- The key_len is only one byte, down from four bytes. This means there is a greater chance of being able to store this entire index in memory, where traversal will be faster.

- The estimated number of rows to be examined on disk after using the index is 42 rows, down from 54 rows.

Tip We chose our words very carefully when we said, "we can speculate that MySQL made this choice because...." There's actually no functionality to be able to export and compare a cost breakdown between query execution plans. The closest feature available is running SHOW STATUS LIKE 'last_query_cost' after executing the query.

MySQL combines all of these factors together to determine what the query cost will be. On every query that the server receives, it weighs options it has available to execute a query and then arrives at the option it determines to be the cheapest.

As a follow-up to Listing 10-5, in Listing 10-6 we can see how the cost of the population index plan becomes cheaper when we start searching for population greater than 500 million.

Listing 10-5. *Comparing the Continent and Population Indexes for Population of 5 Million*

```
mysql> ALTER TABLE Country ADD INDEX c (Continent);
Query OK, 239 rows affected (0.05 sec)
Records: 239  Duplicates: 0  Warnings: 0

mysql> EXPLAIN SELECT Name FROM Country WHERE Continent = 'Asia'➡
    AND population > 5000000 ORDER BY Name\G
*************************** 1. row ***************************
           id: 1
  select_type: SIMPLE
        table: Country
         type: ref
possible_keys: p,c
          key: c
      key_len: 1
          ref: const
         rows: 42
        Extra: Using where; Using filesort
1 row in set (0.00 sec)
```

Listing 10-6. *Comparing the Population and Continent Indexes for Population of 500 Million*

```
EXPLAIN SELECT Name FROM Country WHERE Continent = 'Asia'➡
    AND population > 500000000 ORDER BY Name\G
*************************** 1. row ***************************
           id: 1
  select_type: SIMPLE
        table: Country
         type: range
possible_keys: p,c
          key: p
```

```
    key_len: 4
        ref: NULL
       rows: 5
      Extra: Using where; Using filesort
1 row in set (0.10 sec)
```

Our next example looks at some of the more advanced index usage, with composite indexes spanning more than one column. Before we get to these examples, it's important to make two very important notes.

MySQL will seldom combine two indexes from the same table to execute a query. In MySQL 5.0 an optimization called index-merge was introduced (see `http://dev.mysql.com/doc/refman/5.0/en/index-merge-optimization.html`), but its usage remains limited.

It would be a rare day that you would add all of these indexes in production. In fact, you would be crazy to do so, since an index on (`Population, Continent`) makes the `Population` index redundant. We're just adding a number of possible indexes to demonstrate MySQL's cost model.

In Listing 10-7 and Listing 10-8 we add indexes on (`Population, Continent`) and (`Continent, Population`). While from a glance these appear to be very similar, the optimizer looks at them quite differently and teaches us an important rule: equality to the left, ranges to the right.

Listing 10-7. *Comparing the Population, Continent and Population, and Continent Indexes*

```
ALTER TABLE Country ADD INDEX p_c (Population, Continent);
EXPLAIN SELECT Name FROM Country WHERE Continent = 'Asia'➥
    AND population > 50000000 ORDER BY Name\G
*************************** 1. row ***************************
           id: 1
  select_type: SIMPLE
        table: Country
         type: ref
possible_keys: p,c,p_c
          key: c
      key_len: 1
          ref: const
         rows: 42
        Extra: Using where; Using filesort
1 row in set (0.00 sec)
```

Listing 10-8. *Comparing the Population, Continent, Population and Continent, and Continent and Population Indexes*

```
ALTER TABLE Country ADD INDEX c_p (Continent,Population);
EXPLAIN SELECT Name FROM Country WHERE Continent = 'Asia'➥
    AND population > 50000000 ORDER BY Name\G
*************************** 1. row ***************************
           id: 1
  select_type: SIMPLE
        table: Country
         type: range
possible_keys: p,c,p_c,c_p
          key: c_p
      key_len: 5
          ref: NULL
         rows: 9
        Extra: Using where; Using filesort
1 row in set (0.00 sec)
```

The last index we mentioned is the covering index on Continent, Population, and Name. In Listing 10-9 we can see that MySQL considers this to be the best index. We can see that this is a covering index (with all data needing to be retrieved found in the index) by Using Index; in the Extra column.

Listing 10-9. *Demonstrating All Previous Indexes and a Covering Index*

```
EXPLAIN SELECT Name FROM Country WHERE Continent = 'Asia'➥
    AND population > 50000000 ORDER BY Name\G
*************************** 1. row ***************************
           id: 1
  select_type: SIMPLE
        table: Country
         type: range
possible_keys: p,c,p_c,c_p,c_p_n
          key: c_p_n
      key_len: 5
          ref: NULL
         rows: 9
        Extra: Using where; Using index; Using filesort
1 row in set (0.01 sec)
```

If you've read to this point and you're curious what happened to the index on Name, try it for yourself. As it turns out, the Name index is about as useful as our original population index in that it is quicker to table scan than to index scan and fetch the rows in order.

Note In order to be able to test the name index you will have to drop all other indexes in order for it to be considered and use the FORCE INDEX syntax to insist it be used, that is, SELECT Name FROM Country FORCE INDEX(Name) WHERE Continent='Asia' AND population > 5000000.

Workload-Driven Performance Tuning

The best way to tune a database system is to understand more about the sort of queries that the system will be performing. For example, applications that have more SELECT queries than INSERT, UPDATE, and DELETE queries will often have more indexes, since the cost of maintaining the indexes can more easily be justified.

In database-speak, we call these characteristics a workload. While every workload is slightly different, the following should serve as some generalizations and optimizations that can be made in response.

Tip This section makes heavy use of the command SHOW GLOBAL STATUS, which reveals a number of internal statistics counters inside MySQL. For more information on SHOW GLOBAL STATUS, see http://dev. mysql.com/doc/refman/5.1/en/show-status.html.

Read-Heavy Workload

A read-heavy workload has more queries that read data than queries that write data. A simplistic calculation of reads to writes can be made from the following server statistics:

```
(Com_select + Qcache_hits + Com_replace) versus
    (Com_insert + Com_update + Com_delete + Com_replace)
```

This formula has some limitations, since each of the Com_% counters are only incremented each time the server receives a query, and they do not account for the number of rows affected in each statement. An alternative formula could be one that considers the Handler_read% and Handler_write statistics, which are incremented as individual rows are read or updated.

Many web applications tend to have a few times more reads than they do writes. If in your workload you experience considerably more reads, the following recommendations should serve as a good starting point in optimization.

Find Out Whether You Are Using Indexes Effectively

Indexes can slow down the performance of some of your write operations. But since these are less frequent on read-heavy databases, it's worth checking that you've invested in all the indexes you need and that MySQL is not table scanning in instances it does not need to. The first check you can perform is to see how MySQL is reading individual rows (see Listing 10-10).

Listing 10-10. *Handler Counts Showing Row-Level Access Inside the Server*

```
mysql> show global status like 'Handler_read%';
+-----------------------+----------+
| Variable_name         | Value    |
+-----------------------+----------+
| Handler_read_first    | 7316     |
| Handler_read_key      | 1119968  |
| Handler_read_next     | 446385   |
| Handler_read_prev     | 545      |
| Handler_read_rnd      | 121112   |
| Handler_read_rnd_next | 69949960 |
+-----------------------+----------+
6 rows in set (0.00 sec)
```

These counters incremented as individual rows are read internally inside MySQL (consider Handler a synonym for "Storage Engine API"). If the value of Handler_read_rnd_next is considerably higher than any of the other values, then this probably suggests that you do not have appropriate indexing or that your queries need to be modified to take advantage of indexes.

■**Note** More information on Handler_read_rnd_next is available in the MySQL manual at http://dev.mysql.com/doc/refman/5.1/en/server-status-variables.html#statvar_Handler_read_rnd_next.

Log Queries That Are Slow

MySQL has a feature called the slow query log (enabled with -log-slow) where you can keep track of queries that take longer than a threshold (--long_query_time=N) to execute. The contents of the slow query log can then be aggregated with a utility such as mysqldumpslow or mk-query-digest (recommended). There are two general strategies as to how to best use the slow query log.

The first strategy is that you want to be able identify queries that are exceptionally poor-performing and have the potential to deny service to other queries. As a general rule, we recommend setting long_query_time to a value low enough that you are able to log 1/10,000 queries. However, this formula should be used as a guide as you may want to capture fewer slow queries on systems in very heavy demand or capture more on those under little load or still in preproduction. You can check what percentage of queries you are logging by comparing the status variable Slow_queries to the status variables Com_Select+Com_Update+Com_Insert+Com_Delete.

The second strategy is that you also want to identify queries that execute quickly but far too frequently or that are entirely redundant. These queries are often better served by a caching system than a database server. As part of this strategy, we will normally log into a system, lower the long_query_time to zero seconds, and capture one to two hours of data during peak load. When we've finished recording, we will set the long_query_time back to its original value.

■**Tip** You can download mk-query-digest from http://www.maatkit.org/get/mk-query-digest or visit the Maatkit homepage at http://www.maatkit.org/.

The shortest long_query_time in MySQL 5.0 is one second, which makes the second strategy impossible. To be able to set a lower long_query_time, you will need to either upgrade to MySQL 5.1 or use a third-party release of MySQL 5.0, such as the one offered by Percona at http://www.percona.com/docs/wiki/release:start.

Enable the Query Cache

The MySQL query cache is a feature that enables MySQL to save the results of SELECT statements so that future queries will be able to avoid statement parsing and retrieval from the storage engine. When enabled, the query cache can lead to massive increases in performances for slower select queries, but it is worth noting that this feature also has a number of drawbacks:

- Since the query cache avoids statement parsing, it relies on statements being byte-for-byte identical. For example, SELECT * FROM my_table is not the same as select * from my_table.

- SELECT statements that contain non-deterministic functions will not be cached, for example, SELECT * from orders WHERE date > NOW() - INTERVAL 1 DAY.

■Tip A non-deterministic function means that if you give it the same set of arguments and the data in the table is the same, it is not guaranteed to return the same result. There are actually a lot more non-deterministic functions than you may realize, since any query that makes use of RAND(), time functions, or specific USER() functions is not guaranteed to return the same result if called again at another time by another user.

- Any UPDATE, DELETE, or INSERT statements to the tables referenced in the query cache will result in all of these query cache items being invalidated.

- The query cache does not work with column-level privileges.

- All incoming queries will need to search the query cache before being parsed, which can lead to bad performance when the query cache is too large.

- The query cache does not perform well on systems with many CPUs/cores (improvements are not planned until after MySQL 6.0).

Given what we mentioned in the first three points, on a heavy-read system it's often a good idea to try enabling the query cache and seeing what efficiency it can deliver. To read the query cache statistics, see Listing 10-11.

Listing 10-11. *Query Cache Statistics from SHOW GLOBAL STATUS*

```
mysql> show global status like 'Qcache%';
+-------------------------+-------+
| Variable_name           | Value |
+-------------------------+-------+
| Qcache_free_memory      | 99812 |
| Qcache_hits             | 210   |
| Qcache_inserts          | 8     |
| Qcache_not_cached       | 20    |
| Qcache_queries_in_cache | 5     |
+-------------------------+-------+
8 rows in set (0.00 sec)
```

In Listing 10-11, we can see that there were eight queries that were inserted into the query cache but an additional 20 queries that were not considered. These queries may have had results too large, too small, or incompatible for the reasons listed in the previous list. Of the eight queries inserted, five were still present in the query cache, and over the lifetime of all the items in the query cache, 210 successful hits were made. This means that the application is repeating the queries that it is sending to the database and that we are getting some good usage.

Tip How do you enable the query cache? It turns out to be a very common source of confusion, since you need to set both `query_cache_type = 1` and a value for `query_cache_size` in your configuration file. For more information, see the MySQL manual at `http://dev.mysql.com/doc/refman/5.0/en/query-cache-configuration.html`.

Alleviate MySQL

The fastest query is the one that never has to run. If you have too many queries reading data, particularly in the form of `Qcache_hits` (query cache hits), then the best way to scale is probably to introduce caching such as memcached into your application. See Chapter 4 to learn how to use the extensive caching tools available for your PHP applications.

Write-Heavy Workload

Identifying whether your workload is write-heavy can be done in much the same way as the previous steps to identify a read-heavy workload. The additional considerations you should have with write-heavy workloads should be as follows.

Focus on Your Disk Performance

The most critical factor in a write-heavy load is almost always going to be your hard disks. RAID is the best way to improve disk performance, and by choosing a RAID configuration with a higher number of disks, you should be able to boost concurrency. We cover RAID in more detail later in this chapter.

Remove Unneeded Indexes

The official releases of MySQL from Sun offer no way of being able to check whether an index is no longer in use (normally referred to as a dead index), but the MySQL team at

Google has written a patch to be able to do this. The patch has made it into third-party releases of MySQL (the Percona and OurDelta binaries), which are not officially supported by MySQL. With this patch installed, a utility called check_unused_keys can be run to locate dead indexes (see Listing 10-12).

Listing 10-12. *The Addition of a Third-Party Patch Providing Information on Unused Indexes*

```
shell> ./check_unused_keys --databases=wordpress
# wordpress.wp_ak_twitter.PRIMARY
# wordpress.wp_comments.PRIMARY
# wordpress.wp_comments.comment_approved
# wordpress.wp_comments.comment_post_ID
# wordpress.wp_comments.comment_approved_date_gmt
# wordpress.wp_comments.comment_date_gmt
# wordpress.wp_links.PRIMARY
# wordpress.wp_links.link_category
# wordpress.wp_options.PRIMARY
# wordpress.wp_postmeta.PRIMARY
# wordpress.wp_postmeta.meta_key
# wordpress.wp_posts.post_parent
# wordpress.wp_sph_counter.PRIMARY
# wordpress.wp_terms.name
# wordpress.wp_usermeta.PRIMARY
# wordpress.wp_usermeta.meta_key
# wordpress.wp_users.user_login_key
# wordpress.wp_users.user_nicename


############################################################################
# Unused Indexes: 18
# Uptime: 8964 seconds
############################################################################
```

■**Note** You can download check_unused_keys from the Google Code site at http://code.google.com/p/check-unused-keys/. The patch to the server that makes this possible (often referred to as INDEX_STATISTICS or "userstatsV2.patch") is available in third-party MySQL downloads from both Percona and OurDelta. For more information, see: http://www.percona.com/percona-lab.html and http://www.percona.com/docs/wiki/patches:userstatv2.

Online Transaction Processing

Online transaction processing (OLTP) is the name given to a workload that has a heavy mix of concurrent reads and writes, with most of the working set of data usually fitting in main memory. In addition, most of the queries tend to be based on primary key or secondary key lookups. An OLTP workload is a typical workload for many PHP-based applications. Good benchmarking utilities such as Sysbench (http://sysbench.sourceforge.net/) try to mimic this behavior as part of their tests. Considerations to keep in mind in OLTP workloads are as follows.

■**Tip** A common question is how much is memory to allocate for a database server. The answer is that it depends on the workload and what the working set is (what percentage of the data is actively worked on). While some working sets will only be 1 to 2 percent of the total database size, others may find that they need just as much memory as they do data.

Make Sure Table-Level Locks Are Not Reducing Your Concurrency

Some storage engines (such as MyISAM and Memory) use table-level locks internally while updating rows. While under low load this is not always an issue, under concurrency you may find that table locks have to queue waiting for another lock to be released. If a significant number of table locks are waiting, you should consider switching the affected tables to InnoDB, which uses row-level locking. In Listing 10-13 we can see that 0.625 percent of the time table locks had to queue internally. There is no perfect ratio, as locking contention tends to snowball into worse problems under load. This information is best graphed with a monitoring tool.

Listing 10-13. *Ratio of Table Locks That Waited vs. Table Locks That Were Immediate*

```
mysql> show global status like 'table_locks%';
+-----------------------+-------+
| Variable_name         | Value |
+-----------------------+-------+
| Table_locks_immediate | 52323 |
| Table_locks_waited    | 329   |
+-----------------------+-------+
2 rows in set (0.00 sec)
```

Make Sure the Disk Is Touched As Little As Possible

Some GROUP BY queries and joins on tables with an ORDER BY clause require MySQL to build temporary tables internally as part of their execution plan. While in many cases the temporary table creation is quite fast, it has the potential to become a scalability bottleneck.

Internal temporary tables that contain text/blob columns or exceed both the tmp_table_size and max_heap_table_size configuration variables will result in the creation of MyISAM tables, which are slower than their in-memory counterparts. This item is further explained in the "Online Analytical Processing" section following this section.

Avoid Deadlocks in InnoDB

A deadlock is the name of the situation when two connections are trying to acquire a lock to access information of which the other currently holds a lock for.

You can think of a deadlock as a type of race condition that occurs under concurrency. When a deadlock occurs in InnoDB, the InnoDB kernel automatically picks the least expensive transaction and rolls it back for you (this information can be seen in the command SHOW INNODB STATUS). This is an expensive process. Often it takes InnoDB up to 30 times the resources to roll back a transaction than it would have to commit it.

If you are frequently encountering deadlocks, it's worth investigating whether any changes to business logic in PHP can be made to reduce the risk of the condition happening, or making sure that everything is properly indexed so that transactions are much shorter and less expensive.

Avoid Over-Committing Resources

A frequent mistake in OLTP systems is to attempt too much concurrency at once. When a system becomes loaded, it's normally a better policy to restrict activity to a few simultaneous connections and refuse any additional connections, rather than allow several thousand connections, all being too slow and eventually denied service.

MySQL offers a configuration setting called max_connections to limit the number of connections that MySQL will work on at any point in time.

Tip MySQL doesn't have any pooling options on the server side, so you can't configure a maximum number of connections and a maximum number of connections that are allowed to be actively worked on. It's your job to make sure that you don't overload. One way that you could do this is to limit the number of connections each Apache server allows and limit the number of Apache servers per database server. It's never easy to provide an exact formula of how many Apache connections per MySQL connections to allow, since not all connections will necessarily need a database connection at all times.

Cache an Optimum Number of File Descriptors

As part of its operation, MySQL often needs to keep open many files. Since the opening and closing table events can take a small amount of time and resources, MySQL offers a cache in the hope that files may be able to be reused by another connection. The cache defaults to 64, which is conservatively low, since most operating systems should not have a problem setting this to 512 or even 1,024. The notable exception is MySQL installations on Windows, which have a hard limit of 2,048 file descriptors, so the cache should be left very small. The efficiency of this cache can be determined in Listing 10-14.

Listing 10-14. *Showing Open and Opened Tables Inside the Server*

```
mysql> show global status like 'Open%tables';
+----------------+-------+
| Variable_name  | Value |
+----------------+-------+
| Open_tables    | 0     |
| Opened_tables  | 5     |
+----------------+-------+
2 rows in set (0.00 sec)
```

Set an Optimum Thread Cache

Each connection in MySQL represents a thread internally. As new connections come into the server, it's possible to reuse a previous thread rather than incur the expense of creating a new one. This feature is known as the thread_cache. A small value is normally acceptable provided that it does not increase too much when trending the status variable Threads_created. You can be sure that you have arrived at an ideal cache size (see Listing 10-15).

Listing 10-15. *The Threads Created Inside the Server*

```
mysql> show global status like 'threads%';
+-------------------+-------+
| Variable_name     | Value |
+-------------------+-------+
| Threads_cached    | 0     |
| Threads_connected | 1     |
| Threads_created   | 5     |
| Threads_running   | 1     |
+-------------------+-------+
4 rows in set (0.00 sec)
```

Online Analytical Processing

Online analytical processing (OLAP) is a workload that is used in business intelligence or reporting functionality. It is characterized by expensive number-crunching queries, where there are relatively few concurrent connections to the database but where each take more resources to be able to deliver results.

Increase the Default Session Buffers

OLAP queries tend to be the kind of queries that are run in less concurrency but that individually are more expensive. Given these requirements, it is often a good idea to increase the defaults of individual session buffers.

Sorting Records

Queries that contain ORDER BY statements or GROUP BY statements (without GROUP BY NULL) result in MySQL needing to return the rows in sorted order. MySQL allocates a session buffer called sort_buffer_size to be able to perform this operation. If the buffer is too small, sort_merge_passes is incremented, as seen in Listing 10-16.

Listing 10-16. *Sort_merge_passes, Indicating the sort_buffer_size May Be Too Small*

```
mysql> show global status like 'sort_merge_passes';
+-------------------+-------+
| Variable_name     | Value |
+-------------------+-------+
| Sort_merge_passes | 0     |
+-------------------+-------+
1 row in set (0.00 sec)
```

Temporary Tables

Many GROUP BY statements and some joins on tables without indexes require MySQL to filter results first before they can return them to you. The default is to buffer these changes in memory, but they will spill over to disk if either tmp_table_size or max_heap_table_size is set too small or if the table that needs to be created contains text or blob columns. The number of temporary tables created compared to the number of tables created on disk can be seen in Listing 10-17.

Listing 10-17. *Created Temporary Tables*

```
mysql> show global status like 'Created%tables';
+-------------------------+-------+
| Variable_name           | Value |
+-------------------------+-------+
| Created_tmp_disk_tables | 0     |
| Created_tmp_tables      | 12    |
+-------------------------+-------+
2 rows in set (0.00 sec)
```

Divide and Conquer

Not all analytical queries have real-time requirements. Quite often the best way to return the results for analytical queries is to cheat and have summary tables that are updated only periodically.

If the parent tables are infrequently written to, it is also possible to write triggers that can execute on modification events and update the summary tables automatically.

Note There are some missing features in MySQL, which makes some of the complex queries used in OLAP hard to optimize. Competing database vendors will have parallelism in query execution, materialized views, better algorithms when sorting larger amounts of data, and additional join methods. (MySQL only has a nested loop join.) MySQL also lacks the ability to optimize most subqueries, but this limitation will be lifted in MySQL 5.4.

Data Warehouse

A data warehouse is a workload where a considerable amount of data storage is usually required. In today's typical data warehouses, the amount of data vastly exceeds the amount of system memory, and data is often inserted, never deleted, and quite often infrequently updated.

Table Partitioning

In data warehouses, performance can often be improved by breaking down very large tables into a series of smaller tables. For example, a large sales table could be broken up into sales_2007, sales_2008, and sales_2009. This technique works best provided that the access patterns do not require you to frequently retrieve from more than one partitioned table at once.

From MySQL 5.1 onwards, table partitioning is supported natively, which means that you can have a table appear as one logical table, but MySQL automatically separates it for storage purposes, giving you all the benefits of a manual partitioning without any logical separations. More information on partitioning can be found at `http://dev.mysql.com/doc/refman/5.1/en/partitioning.html`.

Optimization Advice That Applies to All Workloads

The following list of tuning tips is applicable for all workloads and can also be applied to applications where you don't yet know how to classify your workload.

Cache Efficiency

While having good cache efficiency is always a good idea, one of the nice advantages of having a good cache hit efficiency is that you can potentially serve all requests without having to even touch hard disks.

Caching in MyISAM

The main cache is the key buffer, which is responsible for keeping indexes in memory. Listing 10-18 illustrates hits compared to misses, and the number of key blocks unused. The key_reads count is the number you want to be as low as possible, since it indicates that the index had to be read from disk. It is important to note that there will always be some key_reads, since the server will start up with cold caches.

Listing 10-18. *MyISAM Key Cache Efficiency*

```
mysql> show global status like 'key_blocks_%sed';
+-------------------+-------+
| Variable_name     | Value |
+-------------------+-------+
| Key_blocks_unused | 6698  |
| Key_blocks_used   | 0     |
+-------------------+-------+
2 rows in set (0.00 sec)
```

```
mysql> show global status like 'key_read%';
+--------------------+-------+
| Variable_name      | Value |
+--------------------+-------+
| Key_read_requests  | 0     |
| Key_reads          | 0     |
+--------------------+-------+
2 rows in set (0.00 sec)
```

Caching in InnoDB

The InnoDB buffer pool is responsible for keeping both data and indexes in memory. In newer versions of InnoDB, you can see the ratio of buffer pool hits compared to buffer pool misses as in Listing 10-19. The rules for interpreting InnoDB cache efficiency are similar to those for interpreting the key buffer hits and misses. Innodb_buffer_pool_read_requests is a cache hit, and Innodb_buffer_pool_reads is a cache miss. One important exception to note is that because this is data and indexes, you may not as easily fit it all in memory. In addition to reading the SHOW GLOBAL STATUS information, InnoDB will also print a Buffer pool hit rate score out of 1,000 in the SHOW ENGINE INNODB STATUS command.

Listing 10-19. *InnoDB Buffer Pool Efficiency As Seen in SHOW GLOBAL STATUS and SHOW INNODB STATUS*

```
mysql> show global status like 'Innodb_buffer_pool_read%s';
+-----------------------------------+--------+
| Variable_name                     | Value  |
+-----------------------------------+--------+
| Innodb_buffer_pool_read_requests  | 433329 |
| Innodb_buffer_pool_reads          | 93     |
+-----------------------------------+--------+
2 rows in set (0.05 sec)

mysql> SHOW ENGINE INNODB STATUS\G
...
--------------------
BUFFER POOL AND MEMORY
--------------------
Total memory allocated 17433766; in additional pool allocated 888448
Buffer pool size    512
Free buffers        7
```

```
Database pages      504
Modified db pages   309
Pending reads 0
Pending writes: LRU 0, flush list 0, single page 0
Pages read 985, created 1893, written 1683
56.53 reads/s, 107.41 creates/s, 92.88 writes/s
Buffer pool hit rate 998 / 1000
...
```

Binlog Cache Use

When enabled, the binary log records all statements that modified data or could have modified data. It is used for both point-in-time recovery and replication. As part of its operation, it needs to buffer the statements that have been executed in a transaction. This buffer is configured via binlog_cache_size. If the maximum binlog_cache_size has been reached, then the server creates a temporary file on disk, and the variable binlog_cache_disk_use is incremented. If you have a high recurrence of Binlog_cache_disk_use, you may choose to increase the binlog_cache_size to a higher value (see Listing 10-20).

Listing 10-20. *The Binary Log Disk Cache Compared to Memory Cache Ratio*

```
mysql> show global status like 'binlog%';
+-----------------------+-------+
| Variable_name         | Value |
+-----------------------+-------+
| Binlog_cache_disk_use | 2     |
| Binlog_cache_use      | 321   |
+-----------------------+-------+
2 rows in set (0.00 sec)
```

max_used_connections

The status variable max_used_connections shows the maximum number of connections the server has received since startup. This is related to the configuration item max_connections, which restricts the maximum number of connections that can connect to the server (leaving one additional connection free for a user with the super privilege). If you discover that your max_used_connections equals or exceeds the max_connections setting, this indicates that you more than likely had users who were refused connections (see Listing 10-21).

Listing 10-21. *Maximum Connections the Server Has Received Since Startup*

```
mysql> show global status like 'max%';
+-----------------------+-------+
| Variable_name         | Value |
+-----------------------+-------+
| Max_used_connections  | 2     |
+-----------------------+-------+
1 row in set (0.00 sec)
```

Select_full_join

This counter is incremented every time two tables are joined on each other and neither table had an index. In many cases seeing this number greater than zero can be a bad thing, since it indicates very poor use of indexes or an accidental Cartesian product (see Listing 10-22).

Tip A Cartesian product is created by joining two tables but without specifying a where clause, for example, SELECT * FROM table_a, table_b;. This results in the query returning all of the rows in table_a multiplied by all of the rows in table_b.

Listing 10-22. *Select_full_join Indicating a Possible Error in Query Logic via Cartesian Product*

```
mysql> show global status like 'Select_full_join';
+------------------+-------+
| Variable_name    | Value |
+------------------+-------+
| Select_full_join | 0     |
+------------------+-------+
1 row in set (0.00 sec)
```

Tip For more information on this type of tuning, check out Matthew Montgomery's Tuning Primer for MySQL. See http://www.day32.com/MySQL.

For help understanding how to tune InnoDB, a walk-through of SHOW ENGINE INNODB STATUS can be found on the MySQL Performance Blog at http://www.mysqlperformanceblog.com/2006/07/17/show-innodb-status-walk-through/.

Applications with More Than One Workload

It's not uncommon that an application will have a more *hybrid* workload. For example, in an accounting system salespeople create invoices and sell products (OLTP), while management runs reports to judge the salespeople's performance (OLAP).

The optimization order for these two systems (and indexes) can be quite different. One situation you do *not* want is for the overhead added from the reports to impact the sales people, who have real-time requirements. In these situations, it's often a good idea to use MySQL replication and perform the OLTP reporting from a slave. See "Scaling MySQL" later in this chapter.

Using Appropriate Data Types

An often-overlooked topic is the selection of data types for storing basic information. While a saving of *four bytes* of choosing an INTEGER over a BIGINT for a primary key may seem inconsequential on modern systems, and varchar means variable length, when digging deeper we start to learn this is not always the case.

- *InnoDB loves small primary keys*: For an internal row identifier, InnoDB uses the actual primary key value that you have specified (a clustered index). This means that primary-key lookups are very fast, but large primary keys will also result in large secondary keys. Try to use only INTEGER types or very short CHAR columns for primary keys.

- *Sorting data turns varchars to chars*: Internal buffers including when you sort data in MySQL use the full length specified by the varchar definition, not just the space required to sort it. Using varchar(255) can be a disaster and can result in much larger temporary files than required. Try to explicitly specify the maximum number a varchar column would ever reach, such as first_name varchar(35).

- *Memory tables turn varchars into chars*: The memory storage engine does not support variable length columns and stores varchars as if they were char columns. This is especially important, since the memory storage engine is used by default when MySQL needs to create an internal temporary table, for example, if you write a GROUP BY statement and one of the columns you select is a TEXT or BLOB.

Estimating Storage Requirements

MySQL has a built-in method to determine the optimum storage requirements for a given set of data, called PROCEDURE ANALYSE(). This means that while you may have defined the city name as varchar(255), MySQL will look at every city name in the existing table and tell you what the maximum required length is. An example of this command follows in Listing 10-23.

Listing 10-23. *The PROCEDURE ANALYSE() Feature for Identifying Optimal Data Types*

```
mysql> SELECT * FROM City PROCEDURE ANALYSE(1, 1)\G
*************************** 1. row ***************************
            Field_name: world.City.ID
             Min_value: 1
             Max_value: 4079
            Min_length: 1
            Max_length: 4
     Empties_or_zeros: 0
                 Nulls: 0
Avg_value_or_avg_length: 2040.0000
                   Std: 1177.5058
     Optimal_fieldtype: SMALLINT(4) UNSIGNED NOT NULL
*************************** 2. row ***************************
            Field_name: world.City.Name
             Min_value: A Coruña (La Coruña)
             Max_value: ´s-Hertogenbosch
            Min_length: 3
            Max_length: 33
     Empties_or_zeros: 0
                 Nulls: 0
Avg_value_or_avg_length: 8.5295
                   Std: NULL
     Optimal_fieldtype: VARCHAR(33) NOT NULL
*************************** 3. row ***************************
            Field_name: world.City.CountryCode
             Min_value: ABW
             Max_value: ZWE
            Min_length: 3
            Max_length: 3
     Empties_or_zeros: 0
                 Nulls: 0
Avg_value_or_avg_length: 3.0000
                   Std: NULL
     Optimal_fieldtype: CHAR(3) NOT NULL
```

```
*************************** 4. row ***************************
            Field_name: world.City.District
             Min_value: Abhasia [Aphazeti]
             Max_value: -
            Min_length: 1
            Max_length: 20
      Empties_or_zeros: 4
                 Nulls: 0
Avg_value_or_avg_length: 9.0194
                   Std: NULL
     Optimal_fieldtype: VARCHAR(20) NOT NULL
*************************** 5. row ***************************
            Field_name: world.City.Population
             Min_value: 42
             Max_value: 10500000
            Min_length: 2
            Max_length: 8
      Empties_or_zeros: 0
                 Nulls: 0
Avg_value_or_avg_length: 350468.2236
                   Std: 723686.9870
     Optimal_fieldtype: MEDIUMINT(8) UNSIGNED NOT NULL
5 rows in set (0.01 sec)
```

Tip There are a couple of caveats when running PROCEDURE ANALYSE(). The first one is that you cannot take the result too literally while your data is still small. For example, the output recommended a varchar(33) for the city name but decided that districts only go up to 20 characters.

A second caveat is that PROCEDURE ANALYSE() can be quite overzealous to recommend using ENUM and SET data types. In the example we disabled ENUMs/SETs from being considered by adding two additional arguments: PROCEDURE ANALYSE(1,1). See http://dev.mysql.com/doc/refman/5.1/en/procedure-analyse.html.

Just Throw Hardware at the Problem

Although we described at the beginning of this chapter that improving the hardware that MySQL runs on may not improve performance by the same orders of magnitude as will optimizing queries and settings, at some point all the quick wins have been made, and it becomes more cost-effective to just throw money or hardware at the problem.

CPUs

Although work is being done in MySQL 5.4, MySQL tends to be very bad at making use of many CPUs and cores. Benchmarks suggest that MySQL will often fail to take advantage of any more than 8–16 cores. As a result, focus should be made on making sure CPUs are few but fast instead of many but slow. For this reason, hyperthreading should also be disabled.

Memory

Memory serves as a front-end cache for data that is significantly faster than the speed of reading from hard disks. Provided that sufficient memory is available, reads can be served quite efficiently with only writes having to touch the disk.

Disks

When disks are the bottleneck, it's normally essential to group them together with RAID (redundant array of inexpensive disks). When we talk about RAID and database servers, RAID 10 usually provides the best option, as it offers both redundancy and performance.

When choosing a RAID controller, it's important to note that not all are created equally. We recommend focusing on buying a model that supports a battery-backed cache. With the battery-backed write cache in place, the controller can safely be placed into write-back mode, and expensive fsync() operating system commands (required by storage engines such as InnoDB to guarantee consistency) will return almost instantly. In practical terms, this can result in several-times-better write performance, since the RAID controller can still guarantee that the data will be safe but will be able to optimize how the data is written to disk (combining requests and trying to achieve as much sequential IO as possible).

Network

Network is not always a bottleneck in itself, but the round trips that occur between issuing many individual queries to a database can suffer from latency.

For the MySQL Cluster storage engine, it is especially important to focus on network performance. The more expensive switches that have cut-through packet passing (rather than store-and-forward) are recommended.

Scaling MySQL

Most architectures deploying MySQL use a technique called "scale out"—that is, they tend to use many individual machines with MySQL rather than one very big machine running one instance of MySQL (commonly referred to as "scale up").

This technique is used in order to get the best price-to-performance ratio out of hardware. While larger machines are able to offer better performance, they do so at an exponentially higher cost.

It should be noted that a lot of the technology used to scale out an application is not normally provided by any tools released by MySQL directly but by features implemented by the application developer. One common example of this is read and write splitting, where queries that read data are directed to a different set of databases to those that write it (as seen in Figure 10-1).

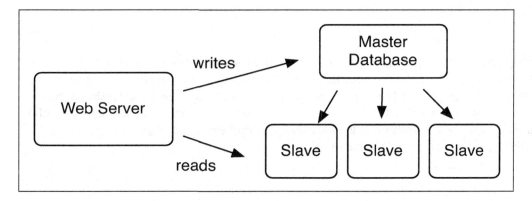

Figure 10-1. *A typical read/write split architecture*

When Replication Scale Out Works Well

Provided that the application is predominantly reads, it's possible to continue scaling via read/write splitting. It's even possible to add slaves onto replication slaves in order to increase the amount of reader machines that are available as seen in Figure 10-2.

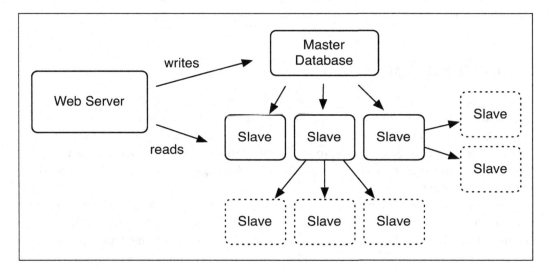

Figure 10-2. *Providing further scaling to a read/write split architecture*

■**Tip** MySQL replication is implemented by replaying the same *statements* on the slave as they were written on the master. One interesting side effect of this is that the master and slave do not need to be identical. Index and storage engine configuration can be different, with the only requirement that the slave be able to process from the *binary log* without error. This means you can have one table you write to using the InnoDB storage engine and a replicated slave that has a MyISAM storage engine (allowing you fast writes without losing the ability to perform full-text search, for example).

When Replication Fails

The dilemma of using a read/write split replication architecture is that each node has to have the capacity available to reply the writes that it receives from the master. If the application is read heavy, this should not be a problem (as seen in Figure 10-3). If the application is write heavy or by sheer growth the theoretical peak of write capacity is reached, then read/write slaves have a diminishing return on investment (see Figure 10-4).

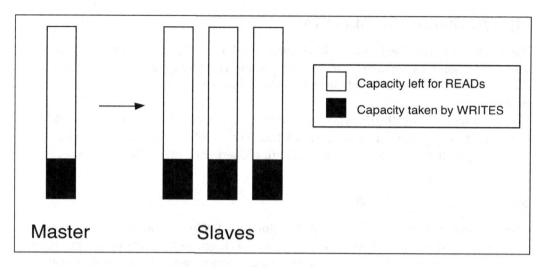

Figure 10-3. *When replication read/write splitting is successful*

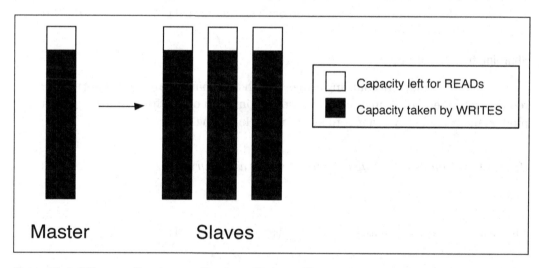

Figure 10-4. *When replication read/write splitting will not work very effectively*

■**Tip** In practice, the slaves tend to have less capacity available for write queries than the master does. While the master can accept write queries from multiple connections at once, exploiting the concurrency available from having multiple CPUs and hard disks, the slave will only apply those writes in a single thread.

MySQL Sharded Architectures

Users who encounter the problem that replication does not scale writes may find that they need to get creative in order to be able to scale. This technique is most commonly referred to as sharding, although more traditional folks may still refer to it as a type of partitioning.

Sharding works by dividing your one large database into a series of smaller MySQL servers and having your application know where to retrieve the data based on some sort of hashing algorithm or directory system indicating where each fragment of data is located.

Sharding by Application Function

One of the most successful methods of sharding is to divide the application by its core functionality. In many cases, some features (such as logging or searching) will not need to join on other tables and can easily be moved off to their own MySQL server. Another example of sharding by function is how Wikipedia can use different pools of MySQL databases for hosting each language.

The downside of sharding by function is that not all application functions are created equally, and the amount of load placed on each shard may become unbalanced.

Sharding by Hash or Key

An easy way to implement sharding is to establish how many shards are going to be required and then distribute the data based on some sort of key, for example, applying a mod on the primary key of a record in a table (as in Listing 10-24).

Listing 10-24. *Sample PHP Code to Shard Based on a Primary Key*

```php
<?php
$number_of_shards = 4;
$destination_shard = ($primary_key % $number_of_shards) + 1;
?>
```

The problem with this methodology is that some shards may receive more demanding access than other shards, and there is no method to be able to rebalance the rows. Place yourself in the shoes of photo-sharing web site Flickr. How much stress would the official Obama photography user generate in the lead-up to the 2008 presidential election?

Caution We can't stress enough that *both* users are not created equally and that it is important that the hashing algorithm spread the data equally among shards. A naïve example of hashing would be to create 26 shards, one for each letter of the alphabet, and store based on the first letter of a username. At first glance it seems reasonable, until you realize that there are a lot more names that start with the letter M than the letter Z and that this a horribly uneven hashing algorithm.

Sharding via a Lookup Service

The most balanced method to implement sharding is to have a user-maintained lookup database for identifying where rows will be stored, as can be seen in Figure 10-5, where data is divided between a main user table and a series of user profile tables stored across multiple shards.

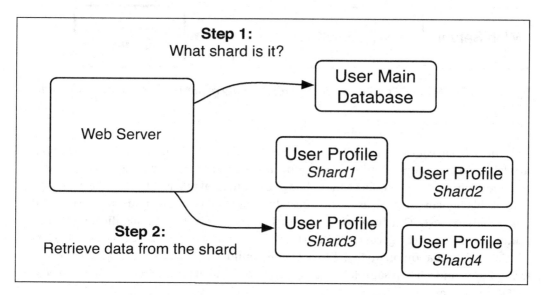

Figure 10-5. *Sharding a user profile database and storing the "shard address" in the main user table*

The advantage of using a directory-service-based sharding mechanism is that scripts can be written to migrate more demanding or higher-profile users to their own shards, and database resources can be adequately balanced.

■**Caution** Sharding is talked about a lot more often than it needs to be done. When choosing to implement sharding into your architecture, beware that separating the data into different nodes will result in the irretrievable loss of some SQL functionality. Basic things like SQL table joins will need to be emulated as part of your PHP application.

Using MySQL Proxy for Automatic Read/Write Splitting

MySQL Proxy is a new product currently in development that can act as a man in the middle between the PHP application and MySQL. One of the core features of MySQL Proxy is a Lua scripting interface, which means that it is possible to intercept, rewrite, and redirect queries before they are sent to the MySQL server (see Figure 10-6).

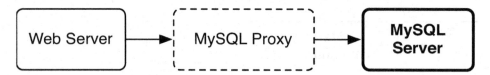

Figure 10-6. *The MySQL Proxy can intercept and modify requests before they are passed to MySQL.*

The only caveat when using MySQL Proxy is to remember that it is not yet a general availability (GA) product. While the product appears stable in basic usage, it is possible that the programming interfaces may change prior to final release. There have also been no credible benchmarks released showing what impact it currently adds under standard benchmarking tests. One blog post suggests that the penalty may be significant: http:// www.mysqlperformanceblog.com/2009/06/09/mysql-proxy-urgh-performance-and-scalability/.

More information on MySQL Proxy can be found at http://forge.mysql.com/wiki/ MySQL_Proxy, and a list of sample Lua usage can be found at http://forge.mysql.com/wiki/ MySQL_Proxy_Cookbook.

Backing Up MySQL

Backup has always been one of MySQL's weaker features, with many different options available but none a clear winner in all scenarios. Before introducing the backup methods available (see Table 10-2), let's cover a bit of theory first on what are the features of the perfect backup.

- *As minimal impact as possible*: The backup should ideally not affect other users on the database system. This is usually defined using terms such as hot (does not block readers and writers), warm (blocks writers), or cold (blocks readers and writers).

- *As up to date as possible*: If the backup takes two days to run, then you will probably not be able to run it as frequently, and any backups will represent much older versions of your data.

- *Quickness to recovery*: Some backup methods will take significantly longer (days!) than others to recover.

- *Flexibility in recovery options*: If you have accidentally deleted a customer's phone number, then it's very painful to justify having to perform a full recovery to restore it.

Table 10-2. *A Comparision of Backup Options for MySQL*

	Engines	Warmth	Flex Backup	Flex Restore	Backup Time	Recovery Time	Binlog Coord
Mysqldump	InnoDB	Hot	Row	Most	Med	Worst	Yes
Mysqldump	All	Warm	Row	Most	Med	Worst	Yes
Filesystem snapshot	All	Mostly Hot	System	System	Med	Med	Yes
InnoDB hot backup	InnoDB	Hot	Table	Table	Fast	Fast	Yes
ibbackup	All	Warm	Table	Table	Fast	Fast	Yes
mysqlhotcopy	MyISAM	Cold	Table	Table	Fast	Fast	Yes
Cold backup	All	Cold	System	Depends on storage engine	Best	Best	Yes

It's important to note that not everything can be compared equally in this table. The following are a few additional notes worth pointing out.

- Filesystem snapshot across all engines first requires a FLUSH TABLES WITH READ LOCK to be run. When this is successful, then the backup can be started, and immediately afterward, the tables can be unlocked. In practice this should only mean a couple of seconds of the operation being not hot.

- For all backup except mysqldump, the restore granularity will usually depend on the storage engine. MyISAM tables (for example) can be recovered individually, but the InnoDB tablespace files and log files will need to be restored together.

- Taking a filesystem snapshot requires InnoDB to run through its crash recovery process upon restart. While no data should be lost, this process can take several minutes to hours when using a larger setting of innodb_log_file_size.

The Rules of Performance Tuning a Database

Before we get into making any tweaks, it is important to lay down the rules of engagement and the process you must take to make sure that your changes do not have any negative consequences.

Be Methodical

Change one setting at a time and record any differences to performance when your application is under load.

Make Any Benchmarks As Realistic As Possible

A lot of developers make the mistake of testing a database change by only testing a small part (or one page) of their application. This can result in queries that reach MySQL having an exceedingly high cache hit ratio that may not be as apparent under real live usage. This also prevents you from seeing issues such as deadlocks, which are race conditions that only show up under concurrent load.

Additional skews of the results can be introduced by not having data in MySQL tables that represents typical production use. As we saw in an earlier section, "Optimizing Queries with EXPLAIN," the distribution of the data will affect the index selection process.

Realize That Every Setting Has a Range

Just because you notice an increase in performance when changing your `sort_buffer_size` from 32 KB to 128 KB that doesn't mean you will see further improvement when you set it to 10 MB. Operating systems are interesting beasts, and allocating larger amounts of memory may take larger amounts of time or cause problems such as CPU caches misses, leading to negative performance.

Realize That Things Change over Time

Some performance-tuning tricks that you read on the Internet are really black magic designed to work around the current limitations of software. As newer versions of MySQL are released, your changes may have negative consequences. One item related to this point (but outside the scope of this book, see `http://dev.mysql.com/doc/refman/5.1/en/index-hints.html`) is index hinting. Use these features with care!

Realize That Some Settings Make Trade-offs

There are settings in MySQL you can enable that will lead to potential performance increases but at the risk of lost data or slower crash recovery time.

Choosing a Larger innodb_log_file_size in InnoDB

A larger log file will mean InnoDB will not need to perform as many implicit checkpoint operations, leading to increased performance. The trade-off is that recovery times after a system crash can be significantly longer, although no data will be lost.

Setting Innodb_flush_log_at_trx_commit to Either 0 or 2

InnoDB allows you to change the behavior of the InnoDB log files so that as they are written they do not demand that the operating system perform a sync operation (to flush the write buffer down to disk). This leads to increased write performance but also the potential loss of data on system crash.

Setting delay_key_writes in MyISAM

On writing data to a MyISAM table, you can choose to not update the index file (since all contents can be recovered from what was in the data file). This leads to better performance but guaranteed corruption on system crash, resulting in an expensive rebuild process when it comes back online.

Realize That Empirical Proof Is the Only True Test

When all seems well at what you estimate to be 10 percent load, don't expect to handle 10 times more traffic. Often when a system becomes loaded, response times start to look like a hockey stick on a graph. You will likely find a bottleneck that prevents you from reaching your expectations, either in MySQL or in your operating system.

Conclusion

In this chapter we started with MySQL's storage engine concept and then dived deep into a crash course on how to performance tune your server. This expands on Chapter 2, where we looked at identifying operating system bottlenecks, and Chapter 3, where we profiled our PHP code.

A database server represents an important scalability challenge in system architecture, since while we can introduce additional web servers to improve our application performance, it is not always so easy to add additional database servers.

Index

You Need the Companion eBook

Your purchase of this book entitles you to buy the companion PDF-version eBook for only $10. Take the weightless companion with you anywhere.

We believe this Apress title will prove so indispensable that you'll want to carry it with you everywhere, which is why we are offering the companion eBook (in PDF format) for $10 to customers who purchase this book now. Convenient and fully searchable, the PDF version of any content-rich, page-heavy Apress book makes a valuable addition to your programming library. You can easily find and copy code—or perform examples by quickly toggling between instructions and the application. Even simultaneously tackling a donut, diet soda, and complex code becomes simplified with hands-free eBooks!

Once you purchase your book, getting the $10 companion eBook is simple:

❶ Visit **www.apress.com/promo/tendollars/**.

❷ Complete a basic registration form to receive a randomly generated question about this title.

❸ Answer the question correctly in 60 seconds, and you will receive a promotional code to redeem for the $10.00 eBook.

Apress®
THE EXPERT'S VOICE™

2855 TELEGRAPH AVENUE | SUITE 600 | BERKELEY, CA 94705

Offer valid through 3/10.